CW00551246

WRITE remarkably

PUBLISH effortlessly

PROMOTE successfully

WRITE remarkably

PUBLISH effortlessly

PROMOTE successfully

How to write a best seller, self-publish, and then keep selling it

Debrah Martin

Published by I.M. Books

www.debrahmartin.co.uk

© Copyright Debrah Martin 2016

WRITE remarkably

PUBLISH effortlessly

PROMOTE successfully

All rights reserved.

The right of Debrah Martin to be identified as the author of this
work has been asserted in accordance with the Copyright, Designs
and Patents Act 1988.

No part of this publication may be reproduced, stored in a retrieval
system, or transmitted, in any form or by any means, electronic,
mechanical, photocopying, recording or otherwise, nor translated
into a machine language, without the written permission of the
publisher.

Condition of sale

This book is sold subject to the condition that it shall not, by way
of trade or otherwise, be lent, re-sold, hired out or otherwise
circulated in any form of binding or cover other than that in which
it is published and without a similar condition including this
condition being imposed on the subsequent purchaser.

ISBN 978-0-9933613-4-0

Contents

Foreword

I have now written and published ten books via both traditional, independent and self-publishing formats. I'm a long way from the day when I held my first book in my hands – but still as excited each time it happens. I've always been an avid reader, and I studied English Literature at university so books have always been an inspiration to me but I didn't start writing in earnest until 2010 after a significant and dramatic change in my life. Writing is both a skill and an art, as well as a wonderful means of learning about both yourself and your fellow companions in this world – or any world you imagine if you write fantasy fiction! As it is a skill as well as an art, a great deal of what it takes to make you a successful author can be learnt. I've always believed there is no point to possessing useful knowledge without sharing it, so here is what *I* have learnt over the bumpy but exciting journey I've taken since I first put pen to paper just over five years ago and wrote *a story.*

Have fun reading it, be successful using it, and above all, love what you do with it …

Part 1: WRITE

Chapter 1:
Getting Started – Finding Inspiration

We all think we have a book in us, don't we? I'd be very, very rich if I had a pound for every time someone has said to me,

"I've had this great idea, I just haven't got round to writing it yet..."

But what happens if you actually *do* get round to writing it? Then the fun really starts. Writing isn't like talking, or eating or breathing – although if you get bitten by the writing bug it could become almost as important as talking, eating or breathing. Writing is a skill, therefore it's possible to learn it – or its constituent parts, at least. It's the skill of putting across nuances and impressions as well as content to your reader in such a way that they become immersed in the world you build for them inside the book. It's done by creating a *believable plot* around a *credible* set of *characters* that will *keep a reader reading* until the plot concludes with a *satisfying outcome,* and using *breath-taking prose* to achieve that. Easy – huh? Maybe. Writing is not only a set of skills, it's an art and art requires inspiration, but inspiration is all around us – so let's start with the skills...

The first skill a writer needs is the art of noticing. How many times have you gone through a whole day barely noticing the details of it? Yet the details are what actually provide the colour and form: the *sense* of the day. As a writer you are now going to start noticing, remembering, recording, considering and trying to recreate those details in all that you write. This is the start of your journey toward success as a writer, and just as surely as when setting out on a real journey you need to know where you're going, how you're going to get there, who the travelling companions are going to be, and what you're going to do when you get there. As an individual, these are simple practicalities. For a writer they are the tools of your trade – plot, setting, POV (point of view) and characterisation; but first of all you need an idea…

FINDING IDEAS

Finding ideas and using them to plan a story can be done in a number of ways:

- Brain storming/spider diagrams and mind mapping – and you can even get apps on your phone and cloud systems to utilise this if it suits you; **iThoughtsHD** and **MindNode** are particularly good for this.
- Open a book, newspaper, magazine, even a dictionary at random:

    - Pick a number of random words from it and combine them. What can you do with them? (This is called 'random word prompting'.)
    - Pick a number of random themes from it and combine them. What can you do with them? (This is called 'random theme prompting'.)

- Use object story generation – collect a number of miscellaneous objects and create a story using them.
- Use an internet idea generator such as http://www.seventhsanctum.com/generate.php?Genname=quickstory
- Solve a problem. Problem solving can initiate a story from an everyday occurrence – take for example:

    - Overhearing a conversation that affects a friend – do you let them know, and if so, how?
    - You crave a bacon sandwich but have no bacon in the fridge – how do you overcome it?
    - Having to shop for a gift for someone who has everything
    - There's a power cut – what do/did you do?
    - A problem often involves a journey or going somewhere to solve it – suppose you have to deal with

a pregnant woman going into labour…
- Finding someone stuck halfway through a window – sash window – is it their home, are they a burglar…
- Getting stuck in a lift/ on top of the big wheel…

- Fairy stories or other well-known folk tales are also a good way to create a tale with a new twist.
- Or try a **fiction square** like this:

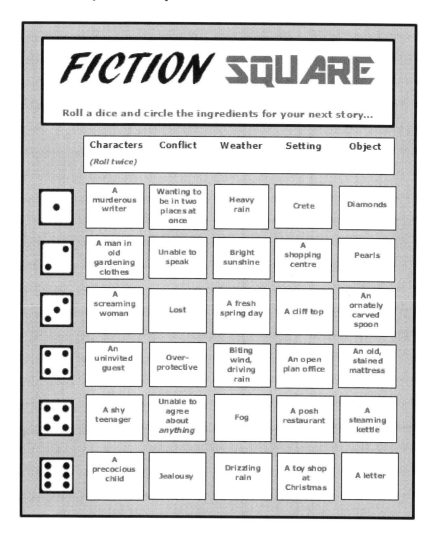

FICTION SQUARE

Roll a dice and circle the ingredients for your next story...

	Characters (Roll twice)	Conflict	Weather	Setting	Object
⚀	A murderous writer	Wanting to be in two places at once	Heavy rain	Crete	Diamonds
⚁	A man in old gardening clothes	Unable to speak	Bright sunshine	A shopping centre	Pearls
⚂	A screaming woman	Lost	A fresh spring day	A cliff top	An ornately carved spoon
⚃	An uninvited guest	Over-protective	Biting wind, driving rain	An open plan office	An old, stained mattress
⚄	A shy teenager	Unable to agree about *anything*	Fog	A posh restaurant	A steaming kettle
⚅	A precocious child	Jealousy	Drizzling rain	A toy shop at Christmas	A letter

Try creating your own with random characters, traits, conflicts, locations and objects.

Objects and themes are wonderful as random story generators because they often have stories of their own, for example:

- Who created it?
- What's it for?
- How did it get where it is?
- How did it come into the owner's possession?
- What is special/unusual about it?

Having something real in front of you makes it easier to stimulate the mind. Two examples of this are *The Hare with the Amber Eyes* by Edmund de Waal, which traces a family's history based on the rare objects collected by the family. Another is *The Conjuror's Bird* by Martin Davies, which tells a story across the years using the extinct bird as the link.

Random word prompts or objects and themes can be used for initial prompts, but they are still only idea generators. An idea needs to be developed in much more detail for it to be worth writing a whole book about. That's where other strategies like spider diagrams, and mind mapping help with story planning. Starting with just one idea, other spin-off ideas can be integrated and intertwined – sometimes in an intensely complex way – to create a plot, which we would otherwise have struggled to imagine all the possibilities for. Your mind is a rich treasure box of ideas, influences, memories, facts, impressions – and sometimes even psychological issues – which can combine to produce an intriguing storyline. By mapping them, it's easy to identify and organise a somewhat random jumble of thoughts into a coherent whole – a plot.

HOW TO CREATE A SPIDER DIAGRAM OR ELEMENTARY MIND MAP

Pick an object and a theme: let's choose a loaf of bread and revenge – two pretty disparate items to mind map with – and see what happens:

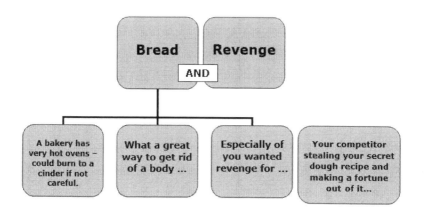

Picking up on an ideas can lead to theme developing, which could lead into a mystery. In this case I think there could be quite a fun 'cozy' mystery in the baking here!

Here's another example of a different kind of mind map, examining the plot of the Harry Potter books courtesy of **Creately**:

http://creately.com/diagram/example/ggvrpcfo1/Harry+Potter

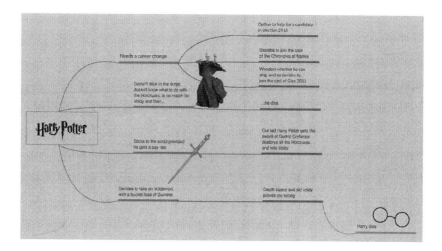

There are a number of other ways to kick-start inspiration, such as:

- Build up a collection of postcards, old birthday cards, images cut from magazines, or photos you've taken that interest you to kick-start an idea.
- See how many stories you can think of relating to just one picture – or who might have just left the picture or be about to join it.
- Collect interesting objects and keep them in a drawer. Open the drawer and pick any one of them for a prompt. Merely keeping an eye out for interesting objects will have your imagination running wild.
- Look at ordinary things as well as extraordinary ones. One of the best surprise tactics is to take something mundane and turn it on its head.
- Write something every day if you can – even if it's only a few sentences.
- Whenever you see or hear or think of something that captures your imagination, record it. It will form your ideas file and be the prompt for writing another day – or even the basis for a whole plot. I often have several ideas simmering away simultaneously. Sometimes they even combine!
- Don't make soup. No – not as crazy as it sounds. I know someone who calls procrastinating 'making soup'. Whenever they have to settle down to something difficult to tackle, they make soup. Soup is warm and comforting and takes time to make and means you can't get on with that tricky thing you were making soup to avoid. Whatever you call it, don't procrastinate if you're short of ideas. Once the words start flowing, they generally keep going. Don't make soup, make sentences.
- NaNoWriMo – never heard of it? It stands for National Novel Writing Month in November and you can find all the details about it here: http://nanowrimo.org/ It's a great tool to get you writing – a lot – and often that's half the battle with getting started at all. Sign up next November and have a look. The challenge alone is good.

8

And if all else fails, here are some other ways to kick-start your first novel:

1. Choose a working title for your book. Write a few sentences outlining the essence of it (good practice for later when you will be pitching it to agents, publishers and potential readers). Have you nailed a theme that intrigues you?

2. Write at least 250 words every day. By the end of the year, you'll have over 90,000 words of your first draft – and this is where NaNoWriMo is excellent for prompting you to write every day. Over 70,000 words is considered a full-length novel.

3. Make a spreadsheet and enter the number of words you write each day on it. As your word count grows, so will your confidence and determination to finish your novel.

4. Make a list from 1 to 30, each being a proposed chapter in your book. Use them as the skeleton to build the flesh of your book around. It also helps track where your plot is going. And if you like having structure with flexibility as you write, with places to store all your ideas in such a way that you can keep track of them and easily move them around, **Scrivener** is an excellent writing tool, although you will have to invest time in learning how to use it to get most from it. It does also have the advantage of converting your completed manuscript into a digital-ready publishing format when you have completed it too. If you want more information and tutorials on how to use Scrivener, there is an exhaustive online course about it which I have listed, together with the link to the Scrivener software, in the downloadable material you'll find the links for in the Appendix.

5. Plot a story outline by drawing a line with the beginning, middle and end marked on it. Add where the significant characters enter the plot, the significant events occur and the climax(es) in the story occur, then start wherever you feel inspired to. This is called a story arc and I will discuss it in more detail in Chapter 3 on plotting.

6. Immerse yourself in your characters and their world.

Think about what clothes they wear, their likes and dislikes, their background, their physical characteristics – paint an imaginary picture of them. Pick a real image from a magazine or newspaper if it helps and base your imaginary character on them – but never refer to this person in the book. The character must become your creation.

7.   Write your character's past history; their 'backstory'. Write it as if you were them – in the first person. What is their motivation for what they do in your story?

8.   Remember, you don't need to start at the beginning – in fact often it's much better to start at another point in the story; the most dramatic point. I'll talk more about this in Chapter 3 on plotting and again in Chapter 4 on beginnings, middles and endings.

SO WHAT ARE THE MAIN INGREDIENTS OF A STORY?

- A main character – the protagonist
- An anti-hero or challenger – the antagonist
- Secondary/supporting characters
- A location
- Events to create the plot
- A crisis (or two…)
- Emotions
- Connections
- Responses to events
- Climax(es) and anti-climax(es)
- Interaction between characters
- Points of view – whose point of view is the story being told from?
- Obstacles to overcome
- Love interests
- Goals
- Motivations
- Experiences outside of the characters' comfort zones
- Transformation of characters
- Learning/outcome
- A moment of truth (or two…)

- What can be shared with society/the world – and will it be accepted?

They boil down to this:

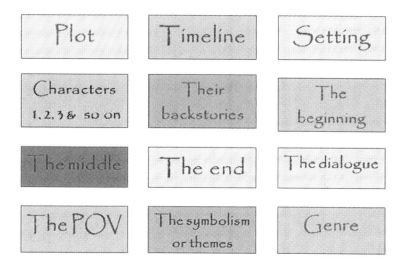

Here's a five-minute fix exercise to try: *Use a theme generator or an object you find round the house to prompt a five-minute story.* Can you expand it? How would you do that? Try mind mapping to see where it might take you.

Now let's start with the last of the boxes: genre, and decide first of all who you're writing for…

Chapter 2:
Finding your Audience

Q: Why are you writing a book? Sounds obvious? To be read, of course!

It's not quite that obvious, actually. Writers write for many reasons and many audiences. You may actually only be writing for yourself, or maybe your family. Writing has long been acknowledged as a wonderfully therapeutic thing to do. By exploring your own experiences and the feelings and behaviour they've prompted, you begin to understand yourself and your own motivations better. Or you may be writing to tell a story for your family – a family history, an autobiography or even a biography. A story based on fact shouldn't lack drama, structure or even intrigue simply because it's true. It can be plotted as well as any fiction, and the people it portrays and the experiences they have should be as 'real' as any you craft in a fictional work. Truth is often stranger than fiction, so use all the tools in the writer's toolbox to make your truth as much of a page-turner as any thriller. So, actually your answer could be any of:

For myself.
For my family (and friends).
For fun.
For personal satisfaction.
Or for readers of…and here we come to genres...

Genre is a category of art, music or literature. In fiction, there are probably more genres now than I could list on this page, so let's look at the possibilities as a kind of overview. Looking at the main genres allows you to narrow down your story style and your readership. I'm going to use good old Amazon's main categories, and show you how they can break right down into quite specialised niches – essential to bear in mind as you write if you are writing a book to sell, because this will have a direct bearing ultimately on promoting and marketing your book.

Let's start with age ranges.

CHILDREN'S FICTION covers anything up to late teens. If you are targeting the US market (which you automatically do since its readership is by far the largest), you will need to break down your audience into 'grades' comparable with US school grades.

- **Preschool** = Picture books (ages 0 to 4).
- **Kindergarten–2nd grade** = Early, levelled readers; first chapter books (ages 5 to 7).
- **3rd grade–6th grade** = Middle-grade chapter books (ages 8 to 11).
- **7th grade–12th grade** = Teen and young adult chapter books (ages 12 to 17).
- **Young Adult fiction** generally covers the age range 14 to 18 and includes the themes of love and some sex – diplomatically alluded to.
- **New Adult** generally covers the age range 18 to 22 and may include quite explicit sexual themes in the context of young people finding out about themselves, their world and their emotions.

Quite a maze, isn't it? It therefore pays to be very specific about the age range you are writing for in juvenile fiction as you will need to target it very specifically in terms of content, vocabulary and theme. It's as essential as the plot that you gauge this right from the outset. Bear in mind too, that children are as complex to write for as adults. Within their lives they encounter equally as many – if not more – metamorphoses as they will as adults. They go from sucking and chewing a book (thank goodness for board books) to being able to recognise the odd word as it relates to a picture, then on to phrases and sentences, and finally, concepts. If you are to engage a child as a reader, you not only have to use the correct images and imagery, but language, story length, life events and emotions they will identify with, without ever patronising or losing their faith in you as a writer writing about something they can identify with. And remember a child is still technically a child until they are 18 – how many almost 18 year olds do you regard as a child? What an enormous range of possibilities to encompass; do your homework well before you even set pen to paper if writing for children!

ADULT FICTION is no easier. Adults are all different, with a huge variety of interests, ambitions and life histories. Some are exceptionally articulate, whereas some have a quite limited vocabulary, but still love to read. Some have very specific reading requirements, and some will devour anything an author writes once they like their style, but there is no point pitching a book to a reader who simply isn't interested in the genre you write in. In Fiction alone in the Amazon Kindle Store I found this top level list:

Adventure Stories & Action
Biographical Fiction
Contemporary Fiction
Crime, Thrillers & Mystery
Erotica
Family Sagas
Fantasy
Film & Television Tie-In
Gay & Lesbian
Historical
Horror
Humour
Lad Lit
Literary Fiction
Medical
Metaphysical & Visionary
Myths & Fairy Tales
Political
Psychological
Religious & Inspirational
Romance
Science Fiction
Sport
Westerns

Let's take just one of these genres and drill down further: Romance – always a popular choice. Romance breaks down further into these possibilities:

Sagas
Historical Romance
Contemporary Romance
LGBT (Lesbian, Gay, Bisexual, Transgender)
Science Fiction
Fantasy
Erotica

And if I chose to pull these apart further, for example in Fantasy I might find:

Paranormal
Apocalyptic
Sword & Sorcery
Metaphysical & Visionary

And so on…

Each of these genres will have a dedicated readership, and even that readership will break down further into male (yes, some men do read romance – think about the LGBT category) and female; young, middle-aged or older, their general social class, educational background, lifestyle and reading capacity. When you are writing a book you wish to sell, you need to be certain you have researched all of those possibilities and understand the kind of reader you are writing for. How do you do that? First by getting a feel for the various genres of books there are out there – browse in bookshops, read blogs, search online, scour Amazon. Secondly by reading widely in your chosen genre yourself. If you've never read a Young Adult book, don't write one until you've read a whole pile of them. If history and romance aren't normally your thing, don't write a Regency romance without having fully immersed yourself in those already written by other popular historical romance authors. Common sense really – and a bit of time, research and reading. As you read you will gain an understanding about style, vocabulary and what has already been done to death. We are constantly told there are no new stories, only new ways of telling them so reading within your genres will also alert you to the ways stories have been told and where the gaps still are. That's where you'll find your new way of telling and your readership. I will revert back to your readership in Chapter 6 when looking at characterisation as there is one other big factor you have to nail when writing successfully in-genre – being credible.

Here are some definitions of the main genres:

MYSTERIES AND THRILLERS, INCLUDING CRIME FICTION:

A plot involving a crime or a mystery which the protagonist must solve – often involving suspicious death, murder or a lethal threat to them. Within this there may be elements of, or a veering towards, police procedurals, serial killers, conspiracies, sagas, psychological suspense, family sagas, young adult or new adult fiction, fantasy, sci-fi, historical or period drama, noir thrillers (very dark) …

ROMANCE:

A plot within which the emotions of love, loss and unrequited love are examined – usually resulting in a happy ending for the protagonist. Within this there may be elements of, or a veering towards melodrama, historical or period drama, erotica, family sagas, chick lit, young adult or new adult fiction, fantasy, sci-fi…

SCI-FI:

A plot in which the protagonist and secondary characters are living within the past, future, on another planet/ universe or encounter technology or events beyond the norms of what we currently accept as reality. Within this there may be elements of, or a veering towards, fantasy, historical or period drama (going back in time instead of forwards), conspiracies, thrillers, crime fiction, romance, horror, young adult or new adult fiction, paranormal fantasy, fantasy…

HORROR:

A plot which scares the hell out of you! There may be violence and gore, or there may simply (but effectively) be only psychological tension – for example, *The Woman in Black* by Susan Hill. Within this there may be elements of, or a veering towards, police procedurals, serial killers, young adult or new adult fiction, conspiracies, fantasy – e.g. supernatural creatures, noir fiction…

SPECULATIVE FICTION, INCLUDING FANTASY:

Plots that cross genres and examine 'what if?' are speculative fiction. What if nuclear war did happen? What if all the women in the world – bar a handful – became infertile? What if our sun started to die prematurely? Within this there may be elements of, or a veering towards, the paranormal, the supernatural, urban decay, apocalyptic fiction, sci-fi, sagas, young adult or new adult fiction, thrillers, noir fiction…

EROTICA:

Erotica includes sexually explicit details as a primary feature, although unlike pornography, erotica doesn't aim exclusively at sexual arousal. The novels of Anais Nin are good examples of well-written erotica – see *Delta of Venus* and *Little Birds*. Within this there may be elements of, or a veering towards, romance, LGBT, BDSM, fantasy, sci-fi, thriller, crime, romance…

HISTORICAL:

The plot is set within a historical period, and beyond that the story line may encompass any of the above – with perhaps the exception of sci-fi.

So what's yours going to be?

Five-minute fix: Make a list of the books you've read in your chosen genre. What do each of them cover – in one sentence only: is there a gap you can identify? How would you fill it?

Is that your genre?

Chapter 3:
Plotting and Structuring

What's in a plot? And why are plot and structure so important?

The main elements of a plot are:

THE PLOT ITSELF – of course: the central strand that impacts on everything. There may well be lesser strands of plot (sub-plots) also impacting on the characters, but the central strand is the biggest and most well-developed element of the story and must have a resolution at the end of the story.

THE QUEST: usually a plot will involve a quest of some kind – to find something out, to solve a mystery, or achieve an end. It is your protagonist's target or goal, and your other character's objective to thwart.

INCITING INCIDENT: a twist or game-changing moment which prompts the protagonist to embark on a challenging path.

THE CONFLICT: the conflict between what the characters want to do and what they have to do is what leads your plot and forces your characters to react. Conflict can be internal – phobias, needs, desires. Motivations or external such as a car running them down or another character hitting them. Along with obstacles and barriers to success or resolution, conflicts – and how characters face or resolve them – are what create a plot.

TURNING POINT: a pivotal moment when something will prompt your protagonist and other characters to resolve a conflict.

THE PROTAGONIST: the main character (or characters – occasionally plural) driving the plot forward. *Gone Girl* has two protagonists – Nick and Amy.

THE SECONDARY CHARACTERS: the other supporting characters within the plot. Your protagonist or central character will interact with them, caring for, or hating, needing, not needing, coming into conflict with them to drive the story forward.

THE HOOK: an event that whets the reader's curiosity to find out what happens next and therefore to read on.

DRAMA: cliffhangers, breathless moments, unexpected twists, pace, intrigues – they all make a book un-put-down-able.

SURPRISE: keep your readers hooked by providing surprises all the way through your plot. Don't go with the obvious, and always end a chapter or a section on a 'hook' – a plot point or a development that will have your reader desperate to read on and find out what happens next.

THEMES: there may well be certain themes you will be returning to in your narrative. Make sure you don't labour it/them with too much repetition or by becoming vague or verbose.

FOCUS: is the ability to sustain the main story line within a mix of other elements without being repetitive or rambling off-topic.

LOGIC: makes sure whatever premise you are putting forward for what happens in your plot is credible and believable. Test it out on third parties if necessary first.

EMOTION: all your characters need to experience and display emotion or they will be 2D and unconvincing. Readers also need to care about what happens to your characters. Always show your characters' emotions, though – don't tell your reader what they are feeling, unless you are writing in the first person and your narrator is going through the process of examining their feelings as a plot development.

CLIMAX and ANTI-CLIMAX: the highest or most intense point in the development or resolution of something or a decisive moment that is of maximum intensity/ a major turning point in a plot – an anti-climax is a point where the expectation of a climax is created, only for there not to be a resolution or turning point after all. Anti-climaxes can sometimes be used very effectively for dramatic build-up leading to a real climax.

RESOLUTION: the conclusion to the story which will clarify and conclude themes, conflicts and plot lines.

And it all hangs around…

THE STRUCTURE: a standard structure for a novel is an opening that includes a 'hook', a middle section that develops the plot, themes, sometimes symbolism, and a satisfying ending. The format may be a straightforward narrative, a two-person narrative, a diary format, in first, second or third person POV (point of view), or even a revolving point of view, in a linear format – starting at the beginning and continuing until the end of the story, or non-linear – in flashback or newsflashes, or even two or more formats running alongside each other. But whatever elements the structure is created from, it will always essentially form a **Three-Act Structure** because dramatic stories fall naturally into three acts – beginning, middle and end. The three acts also directly correlate to the stages of character progression of the protagonist – the hero or heroine – in the story. And every story you read will be repeating this overall structure and one or more of seven basic plot lines over and over again – after all, why reinvent the wheel? There is nothing wrong with retelling a good tale in another way, just as there is nothing wrong with reusing a successful format; the trick is in how you reuse the format or retell the tale. This is how the **Three-Act Structure** works, with a steady rise in tension and drama until the plot line reaches a climax, and a satisfactory conclusion ensues, drawing all the strands of the plot together.

The three-act structure includes:

Act 1 – the beginning where the problem or issue is first aired/ conflict is first set up.

Act 2 – where the conflict rises to a climax (or climaxes), usually towards the end of the second act.

Act 3 – where there is a moment of truth or catalyst to resolve the issue, leading to a resolution.

It looks like this in diagram form:

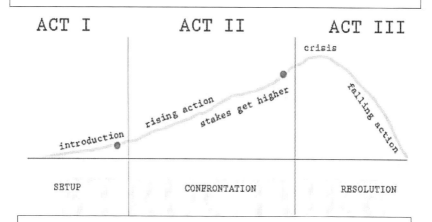

Within the three-act structure, insert characters, their trials and their resolutions, their conflicts and dramas and encase them within a believable premise and you have a successful plot.

A successful plot? So what is a successful plot?

A successful plot not only follows a cleverly planned arc, to which there are several principles that are applied, it also sets up climaxes and anti-climaxes as well as challenges, issues, obstacles and character development – and even a complete transformation in some cases.

According to Aristotle, stories should tell of a change in fortune of a character from good to bad, or bad to good. *Monomyth* by Joseph Campbell, states there is a basic pattern to the majority of narratives around the world, which are based around these themes:

THE DEPARTURE, which forms:

- **The call to action – or inciting incident:** the hero begins in the mundane and something triggers a change.

- **The refusal of the call:** there is a reason for the refusal – attachments, fear, a sense of duty etc and this sets up conflict.
- **The supernatural aid:** once committed to the quest/journey/challenge, an adviser/wise person/mentor arrives to assist.
- **The crossing of the first threshold:** the beginning of the adventure/journey for the protagonist and the departing from their comfort zone.

THE INITIATION, which leads the protagonist through:

- **The road of trials:** introducing the obstacles that will enable failure and learning.
- **The meeting with the goddess:** the experience of true love, power and/or consequences.
- **The woman as temptress:** temptations arise which will distract the hero away from their journey.
- **Atonement:** an initiation which holds power over the hero's life – often in the form of a father or authoritarian figure who has the power over life and death.
- **Apotheosis:** is the death of the old self/ the transformation/ the moving on of the protagonist or hero to a period of rest.
- **The ultimate boon:** the boon is the reward for coming through the initiation or the attainment of a goal.

THE RETURN, which is the culmination of the plot and includes:

- **Refusal of return:** after finding bliss the hero doesn't want to return (more conflict to resolve).
- **The magic flight:** where the hero has to return with whatever they have been searching for.
- **Rescue from without:** assistance from the wise person (from the Departure stage) enables the hero to escape.
- **The crossing of the return threshold:** where the hero returns to the world of 'before the Departure' to complete their quest.
- **Mastery of two worlds:** this is when the hero transcends worlds – like Neo in *The Matrix*.

- **Freedom to live:** the hero has now returned to the world of 'before the Departure' with an insight or truth to share and since they have faced death, they now have the freedom to live. They now live in the moment without regret for the past. They have transcended their challenge/conflict.

Take a look at *Sophie's World, The Lord of the Rings, The Beach, The Life of Pi* and *The Alchemist* (all referenced in the Appendix), which all embody elements of the above. You do not need to place all of these elements within the structure of your plot, but using a number of them from each section will give you a plot with an inherent structure simply through their use.

Five-minute fix: pick some of the elements from each of the sections above and place them in a linear timeline. Once you have created the order you are happy with, write a sentence describing the basic flow of your plot.

Does it have a beginning, middle and end – the three acts?
Do you see how it makes sense?
Good, then let's think about the basic story forms to build around this structure – and there are only seven basic forms of them.

Yes, you did read that right. *SEVEN.* Did you think there were more? Well of course there are as many ways as people to tell a tale, but a little bit of delving around reveals a strange and perplexing truth about storytelling – all the stories anyone ever writes are based around one or the other of the following seven themes:

1. **Overcoming the monster:** Think of St George and the dragon, *The War of the Worlds* – and so topical now – Dracula and his gluttonous vampire army. Monsters represent our fears – dark and dank – that we have to beat to achieve happiness. So of course that is why we are buried under a ton of vampire and werewolves YA (young adult) fiction at the moment. What more dank and drear source of fear is there than adolescence?

2. **Rags to riches:** Oh easy, I hear you say – I'm getting the hang of this now. *Cinderella*, right? Well, yes, of course –

and *The Ugly Duckling, Jane Eyre, Slum Dog Millionaire*. It crosses all genres, cultures and centuries. It gives credence to our belief in ourselves – we may start out mundane, poor, struggling, but we can, through hardship and trial, achieve the pot of gold at the end of the rainbow and return home – bad boy done good etc. It may sound trite, but seeing the underdog triumph does us all good and gives us hope – so we love to read about it too.

3. **The quest:** Another very topical one here – *Lord of the Rings* is the best and most spectacular example of this – and it's an epic journey too, but you could go for *Watership Down* or *Raiders of the Lost Ark* too. There must be a hero, a lure or pull to an all-important goal and thrills, spills and almost death along the way before success brings the conquering hero home again with their spoils. Uplifting, inspiring, escapism – wonderful!

4. **Voyage and return:** *The Wizard of Oz* – I have to choose that one since it is the archetypal voyage and return, or *Alice in Wonderland*, or *The Time Machine* –travelling out of everyday surroundings, the hero(ine) and the group of people travelling with them have to cope with the strangeness of another world, face shadowy threats and make a thrilling escape back to a normality they now appreciate where they had found it boring and mundane before – *'there's no place like home...'* (And of course there isn't!)

5. **Comedy:** Bridget Jones had us laughing all the way here and back with her, and then – if you're a Shakespeare fan, so does *The Taming of the Shrew, A Midsummer Night's Dream* etc. It's all good clean fun where the central character is blinded to the reality of things by their ego, short-sightedness, one-track mind, whereas the reader/audience sees the wider picture and the humour lies in seeing the two juxtaposed. Of course our hero(ine) sees the error of their ways and All's Well that Ends Well but not before they've been led a merry dance along the way. The end result is self-knowledge and reconciliation where there was harmony and unrest.

6.   **Tragedy:** Ironically the same as comedy – and essentially the same as all the other storylines ultimately, where there is a problem to solve, ordeals to overcome and a journey in search of the goal – but rather sadly, the outcome will involve – for some of the characters, at least – death, destruction or disaster. And if you're watching a Jacobean tragedy the body count on stage will probably be higher than the numbers in the audience (I love a bit of blood and guts!).

And finally there is…

7.   **Rebirth (as one would expect after death, destruction and disaster):** Again a journey to achieve self-realisation, but the enemy is often – at least in part – from within. *Snow White*, *Sleeping Beauty*, *The Secret Garden* are all based on rebirth. Often there is a direct confrontation between dark and light to achieve self-understanding and healing.

But if there are no new stories, simply new ways of telling them, how can anyone ever be original? By means of the characters you use to tell your story, their dialogue, the world they inhabit, the events that unfold around them, the trials you make them face their resolution, and finally, the truths you force them to uncover about themselves.

Look at *Hamlet* where the discontented prince becomes the tragic anti-hero, or Lisbeth Salander in *The Girl with the Dragon Tattoo* for a more modern example of the same. So let's not make it easy for the people populating our imaginary worlds. Let's push them to their limits so we can squeeze every last ounce of character development out of them; every drop of passion and desperation – take our readers on a rollercoaster ride and provide not just one incline for them to tumble down to find the ending, but several. *Hamlet* and *The Girl with the Dragon Tattoo* are two good examples of how the same plot format has been reused in a different way. In both the anti-hero seeks revenge and in doing so also finds themselves and changes, in a dramatic way. They are both a hybrid of a tragic and a questing plot, even though the outcomes are quite different. In that they are not new, they are simply a reworking of the seven basic story types.

Taking the elements of any one of these, you will find the basic three-act structure imposed on them, but with clever use of varying levels of disclosure, theme, challenge and development.

Every plot requires characters, of which one will be the main character; the protagonist – the one who will initiate action, face challenges, be forced to change or examine themselves and transform in some way. It also requires an outcome or conclusion, and a series of turning points along the way that lead the protagonist to that conclusion. These turning points need to be carefully placed to maintain the impetus of the story line – to keep the reader hooked, and also to interface effectively with the stage of transformation that the protagonist has reached by the time they occur. Some of these transformations will be on a fundamental level – decisions and the natural results of them. Others will be more subtle – subconscious changes in belief, attitude and motivation. The most effective plot will marry the two to achieve a seamless movement forward – almost of inevitability for the protagonist. Looking at the mechanics of how this works, let's take a best-selling thriller like *Gone Girl* apart.

First, set up the reason for the protagonist's trial:

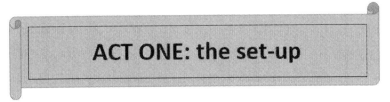

ACT ONE: the set-up

- The dramatic introduction.
- Introduce the protagonist (who might be part of the dramatic introduction).
- Establish the dramatic world.
- Establish the characters' agendas.
- Insert the INCITING INCIDENT – the first twist or game-changing moment which prompts the protagonist to embark on their challenging path.

In 'Act One' of Gone Girl, we meet Amy and Nick and find out Amy's backstory ('what went before') as the daughter of the authors of the Amazing Amy books; spoilt, temperamental, demanding, self-immersed, manipulative.

We also meet Nick – simplistic, self-immersed, bemused by Amy and lacking her intellectual acuity; unhappy and trapped. Not a marriage of equals at all – and not a marriage of contentment either.

Their agendas? Amy's – apparently to make her husband happy despite the fact that he appears surly, unresponsive and boorish to her. Nick's – to just get through the day of his five-year anniversary without upsetting Amy.

The inciting incident? Amy disappears, and as her disappearance seems more and more suspicious, Nick must find her, or risk being accused of being implicated in her disappearance.

Fast forward to Act Two: Amy has been missing for several days now and the police are getting suspicious.

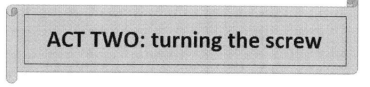

ACT TWO: turning the screw

- Mounting obstacles.
- Uncovering suspects and motives.
- Protagonists are threatened by internal as well as external conflicts.
- The stakes raised by a further twist – e.g. second inexplicable murder.
- The protagonist goes further out on a limb.
- Twist/breakthrough occurs which leads to the final ordeal.

Nick is now the prime suspect in Amy's disappearance for a variety of reasons, but we also now know that Amy isn't all sweetness and light either. Amy is in fact alive and trying to frame Nick for her supposed death. We also know Nick had been having an affair and had grown to hate Amy so both Amy and Nick are clearly unreliable narrators. When the police find evidence which seems to prove Nick has been lying to them, he is on the verge of being charged with murder and feels obliged to engage a lawyer who specialises in defending men accused of killing their wives. Meanwhile Amy – in hiding – has been robbed and is forced to seek help from an obsessive ex-boyfriend. As he becomes increasingly possessive with her, she too is feeling trapped. For Nick, validation of Amy's perfidy finally appears when her diary is proven to be a sham, but how will he get her to come out of hiding?

The mounting obstacles? The evidence accumulating against Nick even though the reader knows it to be fake – dramatic tension between the plot and the story is cleverly used here. And for Amy, being robbed and being forced to ask for help from the obsessive ex-boyfriend.

Internal and external conflicts? Nick's need to prove his innocence against the certain knowledge that Amy is trying to frame him; Amy's need to be in control against her inability to control once her money is stolen and she is obliged to and trapped by her ex-boyfriend.

The twist that proves the final breakthrough? Nick's appearance on TV, proclaiming his innocence and begging Amy to return.

ACT THREE: the resolution

- Protagonist goes beyond the point of no return and stakes everything in a concluding ordeal – JAWS OF DEATH.
- Investigator confronts the villain, reveals truth, and exposes hidden motives.
- Possibly a final twist/surprise.
- Story strands unite in PAY OFF.
- End – emotional resolution.

After seeing the TV interview Amy is convinced Nick wants her back. She murders the former boyfriend, telling the police she had been kidnapped and imprisoned by him as her reason for the attack. She also claims to be pregnant but Nick knows she is both a liar and a killer although he has no proof, so he stays in the marriage hoping to gather it over time.

Amy hopes he will eventually love her the way she wants to be loved, and now it's Nick who's faking it. They both write their own versions of what happened, Nick's with the intention of exposing Amy, but when Amy impregnates herself with Nick's semen from the fertility clinic they attended he's forced to destroy his book or she will keep him from their unborn child and turn it against him. Ultimately Nick chooses to stay with Amy, and continue living the charade, so she won't be able to do that.

The protagonist going beyond the point of no return? Amy murdering her ex-boyfriend and Nick not being able to expose her lies because of lack of proof.

The confrontation – occurs some while before the end of the book leaving Nick and Amy at a stand-off; both of them writing their own version of their story.

The story strands unite in pay-off? Nick and Amy end up together, both hating each other and now with a child further tying them together.

The final twist is that they are now voluntarily trapped together in misery – whether deserved or not on Nick's part; a sick twist indeed fitting for a sick mind like Amy's. Yet for Amy, she still hasn't achieved what she wanted because she knows Nick hates and despises her, and one day, if he ever gets the chance...

Which of the seven stories is *Gone Girl*? Well, maybe a hybrid, a voyage and return, I would say – and also rebirth, because Nick has completely transformed by the end of the book from a self-absorbed, bumbling, blinkered immature man to one tempered and soured by his encounter with duplicity. It doesn't have a 'happy' ending, either, but it does have an emotional resolution almost as stern as any of the epic Greek tragedies – an allegory. This is what happens if you don't take emotional note of your life and the people within it; see what they have become whilst you failed to pay proper attention?

Within the three-act structure there is also some subtle layering. There is what the story appears to be about, and also an underlying truth that gradually becomes more apparent as the plot unfolds. It may be revealed through a number of turning points.

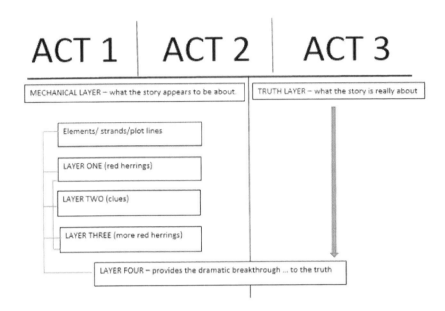

This is a classic thriller/ mystery plot structure. All the layers of the plot are connected, and some of the layers may have other interconnections too – see how the 'red herrings' layers are linked here, but only one – the deepest layer of all – will ultimately lead to the truth. Each layer will be a subplot, involving various characters, and will sit credibly within the overall plot – for example Nick in *Gone Girl* is having an affair. The affair sits at plot level one. It's made perfectly obvious for the reader, but it causes Nick to be furtive and secretive and therefore makes him act suspiciously. It's actually a red herring – a plot device to make Nick secretive and later on a suitable suspect when it becomes public. It's the deeper level plots that provide the truth though – the way Amy's and Nicks diary accounts vary so much, the way Nick is too perfect a suspect to actually be a genuine suspect, the way Amy is *too* sweet in her own early diary accounts. These are all clues that connect to the deeper plot level – and are partially resolved in Part Two when the reader realises Amy is an unreliable narrator. And remember, ultimately all plot levels have to be resolved for all the strands to be interconnected in the final resolution.

The final stages of structuring an effective plot are to:

- Push your protagonist to their limits; take the situation they find themselves in to an extreme, because it's only when a character is at meltdown that they transform and they push through the barriers that have kept them where they have been since the story began. If they're desperately in love but that is keeping them trapped in their old patterns of behaviour, make them feel hatred. If they are upright and respectable, make them face deceit and lies and if they adhere to principles, make them lose their values and ape the bad guys. In the final book in my *Patchwork People* series, the protagonist is a respectable barrister but he is ultimately forced into a resolution that is against all of his principles.

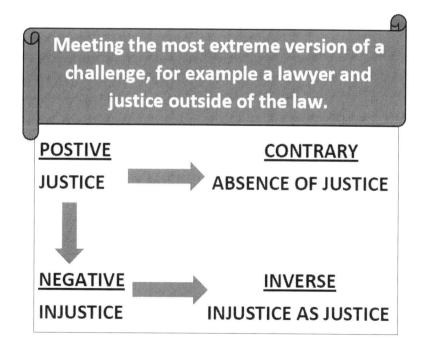

Meeting the most extreme version of a challenge, for example a lawyer and justice outside of the law.

POSTIVE	CONTRARY
JUSTICE	ABSENCE OF JUSTICE
NEGATIVE	INVERSE
INJUSTICE	INJUSTICE AS JUSTICE

As a barrister, his role is to apply justice *within* the law but if that is no longer possible, how can justice still be served? By applying the inverse. Turning ideas on their head like this for your plot and your characters can produce some surprising and dramatic resolutions, but remember:

- Ensure there is no going back for the main or the secondary characters.
- A good plot is all about achieving drama.
- Drama is achieved through dramatic decisions.
- Dramatic decisions come from characters with multiple layers of conflict.
- Drama is given shape by gradual unfolding the process over three acts (or more if continuing into a series of books).
- All plots need structure.
- Play around with ideas to achieve the unexpected – try various POVs, alternating POVs, parallel narratives (two characters telling the same story from a different angle e.g. *Gone Girl* uses alternating narratives (two characters telling the same story but each telling part of it. *The Night Following* uses a diary format and letters (epistolary). *The Perks of Being a Wallflower* and *Herzog* do the same but in a very different way.
- The stakes must be raised when the unexpected is revealed and the rug pulled from under the central character.
- Satisfactory conclusions generally include some element of personal redemption that emerges following an ordeal.
- Suspense should be created through the mental uncertainty of awaiting an unknown outcome and tension from not being able to predict what that outcome might be – whilst sometimes actually knowing more of the facts than the characters themselves.

Enough looking at plots and structures. Try a ***five-minute fix*** instead and do a bit of plotting of your own:

LET'S DO SOME PLOTTING...

Step 1: Choose the idea or concept – spider diagrams, prompts, story charts, and other sources of inspiration.

Step 2: Create the story line – the seven epic tales, adapted as appropriate.

Step 3: Choose the story structure – linear (starts at the beginning and continues straight through to the end), or non-linear (starts at a point before or after the opening event and tells the story in flashback or in fast-forward).

Step 4: Define the main plot and the sub-plots. What are the intended outcomes (don't forget not all sub-plots *have* to have a conclusion, but the main plot must).

Step 5: How do your characters contribute to the plot? Who are your characters?

Step 6: What conflict must your characters contend with? Internal, external (choices), Deus ex Machina (fate), the environment etc?

Step 7: Where are you going to place your pre-climaxes (the ones that occur before the concluding climax)? There should be more than one before the final denouement.

Step 8: What themes are you exploring within the plots/sub-plots, characters, conflict? For example, deception (*Gone Girl*), valuing what you already have (*The Wizard of Oz*), justice (*Slum Dog Millionaire*) etc.

Step 9: The bells and whistles…are you using symbolism, dramatic irony to effect? The dramatic irony in *Gone Girl* is both that the reader knows all about the deception by Part Two but can do little but watch the events unfold. Decide where and how you are going to use it, if so.

Step 10: Write it, then edit, re-edit and edit again…

If it helps, you can set up a spreadsheet a little like the one on the next page, or you can work with a programme like Scrivener.

However you do it, remember to position your inciting incident at the very beginning, the climax at the beginning of act three, after a turning point and a point where the protagonist has gone beyond the point of no return in their quest so transformation and resolution is inevitable as a conclusion.

Some fiction to read for ideas how to plot and structure include:

1. *Dark Matter* by Michelle Paver
2. *Jane Eyre* by Charlotte Bronte
3. *Rebecca* by Daphne du Maurier
4. *The Da Vinci Code* by Dan Brown
5. *Silence of the Lambs* by Thomas Harris
6. *Before I go to Sleep* by S J Watson
7. *Gone Girl* by Gillian Flynn
8. *Skin* by Mo Hayder
9. *Darkly Dreaming* Dexter by Jeff Lindsay
10. *One Day* by David Nichols
11. *Life After Life* by Kate Atkinson
12. *Cloud Atlas* by David Mitchell
13. *The Hunger Games* by Suzanne Collins
14. *The Virgin Suicides* by Jeffrey Eugenides
15. *Possession* by A S Byatt
16. *Tokyo* by Mo Hayder
17. *We Need To Talk About Kevin* by Lionel Shriver

And an example of that plotting table I referred to above is on the next page:

PLOTTING AND STRUCTURING

A useful format to start planning with is:

Ch no:	Timeline/ structure/ POV	Plot point	Notes on plot point: clues &/or info revealed to reader	Character motivation (incl. conflict)	Character development	Motifs and sub-plots (incl. climaxes)	Themes, symbolism and irony etc
1	1935: Nazi Germany	The first hook	The murder, the perpetrat or, the link to 2015...	Blackmail, fear of ruin, hidden Nazi links	Ruthless where family pride concerned – passed on down the line (see later in his grandson).	Greed, fear, malice, ruthless-ness	The golden eagle of Germany, the golden eagle of Rome eg http://www.scots man.com/news/e nvironment/golde n-eagle-symbol-likened-to-nazi-emblem-by-msp-1-3283728
2	2015: Rome	Intro victim's family 80 years on – naively unaware ...	How the 1935 murder links to this family...				
3	2015: London	The other family...					

Chapter 4:
Brilliant Beginnings, Amazing Middles
and Cracking Conclusions

If you've ever read anything about submitting your book to a literary agent you'll know the beginning is the part that everyone insists you have to get right. Of course, that's true – but a brilliant beginning won't carry anyone through a sagging middle or make them recommend a book that has an unsatisfactory ending. A good book needs to sustain a reader's involvement all the way through, so aside from an intriguing plot, dynamic characters, credible dialogue and an astounding denouement, here are some basic ways you can bolster your whole book from beginning to end.

A BRILLIANT BEGINNING

Why is the beginning of a book so important?

Think of the process a reader goes through before choosing to read your book – first they look at the cover and if that appeals, they'll read the blurb on the back. If they're still intrigued, what will they do next? Open it up and read the first page…

Think of the process a literary agent or publisher goes through when being presented with a submission – after scanning the synopsis (more on this in Part 2: PUBLISH), they'll look at the first paragraph, and this is possibly ALL they'll read before deciding whether to devote any more time to it – agents and publishers get hundreds of submissions every week, so yours has to REALLY stand out…

So what will make it stand out, intrigue, and make the reader want to read on?

Opening lines: are the reader's first impression of your book. Think of some of the most memorable first sentences:

"The past is a foreign country..." *The Go-Between* by L P Hartley

"This is the saddest story I have ever heard..." *The Good Soldier: A Tale of Passion* by Ford Maddox Ford

"Lolita, light of my life, fire of my loins..." *Lolita* by Vladimir Nabokov

"It was the best of times, it was the worst of times..." *A Tale of Two Cities* by Charles Dickens

"It is a truth universally known..." *Pride and Prejudice* by Jane Austen

"It was a bright cold day in April, and the clocks were striking 13..." *Nineteen Eighty-Four* by George Orwell

What do they do?

They make you sit up and pay attention.

They make you think.

They make you question.

They make you smile and nod in agreement.

They establish the tone of the book.

They establish the premise of the book.

They evoke mystery.

They evoke surprise.

They evoke curiosity.

They make a promise to be a certain kind of book (and this is where you need to have established your readership well).

They make you want to know more.

Opening lines are iconic, riveting and whimsical. However you start, it has to make the reader want to read on. It also sets the scene for the kind of work you are writing. An exciting opening paves the way for a pacey plot whereas a more reflective start might suggest a more introspective storyline examining characters and their motivations in detail. A novel or longer work of fiction can lead in to the crux of the action over a whole chapter whereas a short story must plunge straight in, setting mood, character and issues within the first paragraph or so. Whichever it is, by the end of it the reader needs to have been hooked and keen to read on.

The first line or sentence is possibly the hardest one to come up with. Many writers (including me) spend endless hopeless hours trying to find exactly the right pitch or format, and it often takes many rewrites to get it anywhere close to something engaging. How long did it take du Maurier to decide on the opening sentence to Rebecca…?

"Last night I dreamt I went to Manderley again…"

Suspense, mystery, a sense of place, the immediate implication that something important happened there, otherwise why would it feature so wistfully in a dream – why, what, when and who was involved? How clever to imply all of that in a mere nine words! How did she do it? I suppose, as with all good writing, she followed some clever rules:

1. Plunge straight in. Put the reader right in the middle of the action.
2. Create a mystery, issue or problem.
3. Don't explain or solve it until you replace it with a worse one.
4. Have a cliff-hanger at the end of the chapter – the 'hook', what happens next…
5. Introduce your main character(s) as quickly as possible – and before secondary ones.
6. Try to keep the reader guessing from the start.
7. Set the mood, tone and style in the opening paragraphs.
8. Edit and rewrite as many times as possible until you feel it is as polished as it can be. Remember, that first line is your reader's first impression – like a smile is a person's.

Plunging straight in works best at the point of change in a character's life. In *Chained Melodies* Tom is about to be released from prison with a decision to make. Add to that the letter and diary which have prompted it, and there are immediately three hooks – the release and what he'll do next, the diary and the decision to make. The first chapter in *Webs* opens with Lily facing the murderer's gun and is immediately followed by being introduced to the unnamed killer afterwards. His thoughts and Lily's, both in first person POV, set the tone of the book – a psychological thriller with a humorous twist. I aimed for mystery and mood as well as hook by the end of the first chapter. *Falling Awake* poses a mystery and an unexpected departure point in the first chapter. The initial hook lies in what is in the strange book of the same name, and why it has such an odd effect on the woman.

I'll admit I always find the first lines the hardest of all to write – the pressure is on to make an indelible impression, especially when trying to convince an agent they might want to read on. Sadly this can tend to make the debut author go over the top in order to grab attention when a gentler approach might have been more in keeping with the writing and subject matter overall. I can only repeat the words of another master in response to this,

"*...to thine own self be true...*" Polonius in *Hamlet*.

In the space of the first sentence – and sometimes in only the first few words – the author is establishing not only the tone of the book but what the book is about. It is the first of many 'hooks' the author will be spreading throughout the book to keep the reader reading on, so consider those first few words well. Read them aloud, read them to someone else, put them aside and look at them again in isolation later, look at them in conjunction with the title, the cover, the book description – do they tell your reader what to expect and lead them to read on? If not, scrap them and start all over again. Those few words are indeed, the most important of the book.

What other strategies can you employ to give your novel an opening buzz?

- Try starting at the end and telling the story in flashback – it adds an intriguing twist if you know the ending but not why it happened.
- Start with the most dramatic scene in the plot.
- Start with a trigger device – someone doesn't want to do something; why?
- Create an atmosphere that lingers; moody, frightening, blissful, or a haunting sense of period if you're writing

historical fiction.

- Start with an overpowering voice – impress the character of the protagonist on the reader with a strong voice or startling dialogue.

However, don't fill the opening chapter with too much information, drama or backstory or the reader may become confused. The danger will then be that they don't read on because they feel overloaded. They do not need to like the characters you introduce in the opening chapter, but they do need to be curious about what happens to them and to like the writing style you employ. It's a little like flirting where less is more; introduce enough to tantalise, but not enough to tell!

AMAZING MIDDLES

Middles have to keep the promise of the opening chapters alive, that's why I will examine next how to avoid the bulging midriff…No, not another dieting attempt, a critical look at the centrepiece of the novel – the middle! Having worked hard at the sprint start and diligently on the startling finish, the main part of the race – the stunning core – remains to be crafted. What do you do to maintain impetus between the bold beginning and the gasping breath at the finish? Maybe the first paragraph of all is the hardest to write, but the middle ones are often the longest, driest, most stumbling and stuck. In fact having finally worked out how to start with a burst and finish with a bounce, I get completely bogged down in between. Here's what to concentrate on to dig/keep yourself out of the mire in the middle.

Pace and plot; that's what.

Pace: is all about timing (obviously), and building the plot to a crescendo, but getting the timing right when doing so is crucial. Unfold it too slowly and you risk losing readers along the way. Allow the denouement to materialise – ta-dah style – too quickly and it feels like someone just burst a whoopie cushion – and the inside **was** wet… Suspense, tension, character development, highs and lows and a few red herrings are all necessary to keep the pace braced. It's a little like a sinus rhythm:

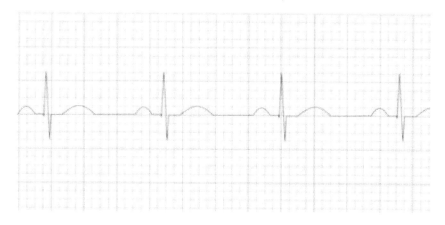

...but don't make it as steady as a heartbeat or the story plods. Make it erratic and surprise your readers. Two or three occasions of semi-climax work to build your readers' anticipatory excitement best (and I'm not talking dirty here). That's why I mentioned climax(es) and anti-climax(es) in plotting and structuring.

Pacey plots: of course the problem with erratic is that it can come across as a series of hiccups making your reader wonder if you've actually lost the plot. Some hiccups I've encountered are:

- Too many flashbacks – flashbacks do run the risk of slowing the story and pace down too much by taking your reader backwards, not forwards.
- Short time spans speed up a story, longer ones extend it. Don't speed through ten years in a 1,000 word piece, but by the same token stretching a few hours over a whole novel can probably only be successfully crafted by the most skilful of writers. *One Day* is a brilliant example of repeat – repeat in a form of flashback – but always driving the plot forward because of what the characters are learning from them.
- If the plot becomes too complex it will become confusing and your reader may well just close the book and leave you to sort it all out without reading to the end.
- Use the middle of the book to allow the characters to develop into rounded people – a useful place to allow the bulging midriff to actually bulge, in fact!

- Layer it – having cross-plot interaction/ layers of the plot or story development increases depth and complexity and improves the quality of the middle.
- Don't get bogged down – and if you do, try a corset…

CLEVER CORSETS TO GET YOUR MIDDLE SQUEEZING OUT EITHER END…

When I get stuck I try to take a step back and revisit the plot and people again to clarify where they're going and why. I have a number of little corset fix-its, such as: *What if?*

Take the characters and plot and try some other possibilities, for example in a murder mystery:

? **What if** Tim murders Kay...

? **What if** Kay disappears, but everyone thinks Kay has been murdered…

? **What if** Tim accuses someone else…

? **What if** someone blackmails Tim…

Try a stream of ideas: take your theme and pick out obstacles, issues and potential turning points:

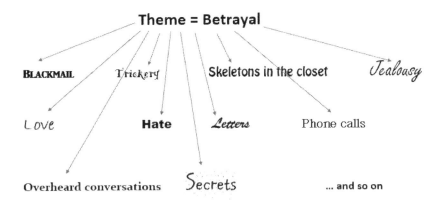

Or create a more visual effect by using the spider diagram format, which is more flexible as you can spin off subsidiary ideas from the main ones, and keep going until you find a series of ideas or issues that you feel could be developed together:

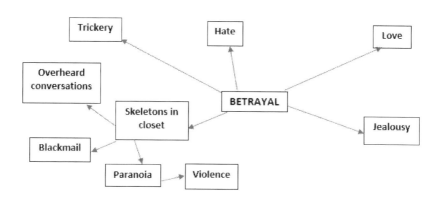

I also like to make sure I have a formal structure to work on to stop the middle ending up in the doldrums. It picks out the main themes, issues and character development points and looks something like this:

Chapter 6	
Main Plotline	Tim realises Kay knows what he has done … etc
Characters involved	Tim
Hooks, denouements or issues	What is the indiscretion?
Character development enabled	Tim's underlying nature – related to whatever the indiscretion is.
Themes or symbols involved	Related to the indiscretion and also to how Tim reacts to Kay finding out – weakness, paranoia, fear, anger, etc.
Chapter 7	
Main Plotline	Kay threatens Tim. She hits him and he retaliates. His ring catches her lip and draws blood. The blood splashes onto the settee cushion and the wall. She leaves angrily telling him he'll be sorry. She

	wants money now or his little indiscretion will find its way to the papers. He follows her downstairs, and although we do not see her going, he will later claim she simply left…
Characters involved	Tim, Kay
Hooks, denouements or issues	Did Kay really leave? What will Tim do next? Accede to the blackmail or not?
Character development enabled	Tim is unable to control his violent temper – leave this open for the reader to wonder later on if Kay really did leave (red herring 1). Kay is manipulative and mercenary.
Themes or symbols involved	Blackmail, betrayal, violence, hate, love (possibly), jealousy (possibly), fear. You may want to pick an image or object to symbolise one or more of these issues and weave it into the plot whenever the issue arises again for layering and depth.
Chapter 8	
Main Plotline	Tim tries to hide the cushion and bloodstains when Joan comes to ask if he knows where Kay has gone off to so suddenly…
Characters etc.	etc.
Hooks, denouements or issues	
Character development enabled	
Themes or symbols involved	

Somewhere in the gamut of lucky white rabbits you've pulled out of your magician's hat will be the string to pull the corset tight, and hey presto! You have a trim, slim and sleek middle, with a climax arriving just nicely before the end of the second act…

CRACKING CONCLUSIONS

Creating a cracking conclusion is what seals the deal for your book. To be satisfying and appropriate an ending needs to address the story goal and it must make emotional and logical sense, whilst still being surprising. And it needs to connect to the novel as a whole so that, in hindsight, it seems inevitable; a tall order, but easily fulfilled if you have in mind a simple plot development tool called story dynamics.

First, establish the overall dynamic of your plot; will it end happily, unhappily, or somewhere between the two?

A word of warning here: be careful when deciding whether the story goal has been achieved as there is a difference between story goal and the theme of the book. The theme of the book is an idea, concept or principle. The story goal is what the protagonist wants to achieve, or the problem they have to solve – there is a difference, so answer the right question. Keep in mind too that there may be goals to achieve on different levels – remember in plotting and structure (Chapter 3) there were levels of plot development – some obvious, some underlying; internalised? An obvious goal could be finding a lost diary. An underlying one could be to face the contents of it because the protagonist knows they are going to be upsetting/ turn their view of the past upside down which in turn may change their beliefs and principles.

Story endings generally fall into four types:

- Comedy: (a happy ending) where the protagonist achieves their goal.
- Tragedy: (an unhappy ending) where the protagonist fails to achieve their goal.
- Tragi-Comedy: (personal triumph) where the protagonist fails to achieve the goal but the failure turns out to be beneficial.
- Comi-Tragedy: (personal tragedy) where the protagonist achieves their goal but it turns out to be a bad thing.

It looks like this as a flow chart:

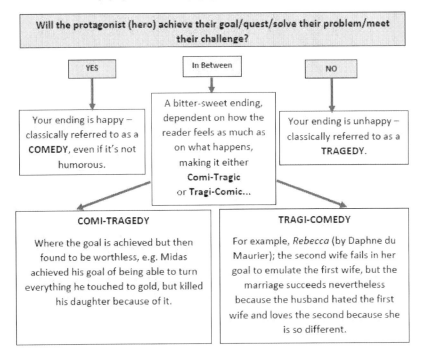

Happy/ Unhappy or In Between?

Will the protagonist (hero) achieve their goal/quest/solve their problem/meet their challenge?

YES — Your ending is happy – classically referred to as a **COMEDY**, even if it's not humorous.

In Between — A bitter-sweet ending, dependent on how the reader feels as much as on what happens, making it either **Comi-Tragic** or **Tragi-Comic...**

NO — Your ending is unhappy – classically referred to as a **TRAGEDY**.

COMI-TRAGEDY
Where the goal is achieved but then found to be worthless, e.g. Midas achieved his goal of being able to turn everything he touched to gold, but killed his daughter because of it.

TRAGI-COMEDY
For example, *Rebecca* (by Daphne du Maurier); the second wife fails in her goal to emulate the first wife, but the marriage succeeds nevertheless because the husband hated the first wife and loves the second because she is so different.

Second, decide how the story goal will affect or involve the other characters. Almost every character in the book will have a stake in the story goal, as well as the protagonist. A single problem might affect a number of people – for example in a war story, one man's decision to be a conscientious objector may affect both those going to war and those staying home and cause others to question their principles where war and killing are concerned too. In a murder mystery, catching the killer will affect the safety of others – and may make or break reputations for police departments. In epic quest stories like *The Lord of the Rings*, the success or failure of destroying the ring will have a dramatic outcome on all the other characters – who are also either trying to destroy or gain control over the ring too. Romantic novels such as *Pride and Prejudice* look at the problem of making a good marriage, and society's strictures where unwise decisions are made for not only Elizabeth Bennet but her sisters too.

Having determined the outcome of the story goal for the protagonist, determine the outcome for the secondary characters too because when you bring the protagonist to their climax and resolution, so the story goal should be resolved across all strands.

WAIT! But you said in Chapter 3 that not all the story strands need to be fully resolved. Aren't you now contradicting yourself?

Yes – and no.

Yes, story goals need to be resolved, but the story strands need not – after all, life goes on, doesn't it? In concluding a story and a story goal, the goal is determined. It's either achieved or not achieved – with the four possible endings outlined above flowing from it – but it does not necessarily end the character's story. In fact, when you finish reading a book, the characters *should* live on in your head, and so should the possibility of their future. John Green's *The Fault in Our Stars* makes precisely this point when terminally ill Hazel's quest to find out what happened to the characters in the book she has so admired is left unfulfilled. She realises, after Augustus dies, that it's not what happens in the future that counts, but what happens in the 'now', because the 'now' makes the future. Her conflict is not to hurt anyone who loves her because one day soon she is going to die. She learns through loving Augustus that being hurt is inevitable, but the joy of loving that precedes the pain of losing is worth taking that chance. We do not know what happens to Hazel – when or if she dies – only that she's satisfied with her choices, but she and her choices live on even as the book ends.

The resolution to a story goal is always preceded by the greatest climax in the book; the biggest game changer of all – to both the situation and in the protagonist's character. To make that both satisfying and credible, the change that occurs has to be entirely in character for your now renewed and transformed protagonist, and that can only happen if you actually live your protagonist. Maybe that's why writing is so therapeutic? Because often we are living through conflicts and challenges that affect us too.

Chapter 5: Characterisation and Dialogue

So now you have a plot you need characters to make it happen. Novel writers basically fall into two camps. There are *plotters*; those who plan their novels from beginning to end before they even write the first word. And there are *pantsers* (or *pantsters*), who simply sit down and start writing on the basis that their idea is good enough to allow them to figure it out as they go along. The name, *pantsers*, comes from the allusion to writing by the seat of your pants, and there's a book about writing this way that's worth having a look at called *Take off your Pants* by Libbie Hawker. I'm a hybrid – I do both; I think that a combination of the two is the best approach and I'll explain why as we progress on through characterisation. Whichever camp you opt for it's still important that each of your major characters fulfils an important dramatic function within the story, and therefore, of course, the plot.

So what is a dramatic function? It's a juxtaposition of qualities, characteristics, conflicts or challenges that force a character or a situation to move on; it creates the plot, and the vehicles for moving the plot along are the characters. Therefore those qualities, characteristics, conflicts or challenges need to be embodied or personified within the characters themselves. This is why there are always archetypal characters that can be found within any novel – even those where the author hasn't intended writing an archetypal character. Some writers start the writing process by creating a set of characters they find interesting, putting them into situations or confronting them with problems that force them to interact and change and out of this a plot grows.

The **characters**, in fact, create the plot. This is what a *pantser* would do. The problem with this is that you can lose sight of where the plot is going – and the characters – and end up with non-essential characters and plot elements which actually detract from the overall plot, rather than move it forward, or fail to include elements of dramatic function which are actually necessary. Others start with a topic they want to consider or a message they want to convey, and create characters who can explore and illustrate it through their roles. Again, this can cause problems because the central character needs to be defined and the dramatic functions of the other characters established by reference to them. Fixing on an issue or a message may stereotype or create too narrow a focus, and that may also limit the credibility and effectiveness of both characters and plot. Either as a plotter or a pantser, you can avoid this by doing a little bit of planning first' by fixing your main character and considering the dramatic functions of all the other characters in relation to them. And this is why all great novels have archetypal characters in them; because archetypal characters perform dramatic functions. So here we go with the archetypal character list.

ARCHETYPAL CHARACTERS AND THE DRAMATIC FUNCTIONS THEY PERFORM

Archetypal characters are essentially stereotypical ways a writer can portray an aspect of a character and assign it a dramatic function. However, whilst they are stereotypical, remember, they do not need to appear stereotypical. We all have some of the stereotypical in us as real, living and breathing people, simply because it represents the basic elements of character – the humour, as Chaucer and his peers would have called it. But we're not composed of only one stereotype or element, and put those elements together and we create interesting propositions, as well as people.

- The **Protagonist** is THE main character in the plot. Their function is to pursue a goal, consider a problem, and/or face a challenge. Set against them the
- **Antagonist,** who tries to create the road blocks for them, making them avoid, reconsider, or anticipate failure, and you have two big characters and a big conflict; perfect for dramatic function *and* plotting.
- There's also the **Guardian** or mentor; whose dramatic function is to assist and encourage when the protagonist weakens. There is also likely to be an
- **Underminer** – representing the protagonist's weakness, confusion or failing will-power in direct conflict with the Guardian, so dramatic tension exists between them.

- **Logic** – or reason, self-control and will-power provide the impetus for the protagonist to move forward. Looking at a favourite movie series of mine, Spock is the archetype of logic in *Star Trek*, compared to Dr McCoy who is the archetype of...
- **Emotion;** as is Ron in *Harry Potter*, against Hermione's Logic. Setting logic and emotion against each other creates not only external conflicts but internal ones too. It can be used to define relationships and people, people within relationships and people as relationships – have a look at *Pride and Prejudice* – Mr Darcy is logic and Elizabeth is emotion, yet becoming gradually tempered by logic – the protagonist caught between the two parallels and only growing as a character when she learns how to combine the two.
- Finally, there's generally a **Support** – a close friend, or a sidekick or a belief/principle, which keeps the protagonist going when all else appears to be failing and countering that,
- Also a **Sceptic**, inserted with the aim of challenging the support – thereby setting up conflict again.

There are no rules as to which characters need to play which roles, and by turning expectation on its head, you actually create more credible archetypal characters. For example, nowhere does it say that a guardian role needs to be played by an adult. Maybe it could even be a child looking out for their parent? An archetype needn't be limited to one function either – how about combining one or more? For example how about a temptress who uses logic to lure the protagonist off the straight and narrow – if you've read my Patchwork People series, you'll find a ready candidate for that role in Margaret. Try dividing up dramatic functions in unusual ways to create a character-driven novel where there is no predictability at all in your archetypal characters, even though they embody stereotypes.

Here's an example:

Rachel (the Protagonist) is faced with a difficult situation at work. She knows Terry (the Antagonist), the MD of Pushy Press Campaigns (PPC), has been steadily stealing customers in preparation for breaking away and setting up his own PR business, but he has also asked Rachel to join him and the opportunity would be incredible. It culminates in a series of arguments, the last of which sees him storming off angrily, leaving Rachel confused and with loyalties torn because Terry is also her lover (Emotion). It challenges everything she ever thought about loyalty – in love and in business.

Louise overhears one of their arguments. She's an old friend (Support), who's already left PPC to make her own way, but works as a consultant with PPC from time to time and is well-respected by everyone. After Louise drops hints that she knows there's trouble in paradise, Rachel eventually asks her advice before she decides whether to side with her employer or her lover. Louise tells Rachel she needs to weigh up her principles (Logic) against her future – after all, this is about her love life as well as her career.

However, what Rachel doesn't know until Harry (the CEO of PPC) tells her one evening when they're both working late is that he thinks Louise (now also an Underminer) could be secretly planning a takeover of PPC but needs Terry out of the way for it to succeed. Whatever Rachel does – as long it's *something* dramatic – will polarise the situation, so either Terry leaves early, undermining PPC, or Terry is fired, also undermining PPC. They discuss the situation and Rachel takes David's advice (Guardian, Logic); to remain true to her principles because overall this will keep her in a job whatever Terry does in the long run.

Rachel is about to go with her principles but sacrifice her personal life when she finds some emails between Terry and David on Terry's laptop when he forgets to close it down one evening. It seems that Louise and David might also be secretly having an affair and that's how Louise has obtained enough information to be able to mount her takeover bid. (The laptop is the Sceptic, but so is Terry.) Louise tells the board of PPC everything – now not knowing who she can trust and it all becomes clear – it's been a test to see how loyal Rachel is as there's a seat on the Board coming up and the other board members wanted to know if she was the right candidate for it. Terry deliberately fed Rachel the challenge and also left the emails open for her to read to prompt her to make her final decision. She's given the seat, but has to agree with Terry that their relationship is not perhaps as strong or truthful as they thought it was – Terry shouldn't have used it to put her in an impossible situation, and she acknowledges that ultimately she chose her career over love.

Rachel is the Protagonist but also her own Underminer and Sceptic.

Terry represents both the Antagonist and Emotion and eventually also Sceptic.

Louise represents Support, Logic and Underminer.

Harry is Guardian, Logic and Underminer.

It's a comi-tragedy, with characters taking on various archetypes to meet the function of their role in the plot. Twisting the roles and interchanging them also provides intrigue, red herrings (remember them from the chapter on plotting) and rounded characters because motives are quite often mixed, confused and mistaken – even in real life. And if you write it and it makes a fortune – please don't let me know!

Jung went even deeper into archetypal characters – naming twelve possible variations, (Jung's twelve archetypal characters: http://www.uiltexas.org/files/capitalconference/Twelve_Character_Archet ypes.pdf), and some TV characters are built around even more layers and possibilities (TV Tropes archetypal characters: http://tvtropes.org/pmwiki /pmwiki.php/Main/ArchetypalCharacter), but I think the eight above are wide open enough to be able to insert whatever layers you like in them to give them light and shade. So let's look at light and shade – making characters not only take on their dramatic role but making them credible. Now this may seem like it's back to front to you – look at what you make a character do or represent before you describe what they look like? Not at all. It's a package, but it's generally better to decide what the core of your package contains before covering it with an outer coating. Starting at the core, there are a whole gamut of personality traits your characters could have. Here's a process you could use to build up your characters to create 4D people – 4D because they not only have to work physically, mentally, emotionally, as a dramatic function(s), but also in time and space too. You have a past, so do they. You have hopes and dreams, paranoia and fears; so do they. You have an intended future. So do they: 4D.

The first point of departure: get inside their head…

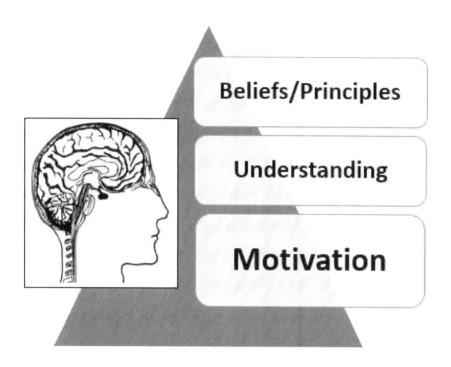

What is going on in your characters' heads?
What do they want to do?
What do they believe in?
What does good or bad/ right or wrong mean for them?
How do they understand their world and the situation they are in?
How does that affect their behaviour?
What is each person's past?

When developing a character, action is born out of emotional response, tempered by their belief system, ultimately resulting in the formation of their personality. Characters don't just suddenly appear, completely formed, at the point of their first entry into your plot. They should have been alive in a 'world' existing in your imagination right up to the point they first enter the plot; their backstory – what is it?

Fears, flaws and failings are perfect examples of the kind of things you could put in your characters' heads, as well as past history (memories), hopes and imperfect perceptions (basic misunderstandings leading to mistaken beliefs).

Moving on to the heart: how do they feel?

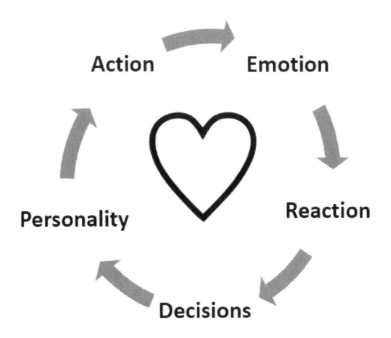

Emotion creates responses, then reactions, then decisions about how the character is going to behave when that particular emotion is next experienced. That ultimately forms the type of personality they have – optimistic, pessimistic, cynical, naïve, kind, cruel and so on. It may also encourage specific behaviour – a little like with Pavlov's dogs, so perfect for setting up your protagonist with an emotional blind spot or behaviour pattern which either makes it inevitable s/he will or won't behave in a particular way but also that allows you, the writer, to set them the challenge of NOT responding that way; the challenge or conflict that will be the catalyst to moving them on.

Then on to the gut – their instinctive reaction – and for this you will need to put our character into a situation to test them out. Think of the best or the worst situation you can think of for them and imagine how this person would instinctively respond to it?

Here's Rachel reacting:

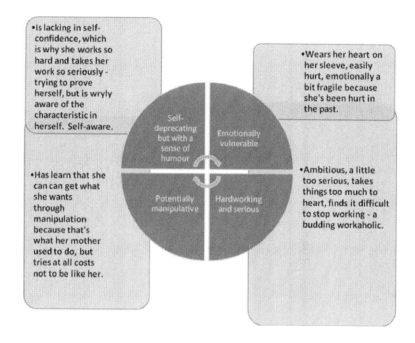

Poor Rachel from the PPC plot is a little lacking in the lighter elements of personality, but if she's lacking in humour how will she react to finding out she's been fooled all along?

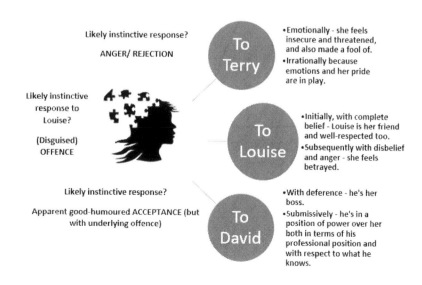

For Rachel, I've created a little bit of backstory to explain her personality traits and they will inform her reactions to hearing from the various people involved that she has been tricked.

Why is feeling that she's been fooled one of the worst situations she could be in?

Because she's lacking in self-belief, emotionally vulnerable, has clearly had a faulty relationship /family background with her mother, works too hard and takes herself too seriously and this situation set career against personal contentment – when she's been let down emotionally in the past.

How will she feel overall? Foolish, relieved, surprised, annoyed, deceived, betrayed, confused, uncertain – and all of these emotions will fuel her reactions. Furthermore, the character of Rachel – if we wanted to take her on into another story – has just collected up yet another bit of past history to reinforce her specific future behaviour patterns; emotionally inarticulate, manipulated as a child and now also manipulated as a woman, she has just learnt a powerful lesson in manipulation and control; what will she do with it? She could become a wonderfully complex character with paranoias, phobias, potentially fatal vulnerabilities and possibly the motives for revenge or becoming one amazingly evil bitch in response. Perhaps *I'll* even write this character sometime in the future!

The range of motivations someone might be driven by are numerous, as are their emotional responses, and physical characteristics, but having determined the core of the person, you may find you want to tailor the outer appearance to imply the inner one. I imagine Rachel would be neat, pretty, well-dressed, immaculate (the hard-worker), small, dark, with somewhat angular features (sharp and over-reactive), quietly spoken (self-deprecatory, emotionally vulnerable) – potentially the perfect victim turned revenge artiste …

Some physical considerations for your characters:

Gender
Height
Build
Weight – under/ over or just right
Clothing
Hairstyle/ hair colour

Facial features
Attitude
Posture
Tattoos
Accent
Hands (you can tell a lot about someone from their hands and nails)
Smell
Age
Do they suffer from any specific ailments?

Some cultural/social origin/ backstory considerations for your characters:

Job
Addictions – drinking, smoking, food, coffee, sex…
Time period born into?
What do they eat/ drink?
Where do they live?
Are they wealthy/poor/in between?
Well educated or not?
Cultural origin
Social origin
Single/ married. In a relationship/ happy on their own/ unhappy on their own?
Do they have children?

Personality characteristics/ backstory considerations for your characters

What are their hobbies?
Who are their friends/ enemies?
What are their ambitions/ hopes/ dreams?
What motivates them?
Have they suffered hard times?
Is there something in their past that has a major effect on them – good or bad?
Who/what would they like to be?
What kind of holidays would they enjoy?
Have they made sacrifices?

How do they cope with stress/ disappointment/ failure?

What is their inner world like, compared to their outer word?

Are they sane and balanced or disturbed?

Victim, rescuer or persecutor?

If they had to confess one thing, what would it be?

What are their quirks?

What is unusual about them?

What are their flaws?

What are their worst fears?

What is the worst situation you could put them into?

Are they falling into a stereotype or a cliché (be careful with the latter)

And finally, here's a list of character traits to get you started. There are many more – try a spider diagram or mind mapping to think of more or delve into a thesaurus.

HAPPY	OPEN	DOMINATING	MANIPULATIVE
CHARMING	RELAXED	MEAN	UNFAITHFUL
FRIENDLY	CALM	UNKIND	VICIOUS
KIND	FUN	SPITEFUL	SLY
POSITIVE	LOYAL	PETTY	PATRONISING
WELCOMING	CARING	CHILDISH	CONTROLLING
CONFIDENT	SINCERE	SARCASTIC	SELFISH
SKILFUL	HONEST	INSOLENT	POSSESSIVE
SWEET	SMOOTH	ARROGANT	BOSSY
GENEROUS	THOUGHTFUL	THOUGHTLESS	SHARP
HUMOROUS	QUIET	LOUD	CUTTING
SUPPORTIVE	UNDERSTANDING	BRASH	INSULTING
HARD WORKING	GOOD-TEMPERED	SWAGGERING	SMARMY
GENTLE	HELPFUL	AVARICIOUS	FRIVOLOUS
LOVING	SELF-DEPRECATING	GREEDY	WASTEFUL
SPARKLING	PROVOCATIVE	HOSTILE	VAIN
KNOWLEGEABLE	NEEDY	BULLYING	MENACING
ORGANISED	NEUROTIC	VULGAR	ABRUPT
NON-JUDGEMENTAL	SHARING	ANGRY	IRRITABLE

SOME WAYS OF GETTING STARTED

- Sometimes a good way to start is to take an image of an unknown that could resemble a character you want to write about and use your visual response to write about them.
- When writing about a character, consider all the senses –

how do they smell, sound, look, feel? Think of the texture of their skin, the impression their clothes give, the vibrancy or maybe even the lacklustre aura which surrounds them.

- Look at the people around you. Don't write about them but consider the personality traits you see in them – how could you combine them to create a dramatic composite?
- Don't forget to create your character's past as well as their present. 4D.
- Don't be stereotypical within the stereotype – a vicious bully could actually live within an ostensibly charming old lady or sweet little girl.
- Don't make them perfect. No one is perfect and a character is all the more credible – and memorable – because of their flaws and failings.
- The outer casing is important but the inner core more so. It's the inner core that will force the action, so always reveal it through their behaviour, not by telling your readers.
- Always push your characters beyond their boundaries – ask that question they least want to hear and write their response in their behaviour.

Five-minute fix: *try this for getting used to getting into character:*

- Set up a situation for yourself – anything will do; a walk in the park on a Sunday afternoon in autumn would be good enough.
- Now set up a range of characters – and make them from one extreme to another, for example:

  - Granny, 67 and delighted to spend the afternoon with her family, a bit bossy – the matriarch.
  - Mum, doesn't get on too well with granny but puts up with it for the sake of peace. Would rather be watching a weepy off Netflix and eating chocolate.
  - Teenager daughter, hates this kind of thing – and texting has been banned for the afternoon because Granny will comment on it otherwise.
  - Six-year-old; the baby of the family – can't wait to kick

all the falling leaves around.
- You can even add in the dog, if you like – who knows what goes on in a dog's head?

- Now write a paragraph about the afternoon experience in each character's POV (point of view). Read them aloud afterwards – forgetting the afternoon outing itself, have you captured the essence of the character experiencing it?

Pantsers write like this all the time – and so do I, at times. Having created my basic structure and knowing the main personality traits and archetypal character formats of my characters, the writing works best if you write in character. It may also mean that sometimes your characters will surprise you and do something completely outside of the plot, but then that's when it's really authentic because your character has come alive and taken charge – now you're really doing what they'd do and your writing just moved up another notch!

Chapter 6:
Setting – a Sense of Time and Place

"The world only exists in your eyes – your conception of it. You can make it as big or as small as you want to." – F. Scott Fitzgerald

Think of setting as part of your novel's skeleton. The most essential parts of the skeleton are the skull, because it houses the brain – the characters – and therefore drives the story forward. Then come the legs, moving the story along; the plot, in other words. In between, however, there has to be something to connect the two; the spine; or setting – the world your characters live in and move through. Without setting your story will lack depth and credibility. How can anyone live in a vacuum? Setting, however, has to be drawn finely and with a clever touch so it neither overpowers, nor under-delivers. It can be used to enhance the portrayal of characters and support plot structure, but it has to be REAL to the reader to do so.

Let's start by defining 'setting'. I've expanded a little in the chapter heading – a sense of place and time, and that probably covers setting in its most basic format. It's the where and when of your story, but that doesn't just mean the geography and the date, it encompasses the mood, the history, the social and cultural expectations of the inhabitants of this particular world, their economy and their traditions – whew! Did you expect to be writing a sociological epic? No – but you can recreate something like it quite easily if you bear in mind the following when determining your setting. The setting you choose is not only describable in physical terms, it's also at the heart of how and why your characters do what they do. It relates to and with them. It's a real world for them and therefore it has to include all the elements above. It also creates atmosphere – the mood of the story.

Time, history and local customs also play a huge part in evoking a particular kind of mood – think of that old favourite film *The Wicker Man* (now translated into book form). The whole mood of the story was set through the locale and the local customs. Or how about Sherlock Holmes? Or even Harry Potter? These are very obvious uses of time, place and tradition/customs but elements of the world the character moves through can also be used to inform the reader of their personality, motivations and conflicts. For instance, a harsh climate can create a suitably stark backdrop to a plot where the character is forced into making equally stark choices in their life, whereas a romantic novel may revolve around a softer setting.

Q: So how to create setting?

"What has fascinated me for a long time now is the relationship between a locale and the lives lived there, the relationship between the terrain and the feelings it can call out of us, the way a certain place can provide you with grounding, location, meaning, can bear upon the dreams you dream, can shape your view of history, sometimes your sense of self." – James D Houston

A: Live it from your soul. And make it possible for your readers to live it too.

Start with the six Ws:

- Where is the story?
- When is the story?
- What's the weather/climate like?
- What are the social/community conditions like?
- What is the landscape like?
- What special details make it vivid?

Here's an extract from my book *Patchwork Man* that picks out all of those themes, introducing the protagonist as a child, and the plot point that made him a man with a patchwork past:

"It was 1959 and I was nine, the day everything changed. Nine, and puny. The aftermath of the Second World War was plain in my rationed frame and our meagre lifestyle, and the Croydon of then was a bomb-

crumbled crater of dilapidated buildings and open spaces, perfect for kids to disappear in when they should be somewhere else. I can still remember it as if it were yesterday. I ran into the room, all skinned knees and flailing elbows, nose running from being outside in the crisp cold of early autumn. I recall even now hastily wiping it on the sleeve of my jumper so Ma wouldn't chide me, and how the snot made a slimy snail trail. It sparkled in the morning sunlight, like someone had woven magic into the jumper's holed and matted dereliction. I remember that almost more clearly than what the woman was saying."

Each of the six Ws is covered in that one paragraph. It is the base line for the rest of the novel, and its theme of hidden poverty and hidden lives. This is the process I followed:

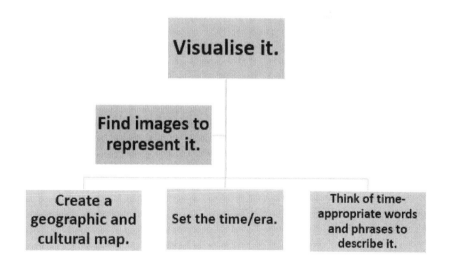

Let's think first what this setting looks like…

Visualising it: most people find it easier to understand something when they see it so why not start the whole process of defining setting with an image? Visualising your setting is also particularly important when building a world your readers may not know. Your readers may not know well-known places like London, or New York or Paris if they've never been there, so your word picture needs to create the experience for them too.

But what if none of your readers have ever been to any of the settings in your book because they don't actually exist? Obviously that will be the case if you are writing fantasy, sci-fi, supernatural or dystopian fiction, but it may also apply if you are writing about another fictitious 'real world' place too – a place in your imagination but not actually on the world map. Now you will have to create from scratch, but you can still draw on real places to unveil fictional new ones.

For example, post-apocalyptic London would have the same geographical features as the London of now, yet it would also be very different if all travel and communication networks were down. Take the visual London you know and superimpose on it the effects of no internet, radio, TV, phones, trains, cars, tubes, buses or planes.

- Everyone would travel on foot or by bike – or perhaps horseback. What would thousands of horses in London do to the state of the streets? Where would they be kept? How? Would it be a privilege to keep a horse? A mark of social status? Would windows and doors be barricaded? Or would doors be open and left unlocked like they were in the war eras? Would people congregate in some areas and avoid others? Would gangs take over and how would that affect the appearance of the city?
- What would the atmosphere be in *different* parts of the city? Would the upwardly mobile and less so merge and simply become one city where everyone was simply trying to survive?
- Would the atmosphere of the city change and become threatening, or more relaxed?
- How would having to communicate by word of mouth or sending a letter change the way the society worked, the way people gathered or didn't gather? How would you know where anyone was at any time – or get away/ get help if the situation was unsafe?
- And how would we speak? Text speak would be gone – or would it? Would there be more 'shorthand', 'signing', slang? Would there be a special language to barter in if movement of goods was a problem?

This is an example of how mapping out your setting – even down to creating a map of the location – is essential, both socially, culturally, politically and geographically; love it or hate it, George R R Martin's *Game of Thrones* series is a perfect example of an exquisitely formed imaginary world.

Your invented setting may be a composite of many places you've known. Combine images to create your own brave new world – Tumblr and Pinterest are excellent for images you can use, but do beware if you are setting your story's world in a REAL place that you DO know the area you're describing. Locals will take exception if you get it wrong so research is another essential here; more of that in Chapter 8.

Let's look at timing next.

Once you've visualised your setting, place it in a historical context.

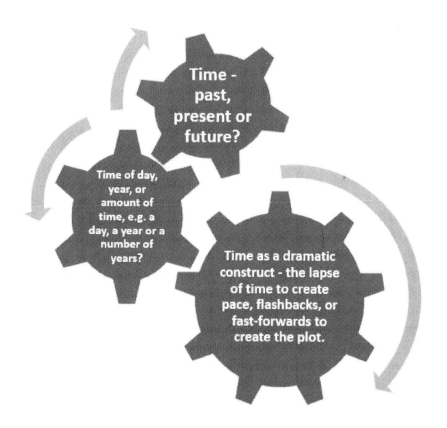

Time can be used in lots of ways to progress both the plot and flesh out the character:

- **Time the plotter** – time can be used to create pace or conversely to slow the pace. Set your book over just twenty-four hours and you can up the ante, and for example, have a detective racing against time to find a killer. Or you could stretch a story over a life time – *One Day* by David Nicholls does this very effectively. *The Curious Case of Benjamin Button* by F. Scott Fitzgerald puts the whole process in reverse but still tells a life story.

- **Time the character definer** – try flashback or fast forward to demonstrate what your character did/knew or how they were at one point in time, and compare it to now. It isn't the plot in a snapshot, but it is a character definer. It also allows you to set up the character's motivations, associations with specific localities and turning points that may have already occurred but which will have an impact later on too. Be careful with flashback or fast forward though – readers can get confused if you don't make sure when this part of the plot is taking place that it is absolutely clear or it can throw them out of the story instead of further drawing them in.

- **Time the mood-maker** – historical settings are the obvious example of this. But historical time is also a character definer – what would characters do five, fifty, a hundred or five hundred years into the past or the future? It may be very different from now because the economic, social and cultural situations of the times would be very different too and they would dictate to some extent what a character could do. Having an illegitimate child would have been frowned on fifty years ago, complete ruin a hundred years ago but barely remarked on five years ago, or now. In the future – who knows? It might be THE way required by society then as in Aldous Huxley's *Brave New World*. Time may therefore also determine a character's motivations and conflicts.

ON TO SOME WORD GAMES TO DESCRIBE SETTING

Pick the core word or phrase that describes the setting you have chosen and mind map to gather together all the other words that are going to form the vocabulary to describe it.

Here's my example; Croydon, UK – the setting for part of my *Patchwork Man*...

What do I know about it?

Well, partly from my own family associations and childhood, and partly from research I had this: *dilapidated.*

More research gave me what the place was like in 1959 and it built in layers too something like this.

Dilapidated place after the war, many buildings bombed and not yet rebuilt.

Post-war society and the Welfare State still getting established - many children still slipped through the net.

Wrecked places to hide and partially demolished areas were children's playgrounds.

Truanting not controlled and families still too large; birth control not fully practised yet .

"...a bomb-crumbled crater of dilapidated buildings and open spaces, perfect for kids to disappear in when they should be somewhere else..."

Eventually the ideas and associated themes brought me the words to make that one sentence, but words are not enough when dealing with setting, and neither is straightforward description. Because setting is the spinal column linking the characters in the skull of your book skeleton and the legs that take the plot forward, it has to be both a conduit and a support. It has to come alive whilst not taking over. Let's go back to my paragraph describing the Croydon Kenny Juss knew in 1959. I used not only words and phrases spinning off of themes and background research, I also used words and phrases to create empathy and mood.

"It was 1959 and I was nine, the day everything changed. Nine, and puny. **The aftermath of the Second World War was plain** **in my rationed** **frame and our meagre lifestyle,** *and the Croydon of then was a* **bomb-** **crumbled crater of dilapidated buildings and open spaces, perfect for** **kids to disappear in when they should be somewhere else.** *I can still remember it as if it were yesterday. I ran into the room,* **all skinned knees** **and flailing elbows,** *nose running from being outside in the crisp cold of early autumn. I recall even now* **hastily wiping it on the sleeve of my** **jumper** *so Ma wouldn't chide me, and how the snot made a slimy snail trail.* **It sparkled in the morning sunlight, like someone had woven** **magic into the jumper's holed and matted dereliction. I remember that** **almost more clearly than what the woman was saying."**

I told a little bit, but I showed much more.

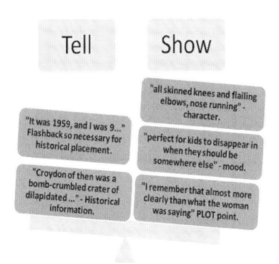

Although the paragraph describes the setting and the time, it also sets the mood, introduces the main character and defines how they were before a plot point occurs and sets up the plot point itself. Here, the plot point is Lawrence/ Kenny remembering the specific event in his past that lead him to the children's home and then to a life half-hidden. However, the balance is tilted towards *showing* what Kenny Juss and his world of then was like; setting a mood as well as a scene. The telling is purely for historical placement. The paragraph falls within a flashback therefore it is has to be clearly established so the reader isn't confused. It establishes an essential point on the time line of Kenny's life.

SHOW not TELL will be reiterated over and over again in any writing-themed discussion. The aim of a good book is to create the sense of what is happening as much as to narrate the facts. It is far more empathetic to enable the reader to feel what the character is feeling for themselves than be told about it. Showing is achieved by putting yourself in the same situation in your imagination as you've placed the character in – so what do you feel? More importantly:

What do you see?
What do you hear?
What do you smell?
If you are touching something, how does that feel?
Can you taste anything?

We experience everything through our senses and our brain translates those sensations to a response – emotion, reaction, thought and decision. SHOW how your character feels or responds by showing what their senses are telling them right at that moment. I could have said *"the snot on my jumper was silvery and shiny, and my jumper full of holes"*, but it wouldn't have had the same impact as, *"It sparkled in the morning sunlight, like someone had woven magic into the jumper's holed and matted dereliction."* You have a window instead into a nine year-old's mind as well as being made aware exactly how close to the poverty line this particular child is.

Think of all the sensations you could experience, for example:

And so on, with as many words as you can think of for all five senses. Use them to breathe life into your characters' senses as they describe the setting they are in, and do the same with any narrative vehicle you use to tell the story. And that leads nicely on to the point of view (POV) of the setting.

Hey – wait a minute, how can a setting have a POV?

Well, the setting itself doesn't but who describes the setting? Whoever is narrating the story at any given time, hence the setting's POV is the POV and voice of the narrator of the moment. Remember:

- Everyone reacts differently to a place – think about the places your friends love but you hate, or vice versa. You can use those differences to create mood, demonstrate character differences and conflicts, plot catalysts, drama and hooks.
- Settings can trigger emotions too. Supposing your protagonist once had a polarising argument with someone close to them in a particular place, which has caused them to feel uneasy or angry when there in the future. Years later put them in the same place and a similar situation and basic psychology alone will manipulate the outcome, making

them edgy, uneasy, argumentative, and anticipating the worst. Their reactions are influenced by what happened there once before. Maybe the setting even defines how they will react simply because of what it represents to them and the emotional response it causes in them. They will also see the place in a certain way, coloured by their feelings about it, whereas a different character with no emotional attachment to the place – or maybe a good emotional attachment – will see it in a completely different light. Maybe that alone will spark disagreement? Two – or maybe many – different setting points of view are therefore possible using different narrators.

- Setting can also be used to enhance a character's inner conflict, which in turn will have cause and effect in relation to the setting, the character and the plot. Use it to create drama, for example in the example above, if you staged the confrontation between two conflicting characters in a setting which had an emotional attachment for one of them, and it is busy, loud, bustling, and distracting, an additional layer of tension is added to an already stressful situation by the nature of the setting. Tempers are fraying, but the atmosphere is tense too, so they fray even quicker.

Some essential DOs and DON'Ts with setting are:

- **DO** tailor your setting content to the plot. The plot always needs to take precedence so **DON'T** bombard readers with enormous amounts of setting description so they miss the impact of the plot point.
- **DO** drop readers through a hole in the page into your character's world – immerse them, in other words, but **DON'T** forget to move them along once in it. The beauty of a summer's evening may be written in enchanting prose but it does need to be leading somewhere, plot or character-wise.
- **DO** focus on what is important and **DON'T** include a plethora of unnecessary detail simply because you've researched it beautifully or you happen to know all about it and it would be a shame not to impart your knowledge.

Yes, books do teach but only as an adjunct to the theme of the book.

- **DO** use the landscape to create action within the plot but **DON'T** use the landscape to simply jump around in, thinking that is creating action. Racing from one place to another is simply moving. You want your characters to move around – within their emotions, their situation of challenge and within their world as it refines and changes.
- **DO** allow characters to interact with the setting to create mood – a gloomy twilight may foreshadow a dark night of the soul or the arrival of fireflies; it all depends on the plot of course, but **DON'T** use the character to describe the setting, use the character's reactions to SHOW the setting. Here is Lawrence – as a child known as Kenny Juss – in my Patchwork series, coming to a decision in a place he calls 'nowhere':

"Nowhere wasn't a real place. It was the idea I associated the place with – Wimbledon Common. The uncultivated expanse of tree and scrub on the edge of the city – not manicured like Hyde or Green Park, but lush and natural, and for me, redolent as much of solitude as calm – what I needed most now. The only time its all-encompassing peace had been destroyed had been when Margaret and I had come across a lone piper deep in the centre of it once on one of our walks. The only time too we'd been in mutual concord other than to propel my career forward. That Margaret seemed a life-time away from the one who'd been leading me by the nose recently, although not on that day. That day she was virtually as she was the last time I'd seen her, only a day ago.

Presumably the piper had been practising for a concert or recital. We didn't ask. The mournful wail of the bagpipes rapidly dispersed wildlife and humankind alike at the time. No peace on the common that day.

'Nowhere,' Margaret had said.

'Nowhere that I want to be right now!' I'd agreed, steering us onto the path leading off the common and back to the car.

'No, the piece is called "Nowhere",' she replied, impatiently. 'It's usually a strings arrangement. Unusual for the pipes.' I raised my eyebrows in mock tribute but ignored her inclination to linger. We found the tree on the way back because I took a wrong turning on one of the circuitous pathways in my impatience to escape.

So nowhere was here, where the Margaret I'd thought I knew wasn't. And indeed, everywhere was beginning to feel like that now. On an impulse I went in search of the tree, retracing what I could remember of our trajectory off the common that day – a short way from the centre, skirting the scrubby lake overgrown with bulrushes and waving grass. It was on a track seemingly leading nowhere too; Margaret had always liked those best. Apt, in fact – then and now. It took several attempts before I found it again but I didn't mind. There was no piper today, and very few walkers. There was space to think, if only I could force my addled brain to work logically."

Nowhere is space for Lawrence – space to think, space to come to terms with what he's just found out (that his wife is a liar and a murderess) and space to make a turning point decision for himself. The piper piercing the peace as he did, some time back, when Lawrence thought he knew his wife, is also metaphorical. Lawrence's peace of mind has been shattered ever since, and he's lost his way several times too – just like he did then. The setting and the memory have been combined to bring Lawrence to the point where he will transform who he was into who he must be. Nowhere is where he's been. Somewhere is where he's going.

Last of all, **DON'T** let setting take over. **DO** use it to enhance the reader's experience. It should always be the backdrop for the characters and the plot; the spine linking skull to legs. It is infinitely adaptable, depending on which character and which POV is currently narrating the story.

Chapter 7: POV

Point of View (POV) is how you present the novel – how it's narrated, in effect. Good use of the right POV is one of the most important elements to making your story un-put-downable. The right POV will draw your reader in, engage them and immerse them in the story. The wrong one will jar and eventually throw them out of it. So what is Point of View? Well there are five of them – with a few intricacies thrown in:

1. **First Person Point of View** – the person telling the story does it through their own eyes: 'I'. It allows the author to develop the inner workings of their characters mind and emotions in fine detail, but can be hard to pull off unless the character is completely 'real'. Wonderful for psychos and deeply philosophical themes as you can really delve into motivations, but be careful not to get caught up in too much *tell* and not enough *show*.

2. **Second Person Point of View** – uses 'you' and the reader is actually positioned as the protagonist of the story. Second person is rarely used because it's incredibly hard to use well. What does second person POV sound like? It's successfully used in *Bright Lights, Big City* (Jay McInerney):
   "You are not the kind of guy who would be at a place like this at this time of the morning. But here you are, and you cannot say the terrain is entirely unfamiliar, although the details are fuzzy."
   'You' is the person actually narrating the story.

3. **Third Person Point of View** – the character's actions are reported 'he/she/they' but can be expanded on by adopting a close or distant perspective – for example a close perspective would give explanation of why they do

what they do: '*she stole him. She thought Carrie must have known that she would steal her lover. Why wouldn't she when she'd always been a bitch to her? It was just too easy not to...*' This POV reports fully, and has the advantage of being able to comment on the motivations behind the characters' actions but is not 'inside the head' of the character as one could be when writing in 1st person POV – a useful mix of show and tell, whereas third person limited – or distant – POV has the characters actions being reported but without the advantage of examining why they do as they do. The author has to really concentrate on showing why, rather than telling, for example, '*She stole Carrie's lover... She just smiled when accused, like she'd done so many times in the past.*'

4. **Omniscient Point of View** – where everything is revealed to the reader but not to the characters – often by a narrator, so the reader knows why everyone does everything, but the characters don't. It's rather like standing on the top of a tall building and watching the people scrabble around like ants below – you know who is about to be squished, and who will run off with the big crumb some other human has dropped, but they don't. Sometimes **Limited Omniscient Point of View** is used. Like the characters, there are hidden parts of the story that the reader doesn't know either – a lot like real life, actually!

They each have their pros and cons, which go like this:

FIRST PERSON POV: UP CLOSE AND PERSONAL...

First person POV is often referred to as close, deep or tight – and it is. It is a limited POV because it puts your reader directly into just ONE head by mimicking the way ONE person perceives what is going on around them, narrating only their conscious thoughts – like being in your own head. If you want a deep but narrow perspective – if you want your reader to really engage with ONE person, it's exceptional.

Using first person POV often makes it easier to capture a distinctive voice too because it is so distinctively that of the character narrating. It's a very immediate form of narrative – especially in close first person POV, and therefore also lends itself to the present tense, although it doesn't need to be. The sense of being in someone's head, and seeing things as they see them is just as immediate if written in the past tense, simply because you are there; experiencing, feeling and transforming as if you were the narrator yourself – which leads me on to another aspect of writing in first person POV: internalisation.

Internalisation is what is going on in your first person narrator's head. It enables readers to connect and identify with the narrator and why they act as they do. It also enables you, the writer to explore some rather less obvious thought and personality processes than if the POV was more removed from the reader. How is your serial killer thinking? Possibly a complete mystery to most people unless you let them get inside their head…

It's not without its problems though:

- There's a danger of **too much internalisation**. Don't record *every* thought your character has – streams of consciousness are very hard to follow and even if you don't go that far (unless you are deliberately showing the ramblings of a madman, for instance), can be repetitive. How many times do you think the same thought over and over again in your head – especially when trying to figure out a problem or persuade/dissuade yourself from a particular course of action? Break up chunks of internal thought with action if there is too much exposition building up from your character.
- **It's limited to the perspective of just ONE person**, so your character has to be present for every scene that is narrated by them, and of course, anything they are oblivious to will be completely missed in their narrative. If the story covers a broad scope or has a big cast of characters, first person POV may be too limiting, unless you use multiple POVs; more on that later.
- **You have to avoid 'telling'**. The danger of being in someone's head is that this can automatically happen because it's an easy trap to fall into, but think about it; a person wouldn't explain something to themselves in the middle of a scene. They won't recount their backstory or

describe what was happening in detail unless you are using some form of epistolary format where it can be used as part of the format itself – a diary, for example. Instead, try to weave information naturally into the POV character's thoughts, feelings, actions and dialogue.

- **Personal pronoun overload** is another risk you take when writing in first person POV. It can be difficult avoiding the use of 'I', 'mine', 'my' over and over again, but too much repetition of them can labour the point. Can you construct the sentence another way? Set yourself the challenge of only using one of those words once in any paragraph – tricky, huh?

SECOND PERSON POV: YOU, OR YOU, OR I?

There is a tendency to confusion in using second person POV. Sometimes a story claims to be told in second person, only to open like this: "*You said you were telling me the truth, but I knew you were lying.*" The 'I' is the person narrating the story, not the 'you', so it's still in first person POV even though another character is being addressed as 'you'. *The Perks of Being a Wallflower* is an example of this, although not claiming to be in second person. I would suggest leaving second person POV until you have successfully tackled first and third – and then you'll probably not even feel the need to try!

THIRD PERSON POV: UP CLOSE BUT STILL LOOKING OUTWARDS...

Third person POV has a far wider scope than first person POV. It enables the use of multiple narrators and POVs and it's also possible to have an omniscient narrator in third person. It's also easier to have a large cast of characters, hence why it's probably the most popular POV to use. A limited third person POV can still follow the narrator's story closely but it has the advantage of being able to include things the viewpoint character couldn't know or wasn't present for. Where the omniscient third person POV is used, *everything* can be thrown into the mix.

Third person POV is more objective than first. It isn't limited to only *one* person's thoughts and experiences so it can incorporate other possible perspectives into the plot, potentially making it rounder and more satisfying. It's also less claustrophobic. If your first person POV character is too dominating or intense, it can be very confining being limited to their bird's eye view for the whole story. It can also be very frustrating and unsatisfactory for the reader to only hear part of the story, especially if the author deliberately manipulates the amount of the story the first person POV character tells so that vital elements of it are excluded. In *Gone Girl*, albeit in first person POV, we have two perspectives. Putting them together we can work out that we are listening to an unreliable narrator on both sides, but if we'd only had one perspective… Do you see the limitation?

Pitfalls and problems of the third person POV:

- Inconsistency is often the biggest one – allowing for variations in narrative distance sometimes means a close third person POV is used in one paragraph but this mutates into a limited one a short while later.
- The intimacy of first person POV inevitably creates a strong voice. This is watered down in third person and can become bland or even absent. The connection is lost along with the intimacy. If this happens to your third person POV, rewrite it as first person to inject character, and then rewrite the enlivened first person voice back into third person. Remember how we explored becoming a character to write? It's a bit long-winded, but great for breathing life into an otherwise dull third person POV narrative.
- Nouns and pronouns – what a mouthful! How many times do you use the character's real name and how often s/he? Also, the more people you have in a scene the more incidences of s/he and the more confusing it can become, for example, *"I saw her on the bridge but she didn't approach me"* makes sense in first, here it is (unedited) in third: *"She saw her on the bridge, but she didn't approach her."* Who? What? Which her? The best way to find these confusing who/which moments is to read it aloud – you'll soon get tangled up in 'hers' and will know when to insert a name instead.

First POV versus third POV:

A deep, 'close' POV doesn't always have to be first person POV, it can be in close third person POV, but it's less easy to maintain, whereas first person POV is more obvious and therefore easier to maintain consistency with. First person POV can also be structured to give a little distance so it's not always uncomfortably in your face. That is the difference between a 'close' and a 'distant' perspective. Here are some examples:

Close POV in 1st: The phone rang, and I jumped up. Who was it?

Distant POV in 1st: I heard the phone ring and, startled, wondered who was there.

Close POV in 3rd: The phone rang, and Jane jumped up. Who was it?

Distant POV in 3rd: Jane heard the phone ring and, startled, wondered who was there.

Here's a thought to throw into the mix: *why not use multiple POVs?*
    Why indeed not! Here are the pros and cons:

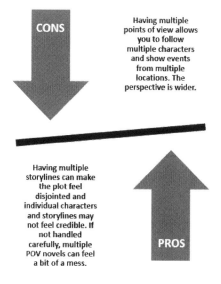

CONS

Having multiple points of view allows you to follow multiple characters and show events from multiple locations. The perspective is wider.

Having multiple storylines can make the plot feel disjointed and individual characters and storylines may not feel credible. If not handled carefully, multiple POV novels can feel a bit of a mess.

PROS

So, how do you avoid the pitfalls whilst taking advantage of the wider perspective?

- **Make each perspective unique:** be in character for each perspective – make the person come alive as an individual just as you would if you were writing only one first person POV. Make sure each character is unique.
- **Make each voice unique:** a reader should always be able to tell which character is narrating from the voice.
- **Keep the pace and the story moving:** switching between POVs can slow or stall the pace of a story because the reader is continuously changing perspective. Counter this by making sure every scene advances the plot without repeating what has gone before, and don't leave one character's part of the story for another's if you will be abandoning all the tension and suspense you have just been building with them. Only use a change in POV to advance the story.
- **Don't head-hop unless it is for a specific dramatic effect:** head-hopping is changing from one first person POV character to another within the same scene. I have only done this once when I wanted to make a direct and immediate comparison between what was going on two people's heads to make the point that they were worlds apart. Luckily, I'm told it worked, but I wouldn't make a practice of it. One POV = one chapter as a rule.
- **No recapping:** don't tell the same story from two POVs. This is repetitive and will slow or stall the story. Instead have one character pick up where the first left off and keep the story flowing, if from a different perspective.
- **Maintain the story line:** fit your characters' story lines together so there is consistency in the plot. How does one POV character's story interweave with another's? Build connections and links even if the connection isn't obvious straight away. This way there is a credibility to using different POVs.
- **Last of all, make sure each POV serves a unique purpose:** each POV must be essential to the advancement of the story – not just for a change of scene. Why do you

need their POV? What do they add to the story? What do they add to your protagonist? What do they explain/show that couldn't be explained/shown through some other medium with just one POV? If they're not necessary for any of those reasons, write them out (sorry!). Remember that investing in a character takes emotional involvement from your readers. They won't invest unless it's worth it.

Once you've picked your POV (or multiple POVs), the trick is to stick to it/them – or rather, the trick is not to get unstuck by it/them and find you've switched POV half way through, without realising it. Here's an example of what I mean:

Jane watched him move across the room towards her, expression brooding. He stood by the table, fiddling with the papers on it.

'You always want things your own way,' he said. 'Is it because that's the way it always was for you?'

'No!' she exclaimed. Why did he always have to bring her mother up? (**Jane: third person POV – close**). *'I just don't think this is right so I can't agree to it.'*

'Then we'll have to agree to disagree for the time being, won't we?' He stopped fiddling with the papers and closed the gap between them. He fiddled with her hair instead. He knew she'd give in eventually. She always did – probably something to do with her evil mother. (**Terry: third person POV – close**).

'Don't Terry,' she pleaded. 'We need to talk about this, not sweep it under the carpet.' He stared at her and then started laughing. She was surprised. (**Back to Jane: third person distant now**).

That's three POV changes in less than half a page – now the reader's head is spinning!

A word on tense changes too:

He watches her approach from a distance, marvelling at the easy way she picks her way through the molehills that had erupted overnight on the smooth green lawn. She was slim and lithe, the way he liked women to be. The old fat woman who ran the site office disgusted him with her rolls of fat. This woman enchanted him.

She in turn was amused by his close scrutiny of her, wondering if he watched all women as closely as this...

'Having fun?' he asks, still enjoying her approach even as she

reaches to within a couple of feet of him.

'Are you?' she would have replied if she'd got the chance.

In the first paragraph, we are in 3rd person POV, which is fine. We are also in present tense – apart from the molehills that *had erupted* – past tense.

In the second paragraph, we are also in 3rd person POV – which is also fine – but it is a different character's 3rd person POV. Finally, the dialogue ends in a future conditional tense, 'she would have replied' – and another change in POV between him and her...

Whoever you start with, stick with them; whichever POV you are using, keep within it, and wherever the story is set – past or present, stay there. Consistency is key. In this case, *oh dear! Looks like we need an editor...*

Chapter 8:
Research, Permissions and
Factual Correctness

But before we look at editing, I want to cover some of the less exciting, but nevertheless, essential, parts of writing a novel: *getting it right*. Let's take them one by one:

RESEARCH

Ernest Hemingway famously advised writers to develop an internal bullshit (BS) detector – probably because, equally, your readers will have their own internal BS detector. The quality of your research, and how it is used in your book will avoid setting it off. Ezra Pound described good literature as news that stayed news, which means you have to be as accurate as a news writer whilst as imaginative as a fiction writer. Even a fantasy world must be a real world for the reader whilst they are in it – and preferably linger on as such in their mind long after they have finished reading your book. Even if our worlds are imaginary and the events in them all made up, still we need to drape the framework of real-life over them, and that is how effective research turns fantasy from fiction into forever. Here are my tips on researching:

1.   **Research early** – preferably before you even start writing, although some areas of research will inevitably only crop up as you are writing and the plot is progressing. Make a comprehensive list of all you want to know before you approach anyone so you don't have to trespass on good will by going back a second time unless it's absolutely necessary. Be efficient and be effective as

well as thorough.

2. **Research on the cheap.** You don't have to visit exotic locations to research – and best not to use them at all if you've never been there yourself. Phone calls to places it's difficult or costly to visit can serve just as well if you've done your pre-research and devised an extensive list of questions you'd like answered.

3. **Research possibilities are everywhere** – online, on the TV, radio, in blogs, on Facebook, Twitter, and even in other's books. And sometimes the smallest snippet can inspire much more. When my mother reminisced one Christmas about how the rag and bone man used to tour the streets in Britain in the 1950s, it sparked a whole series for me. You can read the description of the rag and bone man in *Patchwork Man* – it barely extends to a paragraph, but it just shows how one small piece of information can produce inspiration, so keep a notebook with you at all times and jot down information and ideas whenever and wherever they pop up.

4. **Worried you have no contacts?** Of course you do – maybe not immediate contacts, but remember that notion of six degrees of separation; the greatest in the land are separated from the lowliest by only six degrees – they know someone who knows someone else and so on. Well, the same applies to research contacts. When finalising the *Patchwork* series I needed the details I'd included about court procedures and legal process checked. How was I going to gain access to someone as publicity wary as a barrister – or harder still, a High Court Judge? Answer: six degrees of separation – a friend's brother had gone to school with a boy who'd grown up to become – yes, you've guessed it, a High Court Judge... When I was thinking about writing *Chained Melodies*, I knew no one who was transgender – until I mentioned it to someone I knew, who happened to work with my first transgender research interviewee. Talking to the local LGBT support group introduced me to another – and then my research was well underway.

- Going back to Ernest Hemingway and Ezra Pound, be an investigative journalist *before* you become a fiction writer.
- Ask – most people want to help, especially when they find out why you want to know. Explaining that you're writing a book seems to engender good will even from the most unexpected sources – maybe it's the possibility of that fifteen minutes of fame everyone would like, or maybe its mere altruism, but whatever it is, harness it!
- Use places you can access as a member of the public as a first step – for example, you want to observe criminal behavioural characteristics at first hand? Try a court of law. Want to ask the police for technical advice but think you will be refused? Try the public relations department of the local force first. Want to visit a prison – offer to volunteer as a prison visitor. There are always ways…

5. **Don't BS – EVER.** If you don't know about it, find out. You can never research too much. The art of making research effective, though, is to know when, how much and how to use the fruits of your research.

- Filter technical detail so it doesn't turn into a technical manual within your book. One of the best ways of doing this is to use it in conversation, or overheard, but in small bites.
- Include little details that prove you know your stuff for absolute authenticity – did you know that deep underwater in the filtered light, blood looks green? No, neither did I a short while ago…
- Make sure the research you include plays its part in driving the narrative forward, not bogs it down in a treacle of detail.

6. **What to research?** Facts, dates, technical detail, theories, references, locations, details. Ideas too.

WHEN DO YOU NEED PERMISSIONS?

Or, to start with – what are permissions? Permissions mean seeking permission to quote from or use an excerpt of other people's ***copyrighted work*** in your own. Copyrights are covered in full in Chapter 17 of PUBLISH, but for this section, just be aware that almost all work is copyrighted and it's safest to work on the basis that it only is not if it's specifically stated that it's not – for example where it has a stated Creative Commons License.

To obtain permissions you will have to contact the copyright owner or their publisher or agent. Most publishers will require you to sign a contract and you will be charged a fee for it – varying from a few hundred pounds to a few thousand, so beware if you need permissions…generally you will need permissions if you are using in excess of 'x' – where 'x' is as yet not fully defined. There is no legal definition yet of what it is acceptable to use without permission but usually it's based around either about 300 words, or 10% of the word count. I would be wary of either. The other problem with approaching an author, agent or publisher for permission is that it's a licence for them to print money, courtesy of you, so be careful you aren't taken advantage of.

When do you not need to seek permission?

- When the work is in the public domain – any work published before 1923 is in the public domain, and some works published after 1923 – but still check first. You might find this article on what constitutes being in the public domain useful: http://fairuse.stanford.edu/overview/ public-domain/ or have a look here: https://en. wikipedia .org/wiki/Wikipedia:Public_domain
- If you're merely mentioning the author or the title of their work.
- If you are merely stating a fact – like copying a list of the 50 US states, or the continents of the world.
- When you are linking to something – links don't require permission.
- When the work is licensed under Creative Commons. It will be prominently stated on the work itself that it is so listed. Many sites and blogs come into this category too, but check – a blogger may actually state that nothing from their site

may be used without their permission.

- When abiding by the **fair use guidelines**. You can quote a few lines from a full-length book within the fair use guidelines without permission, but beware here too – see the notes on fair use below.

There are four criteria for determining **fair use** – apparently clear, it seems, but read on, because they're not always!

1. **The purpose and character of the use** – if your use is in a commercial work, you're not automatically in violation of fair use, but your cause will be far less sympathetically viewed if push comes to shove and you find yourself in court.

2. **The nature of the copyrighted work** – facts can't be copyrighted, so creative works are usually more protected.

3. **The amount and substantiality of the part used in comparison to the totality of the work** – there's no percentage or word count cut-off provided by law here because if the part quoted is deemed the most important part of the work, fair use may still be in violation even if you've only quoted a very small section. Usually 200–300 words from a book-length work in an educational context is the arbitrary figure most publisher's guidelines quote.

4. **The effect on the potential market for, or the value of the quoted work** – if your use of the quote means that others may no longer buy the original work, you could be in violation of fair use.

For more detailed information about fair use have a look at this: *A Writer's Guide to Fair Use* http://www.mbbp.com/resources/ iptech/fair_use.html or have a look at good old Wiki's definition: https://en.wikipedia.org/wiki/Fair_use

Some other areas where permissions may not apply:

- Generally permissions apply to copyrighted work on blogs,

- websites and all other digital mediums too but when bloggers and others make their otherwise copyrighted work available on or offline on sites where it's possible to download or access for free, they are often aiming at publicity and will view this more as 'sharing' than pirating, particularly if its for non-commercial (i.e. leisure) or educational purposes. Still be cautious with what you do with any work you have obtained in this way, however, as you should still legally obtain permissions.
- Song titles, movie titles, TV show titles, poem titles, book titles, artist names, band names, names of places, things, events, and people can be used in your work without permissions as they are facts. However: songs and poems are short so it's dangerous to even use ONE line without asking permission. Fair use is not a guideline to rely on here.

Remember, crediting the source of copyrighted material is not enough to avoid seeking permission, but always credit your source regardless of fair use or you are plagiarising.

PLAGIARISM

The definition of plagiarism is:

> *"The practice of taking someone else's work or ideas and passing them off as one's own."*
> (http://www.oxforddictionaries.com/definition/english/plagiarism)

Be aware of the fact that there is software around now which can be used to check on plagiarism – such as Grammarly's. Apart from which, you are a talented and original writer – so simply, **DON'T**…

BIBLIOGRAPHIES

1   What is a bibliography and when is it used?

- A *bibliography* is a full list of all the sources you have consulted and/or referred to in a particular work, although

you may not have quoted (cited) from them all.
- A *reference list* refers only to the sources you have cited (quoted from).

2   What is the format for referencing? There are a number of styles and each is used for a specific type of work:

- **APA is based on author/date,** placing emphasis on the author and the date of a piece of work to identify it.
- **MLA** is most often used by arts and humanities faculties, especially in the USA. It is probably one of the most well-used styles.
- **Harvard** is very similar to APA but APA is used mainly in the USA, whereas Harvard referencing is the most used referencing style in the UK and Australia, particularly for the humanities.
- **Vancouver** system is mainly for medical and scientific papers.
- **Chicago** and **Turabian** are two separate but similar styles, and widely used for history and economics works.

Generally, use the Harvard style. This is the format:

Citing in a reference list: Last name, First Initial. (Year published). *Title*. City: Publisher, Page(s).
Citing after a quote: Last name (year published).

See here for full details of how to use it:
https://www.citethisforme.com/harvard-referencing

Please note that I have not used a referencing style in the Appendix to this book as it is not intended as a bibliography, but as a source of useful suggested links.

And now on to the final challenge: editing.

Chapter 9:
Editing, and the Art of the Rewrite

I'm going to borrow the words of the great Stephen King in his iconic *On Writing* to introduce the final stage of writing:

> *"Write with the door closed, and rewrite with the door open."*
> King (2012)

In other words, when you put down the bones of your story, focus only on getting down the basics. When you edit, focus more on how you can put the flesh on it.

So what is editing? Here's the low-down …

STRUCTURAL OR DEVELOPMENTAL EDITING is the process of standing back and looking at the story as a whole – the big picture. A structural editor will be asking whether all the necessary elements are in place, and furthermore, are they in the right place. It will cover:

- **Plot:** Does it make sense? Is it believable? Does it develop and end satisfactorily or does it leave the reader frustrated – or worse still; cheated?
- **Themes:** Are the themes in the plot handled effectively or are there too many, creating a lack of focus? Do they move the plot forward or hamper it? Are they relevant to the story and the plot development?
- **Characterisation:** Are your characters completely credible? Do they feel real? Are they cast in a role to fit their personality? Do they behave in character?
- **Point of view (POV)/voice:** Is the voice used consistent? Is

there a different voice for each narrator or are they too similar? Is the voice/ voices used ever confusing or confused? Is the voice believable? Have you too many or too few POVs? Are they the right ones to use for this particular plot?

- **Pace:** Does the plot keep moving forward at a good pace? Does the narrative get in the way of plot or enhance/support it? Has the action/climax(es) been placed appropriately to achieve continual momentum? If the pace falters, why?
- **Dialogue:** Do your characters sound real? Do you include too much exposition from them, and too little 'showing'? If you use dialogue to move the plot forward, does it sound authentic, and is it effective?
- **Flow:** Is the natural rise and fall of the three-act structure in place or are there dead ends and cliff faces that can't be scaled because of dead ends or tangents? Is there too much backstory, content, narrative so that the main plot is swamped? Are there missing plot points or inconsistencies?

After a structural edit your manuscript may well come back marked up with major areas to review, constructive criticism and suggested rewrites. It's often best to read it all through and set it to one side before you do anything. The first reading can be a shock; after all this is your baby – the work you've sweated blood and tears over for months, maybe years! After a while, however, you acquire more objectivity and can see the validity of some of the points made. You don't have to agree with all of them – indeed one structural edit I underwent suggested I change a YA humorous detective fiction manuscript back to the somewhat noir adult fiction thriller it had started out as – largely because the editor preferred that theme. That suggestion got a resounding 'No!' from my beta readers and me, and went on to be *Webs*, now happily positioned in YA fiction and the first in a series. The noir elements I edited out I may reuse later – or maybe I won't. The point is you have to believe in what you are doing and a good structural editor will really get that from what they read. What they will do with it is guide you towards the most effective way of presenting it to your readers for maximum impact. If you don't believe in what an editor is suggesting you do, try another editor. Finding a good editor you really gel with is like gold dust.

LINE EDITING is the close focus, compared to the long focus of structural editing, but concentrating on the way you use language to tell your story. The aim will be to make your storytelling as fluid and pleasurable to read as possible by ironing out glitches created by repetition, over-used words or phrases and clichés. A successful line edit will intensify the sense of atmosphere, emotion and tone, and clarify and focus the impact of the story. A line editor will look at:

- Overuse of particular words or sentences.
- Over-long sentences that detract from impact and pace.
- Repetition.
- Dialogue and narrative that can be tightened up.
- Scenes where transition is ambiguous or the author's intent unclear due to lack of focus.
- Tonal disparity, POV shifts and unnatural phrasing.
- Passages that don't read well because of ineffective vocabulary/language – either too complex or too simplistic.
- Narrative digressions and repetitions.
- Changes that can be made to improve pacing.

COPY EDITING is all about flaws on a technical level, and making sure the writing is to industry standards – a high-end proofread, really. A **copy editor will:**

- Correct spelling, punctuation, grammar and syntax.
- Check for consistency in spelling, hyphenation, numerals, fonts and capitalisation.
- Pick outs ambiguous or factually incorrect information.
- Track overall issues, consistency – meaning that there are no inconsistencies within the plot, setting and character traits; for example, Jane doesn't suddenly change hair colour in chapter ten.

There is often some overlap between a structural editor and a copy editor. Most structural editors will point out technical errors or inconsistencies when they are so obvious they can't be missed but essentially they're trying to craft the structure of your story, not check for grammatical errors or typos.

BETA READERS – basically give feedback on a finished manuscript, so it can be adjusted (if you wish) before you release it to the world. I would say beta readers are essential if you are self-publishing, and pretty much so if you are being traditionally published too, after all, this is your precious manuscript – now with even more blood, sweat and tears lavished on it than when it was first handed over to the structural editor. Why spend all that energy and emotion of something if you're not going to complete the road-test process before its grand debut? Derived from the software industry's beta testers of new programs before their release, it means someone who evaluates a manuscript, and tells you of any 'bugs' you may want to fix before it goes on general release. Judicious use of beta readers when planning a book launch can also pay other dividends too – but more on that in the Part 3: PROMOTE section of this book. For now, beta readers also tell you things like:

- The creation of anticipation in a book, but no delivery on it.
- Instances of events or situations that they, with an experienced beta reader's eye, may see but know will not be clear to other readers.
- Times when vital clues or steps in an explanation have been left out or are too vague because you, the author, have got so close to the plot, you're already one step ahead – and anyway, you know what's happening, don't you?
- Characters that are not convincing, either because, like with the clues, we know them too well as writers but have failed to include sufficient for our readers to know them too; like physical description, often ironically.

In other words, if your beta readers are enjoy reading it, it's time to get it proofread and ready for action!

PROOFREADING – so finally you get to the stage of employing a proof-reader; but what else can there possibly be to check on after a structural edit, a line edit, a copy edit and a beta read? This:

- Compare page proofs to the edited copy line by line for typos and errors.
- Check page numbers and headings.
- Check the table of contents against chapter titles, page

numbers and front/back matter, i.e. the appendices, index, and so on.

- Ensure consistency of style, particularly of spellings and hyphenation, by following a style guide supplied by the author or publisher, or by compiling their own after consulting with the author or publisher.
- Look for omissions and inconsistencies in typography, layout or content.
- Judge whether changes are needed, bearing in mind budget and time scale to publication – sometimes changing just one word could have a drastic knock-on effect.
- Identify any changes needed, marking up the proof (on paper or screen) using standard proofreaders' marks (usually British Standard Institution – BSI – marks; you can see them here: http://www.cse.dmu.ac.uk/~bstahl/ CORRECTION_MARKS.pdf).
- Check/insert cross-references where known.
- Eliminate inappropriate or confusing word, column or page breaks including 'widows' and 'orphans' (these are short last or first lines, sometimes just a single word, at the end of a paragraph that appears at the top or the bottom of a page respectively, all alone).
- Ensure that illustrations, captions and labels correspond with the text.
- Check that content is logically arranged.
- Liaise with the author(s) to resolve issues and then collate the author's changes with any others, including their own, to create a finished proof ready to go to print.

As you can see, proofreading really is the final edit of any sort and it is completely pointless to get your manuscript proofread unless everything else has been checked and double-checked first.

BUT WHY DO I NEED AN EDITOR (or copy editor, line editor, proofreader etc – and have to pay for it)? My friends tell me my book's an absolute bestseller in the making and I've checked it over and over again for typos and spelling and grammar mistakes. It's fine.

Answer – some questions to ask yourself:

- Are they publishing experts?

- Are they grammatical experts?
- Are they editorial experts?
- Have they written a best-selling book themselves? (And even if they have, they're not necessarily going to be helpful to you.)
- Are they being objective, or simply being supportive?

There isn't a single book around that wouldn't benefit from a professional edit before going to print (or digital). Anecdotally, it's recounted that J K Rowling's *Harry Potter and the Order of the Phoenix* went to print without a developmental edit and as a result is about one hundred pages longer than it needed to be and suffers from repetition, uneven pacing and side-plots that end up nowhere. It's still a brilliant book – but maybe it could have been better still with an edit? You want to present a professional, slick and inspiring book to your new readers; PLEASE get it edited first and make it the best it can be.

SELF-PUBLISHING ON A BUDGET?

Then maybe you'll have to decide which you prioritise. If, structurally, your beta readers have said the story is basically sound, then go for a line edit and proofreading. **All** books need to be proofread before published. There are also ways you can maximise on your own self-editing before going to a professional, and therefore reducing costs over all as editors and proofreaders will generally charge by the hour or 1000 words. If you're paying by the hour, removing as many tedious and trivial errors will reduce costs dramatically. Try self-editing like this:

1. **Give it a rest**; or in other words leave it to brew for a few weeks so you'll be looking at it with fresh eyes (or listening to it with fresh ears – see below) when you next give it some love.
2. **Print it out, and read it aloud**. Seeing words on paper it's often easier to see errors than on screen, and reading aloud takes you as close as you can be to your readers' experience, bearing in mind you already know what's in your story. If you have to read it aloud, you have to read what is on the page, not what is in your head. If you can't read it aloud yourself – or find a willing victim amongst

your friends to be your personal voice-over, have a look at some of the text-to-speech software around. I've included a list in the Appendix amongst software resources, including *Voice Dream Reader*, *VoiceOver*, and for Kindle devices, *Read Aloud with VoiceOver* (more information on these in the downloadable content listed in the Appendix).

3. **Look for problem words** – admit it, everyone has a word blind spot. Mine is form and from because my fingers run away with themselves, but word blind spots are also those sound-alike words you regularly mix up like 'their' and 'there', 'to' and 'too', 'your' and 'you're'. Here are some of the other offenders:

- affect/effect
- can/may
- further/farther
- good/well
- i.e./e.g.
- into/in to
- it's/its
- lay/lie
- less/fewer
- that/who
- their/they're/there
- then/than
- who/whom
- your/you're

If you're not sure how to use a word, look it up first. *Grammar Girl's Quick and Dirty Tips for Better Writing* is a witty and informative book to use to check on your word blind spots.

4. **Get rid of your irritating frequency words** – you know, those ones you use with irritating frequency when there are other much better options. In fact don't use them at all! What are the most used words in your manuscript other than 'the', 'and' and so on? You can find out by going to "Project > Text Statistics" in Scrivener's top

menu, if you use Scrivener. Click on the arrow next to "Word frequency". You'll then be presented with a personalised cringe list of your irritating frequency words: words you are over-using. If you don't use Scrivener, there's a free *Word Usage and Frequency* add-in for MS Word, and others that I've listed in the useful software download file in the Appendix.

Now you know what they are, go back and see how you can change or remove them.

5. **Check punctuation.**
6. **Run spell check** – the more trivial spelling issues you can remove before sending your manuscript to an editor, the less it'll cost you; things like my 'from' and 'form' could benefit *form* this too (haha)!
7. **Developmental, copy and line edit for yourself before sending your manuscript anywhere**. With the benefit of space, distance and objectivity, you may well pick up on a lot of the points an editor will make to you anyway, leaving them to merely add the cream on the top.

Factors to help you become a good self-editor:

- Read – good, bad and indifferent books. It's only by reading that you'll learn how to distinguish which is which and be able to see either the same flaws or skills in your own work.
- Join a writers' group and get into the practice of regularly attending and regularly contributing. Receiving regular critiquing will help you see how you can improve on a micro level.
- Join a critiquing group or book club – different to a writers' group in that, of course, you are critiquing other authors' books, but in looking at the bigger picture – the whole book – you are role-playing the role of the structural editor.
- Join a beta readers group, or form one from your writers' group. Giving and receiving whole manuscript appraisal is incredibly helpful when developing your style and plotting skills.
- You can find writers' groups in the UK by looking on the

> National Association of Writers' Groups website: http://www.nawg.co.uk and in the US on Writers and Editors: http://www.writersandeditors.com/local_and_regio nal_organizations_57451.html
- Or start your own if there's none in your area.
- Writing magazines and websites such as *Writers' News*, *Writing* and *Mslexia* also have excellent resources on how to self-edit as well as other professional writing tips. A list of books useful in developing writing skills is also included in the appendix to this book.

And last, (but definitely not least), SHOW don't TELL

Reading a really good book plunges you deep into its world and makes you feel like you really know the characters. The story is unfolding in front of your eyes and you cannot put it down until you know what happens next. There are several ways of achieving this, but they all revolve around the principle of SHOW, not TELL by:

- **Using action verbs and sentence structures instead of the passive.** Over-using was, were, are, etc. will keep the action at arm's length because you're telling the reader about it instead of showing it:

  Passive: *The bottle was thrown by the hooligan.*
  Active: *The hooligan threw the bottle.*
  The active sentence plunges you into the action, the passive one just tells you about it.

- **Taking time to choose the perfect word.** Language can be so expressive – why not make full use of a wide vocabulary, but always remembering to tailor your vocabulary to your anticipated audience so they don't lose interest by having to regularly look up uncommon words? Instead of sad, how about miserable, depressed, gloomy, nostalgic, poignant, wistful, down – all expressing the emotion with a moody twist to it. Far more interesting than just 'sad'.

- **Allowing** *the reader* **to make the connections/**

interpretations, rather than you telling them what they are. Which brings the scene to life more?

- Emily was furious with the phone message from her sister.
- Or: As his harsh words hung in the air, Emily clenched her fist round the receiver, choking back her reply. We know Emily is angry, but we don't need to be told it – we can see it in her behaviour.

- **Avoid adverbs whenever possible when describing a character's emotions.** Let your character's behaviour do the work. The same applied to adverbs – yes you can use them sometimes, why not? We designed them to describe, but try to show the character's reactions, moods and emotions by showing instead:

- *"What do you mean by that?" he said angrily.*
- is less effective than:
- *"What the bloody hell do you mean by that?" His hands coiled into fists as he took a step forward.*

- **Add fine detail that focuses the reader on a specific impression.** Most writers have a fine-tuned picture of the situation they are writing about in their head so give that mental image to your reader too by adding the little details that bring it to life.

- *"She took a sip of her wine"* is less indicative of mood and sensation than: *"She took a sip of the crisp, white Chardonnay."*
- I can almost feel that wine slipping across my tongue in the second sentence whereas the first sentence is little more than a bald statement.

- **Use exposition through dialogue and incident rather than narrative.** Instead of telling the reader that something is happening, describe it instead. In *Patchwork Man*, I could have written:

- Kenny waited for an opportune moment to make his move. When the mood was reflective and the old Judge clearly thinking about the future – or more precisely, his lack of it, Kenny applied pressure – just the right amount. Not blackmail, exactly, but as good as.

Instead I wrote:

We talked about aspirations and dreams one evening after I wheeled him outside in the bath chair he'd taken to using most of the time. As one of the oldest boys in the home now – and with Jaggers now gone, life had become more relaxed there. Curfew – since I was visiting such an eminent member of the local community – was extended to nine o'clock for me. The night sky was unusually clear and the stars in it pierced its obsidian depths like tiny diamonds lying on black velvet.
"What's your bright star of a dream, Kenny?" he asked. "You've never really said, but I believe you have one."
"The Bar, sir."
"Oh." He was silent for a while before asking, "But how will you get there, with no money to help you through university?"
"You, sir."
He didn't answer, and we remained looking companionably up at the stars for a while. Eventually he asked quietly, "Blackmail?"
"Gratitude."
"Yes, I suppose you're right."
He died three months later without saying anything more about the conversation, but he left me fifty thousand pounds in his will on the proviso I did what I'd said I told him I wanted to, but never disclosed where I'd got the money from.

The scene comes alive because of the showing of it.

- **Get inside your main character's head and be them.** This tells you about the character's personality without *telling*:

  - *It had been a bad day. A slew of sad songs seemed to be appropriate – let all the emotion out in one hit. Jane selected a suitably miserable CD and collapsed on her bed in anticipation, tissue in hand.*

- Or:
- *God, what a foul day! Jane put on the most mournful of CDs she could think of. Yeah, right – that's me, she thought as the lyrics mourned a lost love. She collapsed on her bed, tissue in hand, and waited for the tears to come. Although hardly a lost love – more a lost cause. She grimaced and screwed up the tissue.*

- Use strong metaphor and simile, but no clichés.

  - A simile is a comparison. It uses 'like' or 'as', such as: *The sky was as dark and dense as black velvet, scattered with stars like diamonds.*
  - A metaphor is a comparison, saying something like:
  - *The night sky was unusually clear, the stars in it piercing its obsidian depths; tiny diamonds lying on black velvet.*
  - That is the difference between **TELL** – which it is easy to slip into doing, and **SHOW**, which will make your narrative come alive.

Here's how I self-edit using my Post-it Notes system (PINS), before I send my manuscript to the REAL editor:

- Print out the manuscript (MS).
- Buy a pack of multi-coloured post-its.
- Allocate one colour post-it to each of:

  - Structure/plot particularly making a note of where acts 1 and 2 end, and any specific climaxes and anti-climaxes.
  - POV – issues/changes/errors.
  - Characterisation and dialogue.
  - Setting.
  - Show, don't tell.
  - Themes and symbolism.

On a read-through, first flag any points in the MS where any issues arise related to the post-it topic. Put a note on the post-it to remind yourself what it was if necessary.

- Now you have a multi-coloured leaf doc. Work your way through it assessing the issues you've identified. When you feel you've revised the MS to your satisfaction removing the issue, remove the post-it. Comparably if you find other issues on the work-through, add more post-its. Continue until all the post-its have been removed.
- NOW, and only now, go through the MS again, refining language, vocabulary, grammar and style.
- Now get it beta read. If more than one beta reader raises the same issue, think again and consider revising again, but remember to also have confidence in what you've written. You don't have to make any suggested revision you're not convinced about.
- After that, send it either for a structural edit, a copy edit, or neither – depending on how confident you are that you've nailed all the problems. Whether this is the first book in a series where the first and/or second have already benefitted from a structural edit may be relevant when deciding which to choose here. A stand alone will almost certainly benefit from a structural edit. A series where you've already established a good format may be able to pass straight on to a copy or line edit if you're happy with the feedback from the beta read stage.
- Last of all, put the MS away in a drawer for a month and then go back to it and reread. Is there anything else you feel you need to change? If so rinse and repeat as per the above.
- ONLY AFTER YOU'VE REACHED THIS STAGE send it to be proofread because proofreading is THE FINAL stage before formatting for self-publishing or submitting to an agent.

And congratulations; you've just finished your novel!

Now the fun really begins …

Part 2: PUBLISH

Chapter 10:
Submitting to Agents and Publishers

So your book is written. What do you do with it now? Get it published, is the obvious answer, of course, but getting a book published can happen in a number of ways.

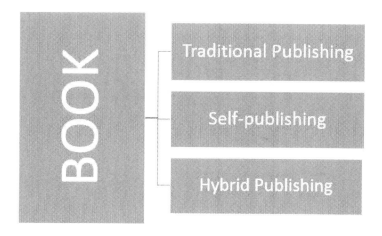

TRADITIONAL, OR MAINSTREAM, PUBLISHING speaks for itself – although remember that you should also consider approaching small independent publishers – independents, or 'indies' – as well as the long-established giants. Some indie publishers will accept direct submissions from authors whereas the big boys will only allow submissions via literary agents, so you have two hurdles to jump before your manuscript even hits a desk.

SELF-PUBLISHING is all about DIY – taking control of what you've done. The new breed of authorpreneur is on its way up the fast lane with names like Rachel Abbott, Joanna Penn, Mel Sherratt, Mark Edwards, Tracy Bloom in the UK and J A Konrath and Amanda Hocking in the US. Self-publishing is also about self-control and self-motivation because you have to be the quality controller for yourself. There is no publisher or agent saying, *"Whoa there,"* if your book isn't as professionally produced as it could be, and no marketing department planning the next sales campaign for you. You have to do it all yourself – with a carefully selected team, if you're wise.

Having said that, as a debut or little-known author in mainstream publishing the marketing and promotion budget allocated to you will be somewhere between 'little' and 'nothing' so you'll still have to plan and promote for yourself – and without the degree of control and autonomy that being self-published allows you. Many of the marketing ploys in Part 3: PROMOTE will therefore be out of your reach, and unless you earn out your advance (earn over and above the advance you were paid) from a mainstream publisher, that two-book deal you signed up for could be dead in the water for all time, because who's going to take on another of your books if the first didn't sell? Now which option seems best?

HYBRID PUBLISHING – as you would expect – is a mix of the two. Maybe you publish your literary titles through a mainstream publisher and self-publish your romance titles (romance is one of the biggest selling genres). Or perhaps you've sold the rights to print and digital books to a mainstream publisher but self-publish audio books (a growing market). Some self-published authors become hybrid authors when their self-published books sell well and a mainstream publisher offers them a contract on the strength of their success. They then retain some rights and sell others – or publish some books traditionally and keep others that they feel are doing well on their own self-published. Self-publishing initially doesn't close off the possibility of being traditionally published with that same book eventually if it takes off.

So which to choose? There's a debate to be had before you opt either way. There are pros and cons to consider for any of them. One thing to remember though is that you do not have to stick with one type of publishing alone. Simply because you self-publish to begin with does not preclude that book being signed to a traditional publishing deal later on if it performs well. Similarly you do not have to sell all rights if you enter into a contract with a traditional publisher. Some authors routinely retain specific rights whilst granting others. Rights are covered in more detail in Chapter 17, but in the meantime, here are some pros and cons to consider when choosing your publishing route:

Traditional Publishing	Self-publishing
'Prestige' – the rubber stamp of approval. If it's traditionally published, it must be good **BUT:** That's not always the case…	Is still stigmatised by some **BUT:** That's now increasingly less so as big names are seen to be delivering good quality – and – popular work.
Access to a professional team of editors, formatters and designers **BUT:** Their decisions will ultimately hold sway over yours.	Have to develop your own team **BUT:** You will also retain control over your work.
You benefit from their distribution channels and far greater reach **BUT:** You will have signed over all copyrights and will only receive a fraction of sales as royalties.	You have less distribution reach via sales platforms like Amazon etc – and almost certainly limited access to bricks and mortar book shops **BUT:** Royalties and copyrights remain yours.
You will join a stable of the publisher's other authors and perhaps gain access to testimonials from them, collect reviews and have advance release coverage **BUT:** You will be strictly tied to both the publisher and the genre and if you fail to perform, the support will all rapidly disappear…	You are not tied to genre so you can write across genre and be more creative accordingly **BUT:** You will have to work hard to obtain reviews, testimonials and coverage – all covered in Part 3 so do not despair!
If you fail to earn out your advance you will most likely be dropped or	If the book falters on the first sales pitch, simply try another

Traditional Publishing	Self-publishing
at the very least allowed to simply fade away **AND:** You will still have signed over all rights related to your book so will be unable to do anything else with it.	strategy to kick-start it – after all, all the rights are still yours…

However, let's suppose you want to open as many doors as possible for your manuscript so you decide to start by testing the water with traditional publishing. Step one will be to get yourself a literary agent and to do that you will need to submit:

- A synopsis of your book.
- An opening or covering letter/email.
- The first one/three/more chapters, or sometimes a specific word count.

You thought writing your book was hard? Now try summarising it, maintaining the 'voice' and making it engaging, intriguing and pithy. All in less than 500 words. Hmm. It's tough – and more so because there is no one way to do it; no perfect format. Hooking a literary agent's interest – or an independent publisher, because if you are submitting to an indie who allows direct submission, the same applies – is as subjective as engaging a reader. What one person likes another hates, what fascinates one, bores another. All that you can do is follow the guidelines which go a little like this:

1. Always submit ONLY what the agent or publisher ask for, and in the format they ask for it on their website.
2. Make sure your first chapter/first three chapters or x thousand words are as polished as they can be. If you haven't used a copy editor or line editor for the rest of the book definitely use one for these.
3. Be professional in your approach – if they take you on, it will be a working relationship so be someone they can

work with. The stories of boxes of chocolates or unusual gifts accompanying submissions to 'sweeten' the recipient are amusing, but also the sure sign of a no-hoper.

4. Approach several agents/publishers at a time. They may take months to get back to you so this is a long process – and one that may take years if you only approach one at a time. Do also tell anyone who expresses an interest if you have had interest from another quarter too. That isn't applying leverage, it's being professional and business-like.

5. Research whoever you submit to thoroughly first. Look first in the *Writers and Artists Year Book* for possible recipients of your submission, then look carefully at their websites and what/ who they represent or publish already. This should give you an idea whether your work would be a good fit for them. You can also look up independent publishers accepting direct submissions here too: My Perfect Pitch http://myperfect pitch.com/ home/

6. Be patient, persistent and professional, and don't remind a publisher or an agent if you haven't heard from them. No reply = no interest. Simply move on to the next names on your list.

HERE ARE SOME BASIC TIPS ON WRITING A SYNOPSIS

Format:

- Usually a synopsis should be between 500 and 1500 words but aim for somewhere in between for preference or your synopsis could become an epic in itself.
- Set up a HEADER (your name, the title of your book, synopsis), e.g. DEBRAH MARTIN/ PATCHWORK MAN/ SYNOPSIS.
- Set up a FOOTER (page numbers).
- Use wide margins (generally 2.5cm all round or you can choose between 'normal', 'moderate', 'narrow' in Word: choose 'normal').

- Double or 1.5 space.
- Don't 'justify' the text.
- Use 12 point font, unless the submission criteria request otherwise.
- Use a serif font (e.g. Times New Roman), unless submission criteria request otherwise.
- NEVER use a fancy font of any kind.

Style:

- Don't write it in the same style as your novel. It's a plan of your novel, but do try to inject the flavour of your novel in to it.
- Use the present tense throughout.
- Write in third person throughout.
- Use the omniscient POV (point of view) throughout.
- Don't embellish it with 'will they?'/'won't they?' type flourishes, rhetorical questions or ellipses.

Structure:

- Don't separate the synopsis by chapter, keep it free-flowing.
- Explain the structure of the book so if there are flashbacks, or fast-forwards in time, explain where they occur in the plot.
- Tell the WHOLE story, including the denouement. You are not giving the game away by doing so. An agent or publisher needs to know the ending to determine whether the book works overall. Refer consistently to the characters by one name only or you will give the impression there are other characters involved, so if – for instance, as with Lawrence Juste in *Patchwork Man* – a character goes by two names, make sure this is made clear, and which name you are using in the synopsis.
- Capitalise each character's name the first time it's used and then revert to lower case for the second and subsequent occasions, e.g. LAWRENCE JUSTE the first time it's used and Lawrence Juste the second time – so that the

introduction of a new character is made obvious whenever that occurs.

- Make it clear whose POV the book is written from by adding (POV) after their name. If the POV changes, show that in the same way by putting (POV) after the name of the other character.
- Start with a summary paragraph.
- Include a character profile for each of the main characters within the narrative. A character profile should include essential elements like the character's appearance, their socio-economic or cultural background, their job (if relevant), anything about them that is striking or unusual, their backstory and where this has brought them to now. Lawrence Juste's character profile might read as:

  "...a wealthy and respected barrister at the peak of his career, some would say he had everything any man could want – success, fame, and a beautiful wife – even good looks. He also carries with him a shameful and unlawful hidden past that could threaten everything he enjoys now."

- Include the sequence of actions, reactions and climactic scenes which form the plot overall from the inciting incident which precipitates the protagonist into their conflict, through the specific plot points that move the story forward and on to the climax and resolution; think of your three-act structure and how you have employed it, including how you've manipulated the story arc to create increases to, and relief from, tension along the way. These are the points the agent or publisher wants to know about.
- Ideally insert a new character profile each time you introduce a new main character, making sure their place within the plot and the story arc is apparent.

Other tips:

- Stick to the essentials. All the finer details are not necessary in the synopsis. A synopsis is essentially for an agent or publisher to be able to see that you have a plot that works and characters that are worth engaging with.

- Generally try to keep to the main characters – the protagonist, the antagonist and the major love interest or sidekick.
- Don't talk about theme – this should be apparent from the plot if the synopsis is concise and focused.
- Don't try to impress – aim for clarity and focus.
- Make yourself a bullet-point list of the major plot points beforehand if this helps.
- Start writing it as soon as you start writing your novel. Yes, it may change as the novel grows, but it is also an excellent way of keeping you and your developing masterpiece on track. If you're deviating from the original summary you've made of your story, why?
- Proofread thoroughly!

Here's an example of a synopsis:

LAWRENCE JUSTE (POV) is the model QC – ultra-respectable, reputable; a winner. He's also emotionally frozen and living a lie because Lawrence Juste is really KENNY JUSS, born in poverty, raised in a children's home, and a graduate of the school of abuse and crime. His first offence? To frame his brother, WIN, for a crime identical to one he is about to defend. His second: to blackmail a homosexual judge. His third, to cover up a major miscarriage of justice as a QC. Now he is glaringly in the public eye after his wife, MARGARET, is killed in an apparently random hit and run and he could do with his hidden past surfacing like a hole in the head. Unfortunately the past has a way of finding its way back to you, and his dead wife has helpfully left a sinister résumé of his to get the whole process under way.

His juvenile delinquent client, DANNY, seems to be the reason everything has kicked off now, and the more he delves into his young client's defence, the more worryingly close his own past misdemeanours become. Add the sudden re-appearance of Win, together with the rest of his abandoned and disaffected siblings and the suggestion that Danny might actually be Lawrence's own son – fathered with his long-lost sister – and the mix becomes explosive.

That's not all. It's not just Win who is out to get him. JAGGERS, the bully who made his childhood a misery and introduced him to the delicacies of pimping, prostitution and blackmail, wants all the money back – and more – that he made out of the judge, who it turns out was Jaggers' uncle. No wonder Lawrence is turning to drink!

The one light in the darkness is KAT, Danny's social worker; half Lawrence's age, black, feisty, and impossibly delectable after a lifetime of emotional denial. Because of her, Lawrence sets about untangling the matted threads that have made him a patchwork man, and re-stitching himself as a whole one. He reconnects with members of his family, some hostile, some neutral, some merely odd – particularly MARY, the sister he thought of as mad, and who now lives in an institution. His instincts tell him Mary knows more than she's saying – but that might just be his own paranoia talking. He does discover that his dead wife, Margaret, and Jaggers may have been plotting against him for years, and the miscarriage of justice was a put-up job designed to trap him, but unless he tells all in court, he can't rectify any of it. But if he does, he'll be ruined.

With the threat of evidence incriminating Jaggers in Margaret's death, Jaggers temporarily backs off, but Lawrence knows he will one day still have to face his arch nemesis, as well as the question of Danny's parentage. A wholly unexpected medical revelation provides Danny's defence and an entirely new dimension to Danny's roots. By the time Danny is cleared, Lawrence has discovered a new dimension to himself too – the ability to care. His belief in the value of truth is sufficiently restored for him to believe that Atticus Finch (*To Kill a Mockingbird*) – his boyhood hero – would have approved of his choices. But how to sustain a relationship with a woman half his age, and work out how the dead can reach the living from beyond the grave – as his wife seems to be doing – are mysteries still to be solved in the second and final books of the series.

While you're at it, also try writing your ELEVATOR PITCH for that moment when you have an agent or publisher within earshot and it's a chance to nail it, right there... Elevator pitch? Try imagining yourself in an elevator – or if you're British, a lift – with Martin Scorsese or Stephen Spielberg and you have just as long as it takes the elevator (lift) to reach the ground floor of the building to convince him he wants to film your book – a minute, maybe three at most. What are you going to say to convince him? That's your elevator pitch; twenty-five words of pure gold outlining your book.

Five-minute fix – try it for yourself with some well-known films or stories. It's great practice for when you're writing your pitch letter and they make great tweets for engaging an audience in the meantime too…

AND NOW FOR THAT PITCH, OR COVERING LETTER…

Some agents read the synopsis first, some the covering letter, and some just dive straight into the manuscript excerpt provided. As with everything, everyone is different and there is really no way of knowing what a particular agent or publisher might do unless you've had the opportunity to ask them – and then you'd have pitched your book right at them already, wouldn't you? The safest way of approaching it is probably to assume that all elements of your submission are equally important in leading them to want to read your whole manuscript, so make your pitch letter as interesting as the manuscript itself. That doesn't mean telling them that your mum loves your book and so does everyone else who's ever read or heard about it. It means making it clear why this book is different, why they would think so too and where it could be positioned in the market – after all, your book may be your baby, but it is now about to become something quite different; a marketable product.

Your letter should be short – maybe around 150 words but definitely no more than 250. That's not a lot. An A4 page with text double spaced is around 300 words, so be succinct. Your letter should fit on no more than one side of A4 paper, single spaced with generous margins, including salutation and sign off (Dear…and Yours…etc). Use a 12-point character size in a no-nonsense font, like Times New Roman – as with your synopsis.

Arrange it as three paragraphs:

- The first paragraph should say what the book is about – in summary. This is where an elevator pitch is useful (see above).
- The second paragraph should describe its genre and style, why it's interesting and important and perhaps liken it to other books in the market for commercial placement. For instance my book *Falling Awake* has been likened to those by Audrey Niffenegger and Carlos Ruis Zafon. The agent or publisher knows precisely the type of book they're about to read having been told that.

- The third paragraph should say something about you, the author, so have your bio ready, include your personal history – age, occupation, life style. Don't regard yourself as uninteresting. If you write racy spy thrillers by night but double up as a science teacher by day, that alone is an interesting twist to you. Include your qualifications to write about the subject – for instance your racy spy thrillers may revolve around industrial espionage and the discovery of a lethal new compound. Finally refer to anything else you've written, and relevant academic or vocational achievements – for example a first degree or masters in creative writing, some published articles or short stories. If you have a publishing history, attach a separate (concise) CV covering it.

THE FINAL HURDLE – DECIDING ON AN AGENT:

- First of all, be organised; create a spreadsheet of agents you have, or are submitting to, including the date submitted and the response.
- Build your list based on careful research. I've included a list of places to check up on agents in the Appendix. They include Agent Query, Query Tracker, Who reps Whom – a good place to trace an agent via their famous clientele and Publisher's Market Place. Do also check the agents you are targeting are reputable. You can do this by looking them up on Preditors and Editors.
- Next, refine your list to remove the agents that are not the best fit for you and your book, for whatever reason. Avoid anyone who reps an author or book too similar to you/yours as they will probably not want to duplicate their list.
- Only plan to query one agent per agency if it's large, and then refine your list again, prioritising the best matches. Query them first in batches of say, five or so, recording the responses you get on your spreadsheet as they arrive.
- Rinse and repeat as many times as necessary. If an agent wishes to read the rest of your manuscript they will ask to. Don't remind them and never send the whole manuscript unless asked. It may be many months before they respond

and patience – like persistence – is a virtue in the world of publishing.

Finding an agent isn't easy. Agents' preferences are subjective, just like anyone else's, and there may be many reasons why they don't offer to represent you even though your book shows great promise. Also remember that even though you may be offered representation, there is no guarantee that they will find a publisher for your book. Many authors languish on the list of an agent who loves their book but cannot find a publisher for it because the publishing world is a tough commercial one, and for debut authors the chances of being a bestseller are minuscule. No publisher is going to risk paying an advance for a risky newcomer when they can put another household name out there and guarantee sales. There will almost certainly come a point for many new authors when you have to decide what your definition of success and 'being published' is. If you genuinely believe in your book, and genuinely believe it is the best you can make it, and genuinely want to see it in print, then maybe self-publishing is for you? If you have an agent, then Amazon's White Glove publishing programme may be for you. Designed essentially to provide additional technical support for self-publishers, it has been adopted by some agents as a means to getting their authors' work out there, and occasionally with some additional promotional help from Amazon, but you will be signing up to exclusivity and a percentage royalty only if you do so. Check the contract first and limit the amount of time it binds you – perhaps a year? By then you will have investigated other options whilst also having gathered a following. Then the world really is your oyster, and you are master of your destiny (or something like that)…

Chapter 11:
A First Look at the World of Self-Publishing

I've mentioned the pros and cons of traditional versus self-publishing in the previous chapter, but if you think it might be for you, the rest of the chapters in the PUBLISH section of this book are especially for you. Let's start with a review of who does what and how they do it.

First of all WHO will help you self-publish?

- **CreateSpace**: http://www.createspace.com/ for print distribution on Amazon (zero upfront cost).
- **IngramSpark**: https://ingramspark.com/ for print distribution to the universe outside of Amazon ($49 US/ £29 UK set-up costs)
- **Amazon KDP**: http://www.kdp.amazon.com/ for ebook distribution on Amazon; i.e. Kindle (zero upfront cost).
- **Draft2Digital**: (https://draft2digital.com/) for ebook distribution to the universe outside of Amazon (zero upfront cost).
- **Smashwords**: (http://www.smashwords.com/) also for ebook distribution to the universe outside of Amazon, but with slightly complicated file formatting (zero upfront cost).
- **eBook Partnership** (http://eBookPartnership. com) also for ebook distribution to the universe outside of Amazon, but with upfront costs.
- **Crowd Funding e.g. Unbound:** https://unbound.co.uk/
- **Lulu**: https://www.lulu.com/

- **BookTango**: http://www.booktango.com/
- **Bookbaby**: http://www.bookbaby.com/
- **Vook**: http://pronoun.com/
- **Pressbooks**: http://pressbooks.com/
- **eBookIt**: http://www.ebookit.com/index.php
- **Nook**: https://www.nookpress.com/ebooks
- **Gumroad**: https://gumroad.com/
- **Sellfy**: https://sellfy.com/

I've included a full summary of all the self-publishing options I am aware of as at December 2015 in the downloadable material referred to in the Appendix, so please subscribe to my list and help yourself to this. I will be endeavouring to keep the downloadable material regularly updated.

Each publishing platform/provider has their pros and cons and it's best to spend some time reading through the site information and familiarising yourself with their differences and similarities. Which is best to use? A personal choice – and somewhat influenced by marketing and promotion choices later on. For simplicity and range when first starting out, I would possibly go with KDP (Kindle Direct Publishing for Amazon) but review everything again a little further down the line, however, each book and each author is different so you must carefully consider what it is you are publishing and how you want to approach that before making any decision.

For example: *what if someone wants to buy your book but has a Kobo reader, or a Nook (Barnes and Noble) but your book is only available on Amazon?* Amazon with its massive reach is a tempting option, but if you are signed up to KDP Select (discussed in detail in Part 3: PROMOTE), you do restrict readership possibilities. Alternatively, what about libraries? Libraries are now offering ebooks too. Or Google? Google is a powerful tool and will almost certainly continue to look for ways to make use of their vast user database to buy via Google Play. Add to this the changes Amazon has now introduced in the way authors are remunerated with the advent of Kindle Unlimited (KU), and we're into a whole new ball game. Kindle Unlimited is a recently introduced service that allows Amazon customers to read as much as they want on any device for a standard fee per month – thereby eliminating the need to buy individual books. Currently standing at £7.99 p/month (correct as at December 2015) in the UK and $9.99 p/month in the US, that means an avid reader of ten books at say £ $2.99 (roughly £1.99 in the UK) with 70% royalties payable to the author if enrolled in KDP Select – would only pay $9.99 or £7.99 instead of $29.99 or £19.99 per month. That also means the author would only receive a fraction of the 70% x $29.99 or £19.99 they would have received because now they are paid for 'pages read' in the KU programme.

But hold on, if Kindle Unlimited pays an average of $0.005779 (the stats for July 2015) per KENP (Kindle Edition Normalized Pages) read then on a 400-page book the author would be paid $2.31, and if the book had been sold they would have earned $2.99 less 30% = $2.09 so they're actually being paid more under the new system...unless of course their book was only 50 or 75 pages long (a practice some of the Kindle sharks rising out of the Kindle boom got into) when of course read, their $2.09 royalty would only amount to $0.005779 x (say) 75 pages = $0.43.

It's to remunerate the real authors, and limit the sharks, Jeff Bezos says – maybe it will overall, and maybe it won't, but it is another consideration to bear in mind when deciding which platform to use to publish your books. You see the complexity of the arguments now?

Here's another one to add to them:

Maybe a mix works best?

For example if you choose print-on-demand (POD) – always recommended over ordering a print run though a printer because then you won't have a stack of thousands of physical books to physically sell, as in the old way of self-publishing – then consider:

- Using Ingram Spark to produce a POD edition for all markets other than Amazon. This will ensure your book is listed and available to order through the largest and most preferred U.S. wholesaler (Ingram).
- But also using Createspace to produce a POD edition for Amazon – and thereby maximising your profits as you would lose a slice of them if you use Ingram to fulfil Amazon orders.
- Bricks and mortar book shops are also more likely to stock books via Ingram than Amazon (no sale or return). This also saves having to have that enormous print run and physical booklog that used to be the only way to get physical books into physical book shops. Ironically, Amazon opened its own bricks and mortar book shop in

November 2015, but that's another story…

The same applies, without physical book stocks, to digital books – where one distributor works well, another may work less so in that area, but better in another. For example Smashwords and Draft2Digital distribute to Barnes and Noble, Apple and so on, whereas KDP only distributes to itself.

All these services are more or less DIY, although you may need specialist help with getting your book past the Autovetter in Smashwords, but there are services you can access quite cheaply for help with this on places like Fiverr (https://uk.fiverr.com/), an online source of just about every service you could think of buying for – as its name suggests – multiples of $5. This means that you will need to prepare and upload your files for publishing and distribution yourself. If you need help with uploading and publishing or a one-stop shop to help with print and ebook formatting, design, and distribution:

- Bookbaby is reputable and helpful.
- CreateSpace, and
- IngramSpark will offer paid service options too.

So, as you can see there *are* choices – not only in 'how' but also in 'what' you want to publish. Give some serious thought to WHAT you're going to publish because it may well influence your publishing decisions in the long run. Consider:

- Will your readers prefer print or digital? With readers reading so much online now – even on their phones – digital publication is really the thing of today. If your book isn't available in a digital form then you are probably missing out on 90% or more of your possible market. This is why if you don't definitely know that your readers would prefer a print format, you should release an ebook first to test the water.
- When is an ebook not such a good idea? If your book contains a lot of coloured and detailed illustrations. Be aware that there may be significant challenges to creating and distributing an illustrated ebook across multiple platforms. It can be done but requires more technical skill

in formatting.

- You also will have to think about how you are going to promote your book. With something like 44,000 books being released on KDP (Kindle Direct Publishing – Amazon) daily, how is anyone going to find your book, let alone be persuaded to buy it? People who buy ebooks will probably only find out about your book online, and self-published print books rarely make it in quantity into bricks and mortar shops. The world of promotion is online. Only an author who is prepared to tackle the savvy world of online marketing is likely to succeed in selling their books so you'll need to master the techniques not only of formatting and uploading but also promoting and marketing. Luckily for you, that's all covered in Part 3: PROMOTE – but do also prepare yourself for the fact that succeeding at self-publishing is all to do with patience and persistence, not overnight bestsellers.

So how does self-publishing a book actually work?

1. First of all there is usually no actual cost to uploading your book, unless it is via a distributor like BookBaby.
2. If you do pay an upfront fee, (like with BookBaby), you'll earn 100% net; that means net of the cost of printing the book. If you don't pay an upfront fee, then a percentage of your sales will be kept. KDP, for example, will pay over your sales at two rates – 35% for non-exclusive sales and 70% if you have enrolled your ebook into KDP Select so it can only be sold via Amazon.
3. Next, note that I referred to BookBaby as a distributor. That is all any of the publishing options referred to above are, essentially. They are not publishers in themselves, although Amazon does now have a number of its own publishing imprints and does also accept submissions to them in pretty much the same way as the traditional publishers do – via an agent.
4. With all ebook retailers, you can upload your book files at any time and make your ebook available for sale. You can also take it down at any time too. If you want – or need to

– you can upload new versions. You can change the price, the cover, the description and you can sell it through multiple channels (if you haven't enrolled it in KDP Select). It is yours to do what you want with.

5. All copyrights remain yours. The fee that is charged by KDP et al is merely that – a distribution fee for hosting your book and making it available for sale through their channels.

6. It's DIY. In other words you do it yourself – albeit at times with a little third-party help. Most also offer automated tools for converting, uploading and listing your ebook for sale, as well as guides and tutorials to help you ensure you get it right – all free. They are actually very helpful, and once you've done it a couple of times, it is really very easy – as you'll see.

Distribution bears more explanation as it affects where and how you make your book available. For ebooks there are two types of distribution available: single and multi-channel.

A SINGLE CHANNEL DISTRIBUTOR is a retailer who sells your book through only one channel or device. KDP (Kindle Direct Publishing) and Barnes and Noble (Nook Press) are examples of this.

A MULTI-CHANNEL DISTRIBUTOR introduces the middle man to push your book out to multiple retailers and other distributors. The biggest multi-channel distributors are Smashwords, BookBaby and Draft2Digital. In exchange for multi-channel services you generally have to pay an upfront fee or allow deduction of a percentage of your sales income.

Quite often a self-published author may start with KDP and then opt out of KDP Select so they can also sell/distribute through a multi-channel distributor like Draft2Digital, which will be able to distribute to all other major ereader retailers too. There are a number of marketing strategies that can be used if doing this – all covered in Part 3.

BIBLIOGRAPHIC DATA

Distribution is largely taken care of via the platform you have chosen but you should also know the background to know how it all works and how you can capitalise on that, or maximise your books exposure to customers. I'll talk more about ISBNs below, but basically an ISBN is the way a book is referenced in a database of books worldwide called BookData, maintained by Nielsen in the UK. It is the life blood of the book trade since it contains the bibliographic data of every book that has been released for general sale since its inception and is therefore also the go-to place for the trade to order. It is also a requirement of law for any book with an ISBN to be recorded on there – print, or ebook. In the US, this facility is provided by Bowkers. Children's books are also catalogued at: www.bic.org.uk/8/children'sbooks

You can personally add bibliographic data to BookData in the UK by registering on www.nielsentitleeditor.com if you are not using a publishing service that does it for you (always check as it is your responsibility). In the US, data is provided to Bowker. This also raises another point that is worth considering in relation to ISBNs and who your book is published by…

YOUR RESPONSIBILITIES AS 'PUBLISHER'

If you supply your own ISBN, you have the option to register yourself as owner of the ISBN with Nielsen or Bowker as a *publisher*. If you register them under your name, the book will be published by 'your name' where your name is your name. If you don't provide an ISBN at all and use the courtesy one provided by the distributor/online publisher (e.g. CreateSpace, Ingram etc) your book will be published by CreateSpace or Ingram, etc. What is wrong with this? Well, a book published by CreateSpace or Ingram IS undoubtedly a self-published book. Some sellers and buyers will still turn their nose up at this. If the book is published by [you], even worse. Definitely an amateur. If it's published by [Publisher name], then who is to say – without a little research – whether this publisher is mainstream, independent – or you? It creates a gloss of professionalism – which will be carried through the rest of the book anyway, right?

WHOLESALE DISTRIBUTION is organised via a number of routes, depending on who your publisher is and how big they are.

Large traditional publishing house – direct sales reps (on commission)

will go to distributors to sell to bookshops and wholesale traders.

Smaller and/or self-publishing businesses – send copies direct to a wholesaler.

Self-published Indies – rely on the publishing platform they have chosen – e.g CreateSpace.

Distributors and wholesalers are the middlemen – taking, jointly, anything between 65% and 75% off the cover price, and selling to the public at an increased retail price on top of that. This means publishers often only end up with between 25% and 35% as a return on the sale. Out of that, you, the author, will be paid your royalty – often not a lot! Big bulk buying outlets like W.H. Smith and supermarket chains can negotiate good deals and small, often independent, book stores struggle to compete. This is why books are often only taken on a sale or return basis, especially in the small book shops whose budgeting can't afford to risk buying a flop with no way out of the expense if necessary. Big retail outlets will also require contracts in the thousands so for a self-published author – even if you get your foot through the door – you will have to take an investment risk in a print run of similar quantities to stand a chance of being stocked by the big boys.

The main wholesale distribution warehouses in the UK are:

Gardners
Bertrams
Marston
Orca
Grantham
TBS
Amazon (not really a wholesaler but the biggest distributor of all)

In the US, the main wholesale distributors are:

Baker and Taylor
AK Press
Alibris
Barnes and Noble
Amazon (not really a wholesaler but the biggest distributor of all)

It is a good idea to know through which of these, and in what quantities, your book is being ordered and sold. You can find out where your book is being stocked by going onto their websites and searching for your book (by ISBN). To find out how many are being stocked you will have to contact the distributor direct, and even then you may be refused this information.

All very unfair? Maybe, but unfortunately it's still the system and the traditional publishers still have a stranglehold on it. However, that doesn't mean to say that the self-published author stands no chance. Indeed, this is possibly where they score because they don't suffer from the same deep trade discounts so nearly all the profit on sale goes to you when you sell.

Even though an ISBN isn't necessary to distribute an ebook, most distributors and service providers *do* require one. They may provide you with a free one as part of their service, but this does then tie your book to their service. I would always advise acquiring and using your own ISBN because your book will be independent of distribution ties.

An **ISBN** can be obtained in the US through Bowker or Nielsen in the UK (See downloadable info sheets for URLS). An ISBN is an International Standard Book Number. Until 31st December 2006 it consisted of 10 digits, and since 1st January 2007 it consists of 13 digits, identifying the data relevant to the book for publishers, booksellers, libraries, internet retailers and others for the purposes of ordering, listing, maintaining sales records and stock control data.

An ISBN is made up as follows, using the ISBN for *Patchwork Man* as an example:

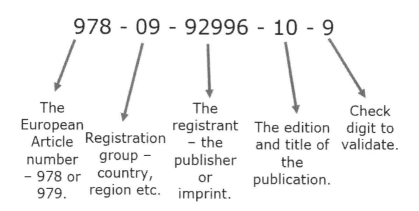

978 - 09 - 92996 - 10 - 9

The European Article number – 978 or 979.

Registration group – country, region etc.

The registrant – the publisher or imprint.

The edition and title of the publication.

Check digit to validate.

Whichever service you opt for you will have to upload your book file in the appropriate format for conversion to read on the electronic reader device it is destined to be read on and there are commonly used formats for these as follows:

- **EPUB** is the global standard format for ebooks as it works on most devices. You can't create an EPUB file direct from a Word document (what most authors use) but you can save your Word document as a text (.txt) file, and then convert/format it using software mentioned below and in the Appendix.
- **MOBI** is Amazon Kindle format, although you can upload an EPUB file too.
- **PDF**: a PDF can be converted to ebook formats but it doesn't display particularly well on reading devices so EPUB or MOBI are better formats to use.

Some of the distributor-retailers will convert your word document for you, but you still have to 'unformat' it to an .html document for best results. You also need to ensure that it includes a table of contents or a table of contents will be created in the conversion process as this is the way ereaders will navigate through the book, and be aware that even though a file may *convert* to a new format, it may not be *formatted* so that it looks like a professional ebook. Formatting is covered for both print and ebooks in the next chapter unless to want to invest in the following software that will format and convert to an ebook for you:

- **Calibre**: is free software that converts and helps you format ebook files from a variety of file types.
- **Sigil**: is free software for editing and formatting ebooks, and converting to the EPUB format. You use a plain text file from Word in the process.

Details of both are given in the downloadable material referred to in the Appendix.
I would suggest you might initially want to take advantage of the formatting information in the next chapter and then the free conversion services offered by Draft2Digital and maybe Smashwords. However Smashwords does have a tricky little tripwire called the Autovetter which

your book has to pass through in order to make the grade, and there are a variety of little snags that could trip you up before you manage that. I would try Draft2Digital in the first instance and see how you get on; always best to try something that costs nothing first, isn't it?

Three other publishing options should be included here for completeness' sake:

1. **Using a self-publishing service, print only:** some self-publishing services offer the full whack – editing, proofing, print, ebook, marketing and distribution, at a price. Some offer lesser variations on this, at less cost, and some will proved a print-only service, where you buy copies of your book in bulk at a far lesser cost than if you'd used one of the other POD self-publishing services. Please be wary of any and all of these services, but particularly those where you buy a print run – anything between a few hundred and a few thousand copies. You need to be very confident that you are going to be able to sell all those copies, added to which if you subsequently find there is something you want to change either on the cover or inside, all those copies will be wasted.

2. **Crowdfunding:** is a way of getting your book published using other people's money – the 'crowd' that funds you. Unbound (https://unbound.co.uk/) is a good example of it. Your book (project) is featured on the website for interested parties to offer donations to 'fund' its publication – anything from £10 to £500. It sounds an excellent idea, but don't be fooled by the simplicity of the concept. It takes a huge amount of work to find, encourage and persuade people to donate. The one good thing about the process is that it does force the author into doing an enormous amount of promotional work even before the book sees the light of day – which can't be anything but good (see Chapter 20 in Part 3: PROMOTE).

3. **Amazon's White Glove Programme:** is available only to authors who are already represented by a literary agent. The premise is that the books they are represented for

have already passed the quality gatekeeping test by being accepted for representation. The White Glove Programme provides a form of assisted publication, helping agents and their authors with technical issues in order to get books that might otherwise languish in the shadows waiting for a traditional publisher. In return for implied, but not specifically promised, additional publicity by Amazon in the first 30 to 90 days after publication (the honeymoon period for newly released books) and some extra deals not otherwise available to independently self-published authors using KDP as a platform, the author enters into a contract for royalties at a specific percentage and complete exclusivity for Amazon for a specified term.

Does it make a difference how you self-publish? Difficult to say, but no doubt some of those books you are seeing popping up in front of you so regularly, either pre-release or immediately afterwards, with a ton of reviews and a high ranking with the publisher designated as 'Amazon Digital Services' are in the White Glove 'club' – and for some it definitely has 'bestseller' stamped all over it. Definitely worth thinking about if you are already represented but haven't found a publisher yet.

Chapter 12: Getting Digital

Creating a digitally formatted book is a little different to creating a book ready to go to print. What you see on your screen for a print book is not what you will see on, for example, a Kindle. There will be extra spaces where you've hit the space bar more than once when typing and the text won't be formatted so it flows the way it should on an electronic device. Remember, readers can adjust the size of text on an electronic reading device so it has to be fluid, not rigidly formatted as it is for a print book. Start, therefore, with a bit of housecleaning on your file to get rid of anything that will stop the flow.

Hit the show/hide button on your toolbar – the one that looks like this:

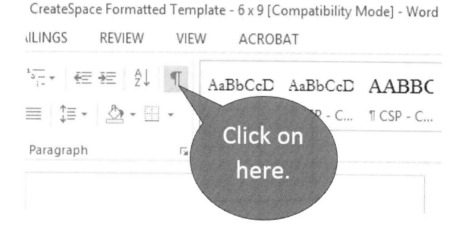

This brings up all the formatting. Now check for glitches, and amend:

- **Wherever you see a double dot at the end of a sentence** you've hit the space bar twice so backspace to remove one of them. A quick way of finding all the instances of this is by going to "Find/Replace" and hitting the space bar twice in the "Find" entry space and then hitting the bar once in the "Replace" entry space. Click "Replace all" and you've eliminated all of them in one fell swoop – if only doing the dusting at home was as easy! Do check you haven't eliminated any spaces you did want though before the final conversion.

- **Paragraphs are usually indented** by hitting the tab key when typing, but Kindle doesn't recognise this, so you will have to manually format the indent on a paragraph. Instead adapt the "Normal" style by right-clicking on it, and in "Modify" (from the drop-down menu), go to "Format" at the bottom of the screen and select "Paragraph". In "Paragraph", make sure the alignment is left, and that the indentation space is "0". Then look for "Special" on the right-hand side and in "First line" change the figures under "By" to read 0.5 cm, or 0.4cm if you prefer a smaller indent. Hit "OK", to all the screens until you are back to the main top menu of MS Word and now all your new paragraphs will indent automatically, but with no manual formatting to interfere.

- **Alignment should always be** left and don't 'justify' (centre text to the page). On eReaders, as in print books, the right margin is justified but on Kindle, the reader is in charge of font size, and every time the font size is changed the right-hand margin will change too. If you justify your file, it will simply be a mess when it converts to Kindle.

- **Spacing** should have zero in both boxes in the style sheet for "Normal" (I recommend Times New Roman as the font, 12 point) – i.e. nothing before, and nothing after and the spacing should be single. Kindle automatically puts a good space between lines, for easy reading, so you don't have to worry about it.

- **You can get rid of all manual page breaks** by running through the document and manually deleting them all, but another style sheet will deal with the problem for you far more effectively – see below.
- **Chapter headings** – choose "Heading 1" and right-click to get to "Modify". Keep the same font as you have used for "Normal" but change the font size to 16. Then go to "Format" and hit "Paragraph" again. In "Paragraph", change the alignment to "Centred" and the special to

"(none)". Now choose spacing of 42pt in the "Before" line and18pt in the "After" line, but still keeping the line spacing single. Finally at the top of the screen, click on "Line and Page Breaks", and you'll get the screen below.

Click the box by the fourth option "Page break before" and the "Widow and orphan control" box to ensure the last line of a paragraph doesn't slip over on to a new page all on its own. Then OK everything and this is now your style sheet for chapter headings. You can easily update all chapter headings by using the "Find" facility (I suggest you preface your chapter titles with 'Chapter' initially in order to do this, even if you decide to delete the 'Chapter' later), highlighting the chapter head and clicking "Heading 1".

- **If there are sub-sections within your chapters**, which you might have separated with a double hit of the return key, making a line space, create another style sheet called 'Subtitle'. Denote the subtitle in your manuscript by using a symbol instead of a double return – for instance, hit one return then use ### and then another return and format a style sheet to use on all instances of this in your document. Name the style sheet "Subtitle". Go to "Modify" and then "Paragraph". Make the alignment "Centred" and special "(none)". Put 3pt in the "After" box at "Spacing" and OK everything to close the style sheet. Now, find all those triple returns (using the find facility and the symbols you've used), highlight all three symbols and click the "Subtitle" style sheet.
- **You can do the same for 'quotes'** if you have included quotes in your book too. Create a style sheet called 'Quotes' and format in the same way by using the modify option in "Paragraph" but this time, you are allowed to 'justify'. Do adjust the indentation though – probably to 1.5cm to set the quote off from the rest of the text. Make sure that the special is "(none)". In this instance you may also want to add a double hit of the enter key before and after to distinguish it further. If your quotes aren't poetry, put 6 in the "Before" and "After" boxes to put spaces between the paragraphs in the quote.
- **Front matter:** always insert two blank pages at the front of your document. The first will be your title page, the second your copyright page.
- **Title page** – create another style sheet called 'Title' and this time use Times New Roman, in bold, and a font size of 28. Make the alignment centred and make sure that special

is "(none)". Use 42pt in the "Before" box and OK to complete the style sheet. Next bring up the first of the two blank pages you have created at the start of your document and type in the title of your book and the author's name underneath (Kindle insists it's done this way). Highlight both, click the 'Title' style sheet and you will have created your title page.

- **The copyright/rights page** is created in exactly the same way and comes after the Title page. Create a style sheet called 'Copyright' and modify it in the same way as before, with alignment centred, special "(none)", and 6pt both "Before" and "After".

- **There are a couple of additional pro tips** you may want to employ, but are not absolutely necessary to the health of your book:

- You may have noticed that in traditional print publishing, the first line of every chapter is not indented. If you want to follow this in your book, click the first letter of the first word of the first sentence of the chapter, and go to "Paragraph" within "Normal". Go to "Special" and change the box to "(none)" then hit OK to return to the top menu. Now your first line of your first paragraph in each chapter won't be indented but those in the following paragraphs will. You will need to do this for every chapter.

- The other is where you use an ellipsis (…), or ends abruptly with a long dash (an em rule) — (often used when speech is cut off). On Kindle the ellipsis or the long dash can leak over to the next line and look odd. Go through your document and close up the gap between the last letter of the word and the dots or the dash, so instead of:

"But the dog kept howling like a mad wolf to the moon …"

It becomes:

"But the dog kept howling like a mad wolf to the moon…"

and the problem will be fixed.

- **Now save your document as .docx** ("Web Page, Filtered.") and it will be ready for conversion. You can either upload it onto Amazon, and let Amazon convert it for you, or you can use the services of a formatter, and pay for them to format your file to Kindle and ebook, or use one of the other digital platforms like Draft2Digital. Upload your whole project, convert to Kindle or EPUB and then download the files; don't publish them (although you can do later if you are employing such strategies as 'perma-free' – see PROMOTE).

Chapter 13: Getting into Print

Even if you don't particularly want to publish your book as a print copy, it's still a good idea, despite maybe not anticipating actually selling many print copies. The print price will show up as a direct price comparison to the Kindle price, and of course the Kindle price will be much less, therefore making the Kindle version look an absolute bargain – for example, like this:

Turning your manuscript into a print book is actually relatively easy – more painstaking than difficult. Here are the guidelines, aiming for a professional and easy to read finish – no fancy fonts, dropped caps or unusual flourishes, starting with some terminology and tips:

- **Book size:** CreateSpace and its alternatives will offer you the choice of a variety of finished print book sizes, but probably the most used are, 5.06in x 7.81in (normal paperback size – which is 12.85cm x 19.84cm in metric) or 'Royal', which is 6in x 9in (or 15.24cm x 22.86cm in metric). I usually choose 6in x 9in mainly because, although it is slightly larger than the average paperback, it is still a popular standard size and because it is larger, the overall page count is less – a serious consideration when doing the sums for the costs of POD (print on demand). Fewer pages = less cost = higher royalty. A 6in x 9in book size also gives you more room for cover art – another bonus when considering what the thumbnail of your book will look like on Amazon or other sales platforms – more on that later in cover design.

- **Page margin** is how far away text is from the edge of the page. 0.6in to 0.8in is generally fine.
- **Gutter** is the extra space on the edge where the book is held together by its binding, and also where the margin needs to be slightly bigger than the standard page margin – say 0.3in more, so the gutter should be in the region of 0.9in to 1.1in.
- **Font** is the typeset used. Unless you are publishing a children's book, use a serif font. Some popular ones are Adobe Caslon Pro, Sabon, Dante, Minion Pro, Adobe Garamond Pro, Goudy Bookletter 1911, ITC New Baskerville, Cardo, Janson, Bookman Old style, Palatino Linotype, Bembo, Theano Didot, Tryst, Fournier, Filosophia, and Electra, but Times New Roman works perfectly well for me. Do not use a sans sans serif font (like Arial, Geneva or Helvetica).
- **Point** is the size of the font. If you choose a non-standard font, such as one of those off the list above, play around with it to check on size as some come up smaller and some larger. Aim for between 11 and 12 point, with 12 point for YA fiction and possibly 11 point for academic or non-fiction.
- **Spacing** is the distance between lines of text. Note: when submitting a manuscript to agents and publishers generally you should use double spacing (2.0). When formatting to publish, use around 1.3, with possibly 1.5 for self-help or spiritual genre books. Overall aim for 350 words per page for a 6in x 9in book and 300 words per page for a 5in x 8in.
- **Styles** are the formatting options for the bodies or types of text within your document. Make use of this feature to set up consistent formatting throughout your document, for example in MS Word, click on "Styles",

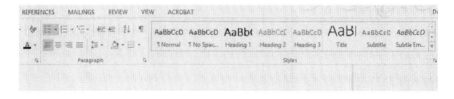

and it will automatically change the selected text to the font, size, line height, colour and spacing of that style. You can adapt the style by selecting the style you want to use/change and then right-clicking and selecting "Modify". In this screen you can change font, point size, justification (text position on the page), colour, spacing and so on, and if you drop down to the "Format" box at the bottom of the screen, you can drill down further to modify specific aspects even more. Choose "Paragraph", for instance, and you can set up whether you want to indent the first line of the paragraph, and by how much. Use the styles you have selected and modified to format your manuscript prior to conversion to digital format or PDF. Using styles will also make creating a Table of Contents for your digital book simple. These are the styles to set up:

- **Header:** for chapter titles. Use 'Header 1' to easily create a table of contents later and chapter titles are usually left-justified rather than full-justified (they are to the left of the page, not the centre).
- **First Para:** for the non-indented first paragraph of each chapter. Type a paragraph, setting the font, point size and line spacing to how you want them for the main text, then drill down to the "Para" section when in "Modify" and remove indentation in the settings. Save this style as "First para". A non-indented first paragraph is standard in all print and digital works.
- **Normal:** Copy your "First para" text and save as "Normal" but this time using modify to drill down to paragraph again and add an indent of 0.3in so that all paragraphs apart from the first paragraph will be indented.

- **Subtitle:** use if your book has a subtitle – to the main book title for instance, or the chapter titles. Typically, subtitles or subheads should be no more than 16 points in size, but you may need to go larger if you have several layers of subheads; you can also use italics and even underlining to set off sub-sub-heads.
- **Quotes:** if you are quoting from other works.
- **Foreword/Preface/ Introduction:** written by the author, explaining the purpose of the book.
- **Acknowledgement/dedication or a 'to/for' page:** dedicating the book to or acknowledging the particular input or help of specific individuals or bodies.
- **Epigraphs:** where the author includes a quotation at the front of the book.
- **Table of contents:** also known as a contents page and less popular now in general fiction, (but always present in digital formats).
- **List of figures:** where a book contains a number of illustration which may be referenced by a numbered list for ease.
- **List of tables:** where a list of tables is used for reference – much like a list of illustrations.
- **Page numbers:** for standardising page numbers when finalising before converting to PDF format.
- **Footers:** if adding notes in footers (academic and non-fiction works).
- **Headers:** manyprint books have the book title and author name in a header on alternate pages.
- **Title page:** the main title of your book.
- **Copyright page:** the copyright notice, ISBN, edition, publisher, date of publication and other cataloguing information.

When you want to edit your manuscript prior to formatting it will also be easy to edit any specific blocks of text without having to hunt through the whole manuscript for specific items. For instance, if you decide to change the chapter title format, change one title and modify it in styles. It will then update all other chapter titles to match. I have covered creating style sheets in Chapter 12 but remember that the style sheets you create for a file ready for conversion to EPUB or Kindle will be different to those you create for a print copy so simply repeat the process with the necessary adjustments for Kindle. Text will be justified to fit the page and margins and gutters are necessary in print where they are not in a digital format. Create separate style sheets for the two types of format.

Formatting

CreateSpace very helpfully provides a template for you to use if you want – a handy help as it is already formatted with gutter and margins, as well as a Title Page. When you choose the size of your print book, with it you'll get a clickable link to download an MS Word blank or formatted template. Choose the formatted template and you will get one formatted to the book size you've chosen, but before you do anything with it make sure you have turned on the "Show formatting" by clicking here:

Then your template will look like this:

Don't panic. The formatting won't show up on your book when finished. It's purely for you to see where the spaces and line/page and para breaks are for layout.

Add your book title and author name (no 'by'...please. It's not professional) and then add content to the copyright page.

I have a standard format copyright, but you can find guidance on copyright text from CreateSpace in their 'Help'section, and it should include this as standard even if it includes little more:

Copyright © [Year] by [Author Name]
All rights reserved.
ISBN:
ISBN-13:

Information about ISBNs was included in Chapter 11.

If you have a dedication or foreword to include, add them after the copyright page, but they are not mandatory. After this it's simply a case of putting your own text into the template. Copy the text in your document and then paste it into the template. The style formatting from your document should be preserved, but do a double check on things like italicised text.

You may decide to amend the margins slightly on the template, depending on how much text you want on a page – remember fewer pages = less cost so higher royalties on copies sold. On the other hand, a difficult to read page may be abandoned by a frustrated reader so don't cram a page; remember – aim for a good, easy reading experience. If you want to amend the margins, go to "Page layout" on the template, then "Margins" and then "Custom margins". The custom margins screen looks like this:

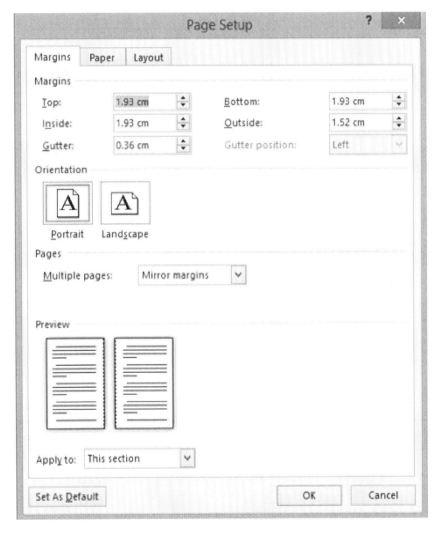

You can adjust the margin sizes so perhaps your gutter is slightly larger, and your header, but perhaps the bottom is slightly less. Test what you set up by looking at a two page view to see if it's easy to read before standardising to it, so make a note of what the original settings were before making modifications in case you want to go back and make further modifications or revert to the original template settings.

On to some more technical aspects now the main text is in the template: page and line breaks, headers, footers and page numbering. Your template should already be set up with alternate odd and even pages, but you will need to delineate within the document:

- **Where one chapter ends and another starts** using section or line breaks: place your cursor at the end of a chapter, and then in the top menu, select "Insert > Break > Section Break" and your next chapter will start on a new page. Note a section break is different to a page break – you'll see why in the part about headers below.
- **Chapter headings should all use the same MS Word style** and should look right in the context of the page so check first they are all formatted to this style and then adapt the size and font to suit. If you make a change when you are reviewing a page in this way and want to apply it to all chapter titles, simply reapply your 'Header' style and you'll get an option to update all style text to which 'Header' has been applied with the recent changes.
- **Number of pages in the book?** You will need to add some blank pages in the book so that overall the number of pages divides equally by four (two print pages back to back = 4 overall). Remember total pages includes the title page, copyright, dedications etc pages too. To add a blank page use "Insert > Page Break".
- **Headers and footers** are the trickiest bit of all if you want a professional finish. I've devoted a whole section to this below.

Headers, footers and page numbers:

Open a print book and you'll often find the author's name appears in the header on the left-hand side and the book title – or sometimes there are variations to this where a chapter title is used instead – on the right-hand side.

Why? Surely you know which book you're reading?

Of course – it's simply a bit of branding going on by the publisher but if you want your book to have that professional polish to it, you need to be branding too. By the way, these are called 'running headers' and here's how to set them up:

- Use a section break to mark the start of each chapter.
- Start each section on an odd page – your layout should already be set up for alternate odd and even numbers if you are using a CreateSpace template – like the image below, but if for any reason it's not, go into the custom margins section and click on layout to get this screen up then alter it to match the above.

- Blank pages should have no header, footer or page number.

- The first page of a chapter should have no header, footer or page number.
- Make each chapter a new section by adding a section break. Do this by positioning your cursor at the beginning of the chapter. Then go to "Page Layout", choose "Breaks", and then "Section Breaks". Choose the option of starting a new section on a new page.
- Now add the headers, footers and page numbers: go to the "Insert" menu, and at the beginning of the first page on which you wish a header to appear, click "Header". This brings up the header/footer menu.
- Click "blank" ([type text]). Under options, select "Different First Page" and "Different Odd and Even Pages".

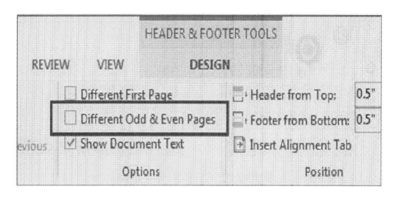

- Now, click "Page Number". For your even (left-hand) page, select the option to position the page number on the left and type in the book title, and format as desired.

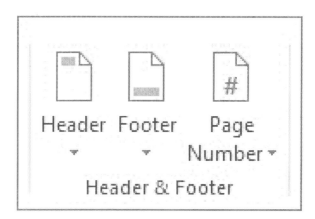

- Using the same font as you have used in your main text, capitalise the text you are inserting into the header, (where you see the words "type text", delete them or type over them to replace them with your text), or add the note you want to add in the footer non-capitalised text.
- Then, go to the next (odd/right-hand) page and repeat the same process, this time positioning the page number on the right and entering your author name or chapter title (whichever you are opting to include).
- Now go to the first page of your chapter; if you see the words "type text" at the top of the page, delete them.
- Finally, click the red "Close header and footer" button to return to your text and to check your headers.

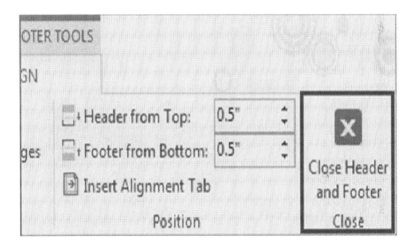

- Repeat this process for each chapter throughout the book.
- If you are using a chapter title, when you start a new chapter, click the "Link to Previous" button under the header that you want to change (for example your chapter title). This enables you to specify that you do not want to pick up the header from the previous chapter for that page.
- Word offers a variety of preformatted headers including some listed specifically for odd or even page layouts, but keep it simple.
- In the header/footer menu of Word, if you click "F1" you will get a help menu for additional guidance if required.
- Remember also to unlink the start of chapter one from the

front matter in the book so no headers or footers appear in the front matter.

- The front matter and back matter is generally not page numbered either – but if it is it will be in roman numerals, and remember when looking at page numbering that when you look at a double page spread in layout, odd numbers will appear to be on the left-hand side and even numbers on the right, but when the book is in print, it will be the reverse, so check carefully that you have identified the correct odd and even/left- and right-hand pages when creating headers and page numbering.

- Note also that if you created different first page or odd/even headers or footers, or if you used sections that aren't linked, you will need to manually remove the page number from each different header/footer for each chapter. First pages of chapters are not usually page numbered.

Some excellent and detailed guides covering formatting and formatting in MS Word are included in the Appendix so if you get stuck, have a look at them and follow them step by step if necessary. Failing that, formatting your files to print ready is one service I would definitely consider buying in from a freelancer. Fiverr (http://www.fiverr.com) is a good and inexpensive service to use.

Once completed, save the document as a PDF as you will have to upload to CreateSpace in this format. I will cover setting up an account and uploading to CreateSpace, including all the administrative issues you will need to address, in Chapter 15.

Chapter 14: Titles, Covers and Blurb

So your book is formatted and ready to convert, but it still needs a cover. CreateSpace enables you to create your own cover using their own templates, and to convert it to a Kindle cover too; a generous offer and you may wish initially to try this as it is free. However, you will need to supply your own imagery, and beware that your cover doesn't look amateurish as nothing potentially brands a book as self-published more than an amateurish cover. Cover creation on CreateSpace is quite simple, just follow the steps and it will more or less do it all for you, but the style and formats are also quite limited/limiting – and your cover will essentially look similar in style to every other CreateSpace cover. Much more creative and original is to upload your own cover, so let's look at how this can be done.

IMAGERY

First you will need to find an image, or images, for your cover. There are a number of places you can find suitable imagery, some entirely free but with attribution required, others paid but with licensing available. I have included a full list in the Appendix. There is also a list of cover designers – by no means comprehensive, but some who have been recommended or mentioned by other authors, and fonts for if you are intent on a DIY cover (from which you can gather I'd err on the side of a professionally designed one).

The point of an image is to attract the attention. The point of a good cover design is to hold that attention long enough for the viewer to take in more about the book and as a result be tempted to buy it. It needs to convey the genre and a sense of the book as well the story line, but in a dramatic and memorable way. A good cover should haunt you as much as the characters haunt you once you've read the book inside the cover. If it captures fundamentally and possibly in an unexpected way, what is inside, it's done its job well, therefore don't simply go for the obvious. If the book is about a man and a woman and a challenging love affair, don't simply opt for two figures and a dramatic backdrop. Look into the heart of what the book is about – its themes – and wrap them into the cover imagery.

Some other tips on imagery – tailor it to the current trends in the genre. Romantic literature tends to feature people, mysteries and thrillers atmospheric places (and often, people) indicative of the nuances in the plot or the setting. True crime is hard-hitting and often features the instruments of death – or the victims. Fantasy is almost certainly other-worldly, but often featuring its fantastical hero or heroine, and horror is dark and sinister, again often portraying its victims or villains. YA and new adult fiction – if not in the paranormal or dystopian veins – is real life to the core, and children's fiction often whimsical, caricature-or cartoon-like. Where does yours fit in there? And once you've determined that, does the image you have in mind really hit you between the eyes? You see the problem? That's why I tend to go with professional cover design – money well worth spending, but if you wish to look into a self-made cover, here are some ways of creating one.

- Photoshop Elements is good if you're doing lots of your own covers. The downside is that you will need to learn how to use it properly and you will have to buy the software first.
- You can download free software from Gimp (www.gimp.org) but I'm told there is a steep learning curve to using it.
- Canva (https://www.canva.com/create/book-covers/) can be used to create book covers but you will have to subscribe to it.
- PowerPoint can also be used;

  - Open up PowerPoint and on the "Home" tab, create '"New slide", choosing "Blank" for the layout.
  - Change the page setup to "Design" and on the far left you will see "Page setup". You will then get this screen:

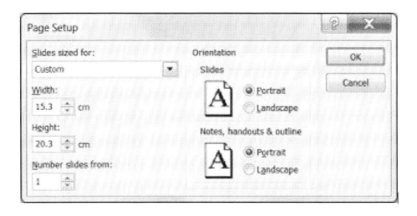

- Click "Portrait" beside both letters A and on the left-hand side, choose "Custom" for slide use. The width and height are trickier. The ratio should be 3:4 and in metric, this is a height of about 20cm and a width of about 15cm. If you have inches on your screen, use a height of 8 inches and a width of 6 inches. Click "OK" and insert the image you have chosen for your cover and you'll get an idea of how it will present. One advantage with using PowerPoint is that you will also be looking at a thumbnail on the left-hand side of your screen throughout the process – very useful for considering whether the cover you are designing will have sufficient impact on Amazon or any other sales platform in due course as this is all any potential reader will see initially.

- Insert your image by using the "Insert" tab in the top ribbon of PowerPoint, clicking "Picture", and browsing for the image saved in your library.

- Next add the author's name and the title of the book, using the insert tab again. This time hit "Text box" and click on the slide in the place you would like the words to appear. A box shape will appear for you to type your text into. Do this twice if the title and author's name are going to be placed on different parts of the cover.

- Play with fonts and effects, adjust the size, italicise, make bold or not etc until you achieve the effect you want. You can do this using "Text effects" – highlight your words and "Format" will come up. Hit this and "Text effects" will appear. Use them to bevel, add glow, outlines, change colour, and so on. Remember to keep checking the thumbnail on the left for the overall impact.

- Save your cover as a jpeg (Jpeg file interchange format), not a PowerPoint slide. When a box comes up saying "Do you want to export every slide or only the current slide", choose "Current slide only".

- If you tinker with it again, do it in PowerPoint on the slide you have created as every change you make to a jpeg degrades it a little more, losing quality. Save it as a separate jpeg each time until you are satisfied you have the final image then resize it, making sure the longest side of your cover is at least 1000 pixels to meet with Kindle's cover size requirements. Save it again and your cover is ready to upload to Kindle.

Note: I said your cover is ready to upload to Kindle, because this is only a front cover and if releasing a print copy of your book too, you will need a spine and back cover too.

- Word can also be used to create a basic cover for Kindle but the same limitations apply – it is not a full cover for a print book. To use Word to create a Kindle front cover:

  - Open up a new file in MS and adjust the size to 6in x 9in (or 5in x 8in if you've chosen that size for your print book). You can do this by going to "Page Layout" and "Size". Scroll down to "More Paper Sizes" and type in 6in and 9in in the relevant boxes.
  - You don't need the margins so big, so click on "Page Layout" again, select "Margins" and then set them to "Narrow" all around.
  - Add your pictures by using "Insert>Picture" and then selecting the image you want to use. When the picture is dropped in it will automatically stretch to fit the page up to the margins but you can't move it around. If you double click on the picture and go up to "Wrap Text"

and choose "Behind Text" you will be able to scale it, move it around and resize it to suit. Zoom in and out on detail using "View" and then "Zoom" if you need to.

- If you are using more than one image, select it in the same way, choose "Behind Text," and place it where you want it to be. If the picture is big, you may lose some of it under the other one, but that can be fixed (see below).

- If you click on "Page Layout" and open up the "Selection Pane" you can see all the layers in your document, making it easier to keep track of them. This is a little like Photoshop, where you will manipulate layers too. Whenever you want to hide one of them temporarily, click on the "eye" button to hide it, and click on the "eye" button to reveal it again when you want to see it. If you build up a number of layers, try right clicking on the *border* of the picture to select the right layer.

- You can also remove areas you don't want by using the "Remove Background" button on the top left. You can also use "Mark areas to keep" and "Mark areas to remove" to be ultra-selective. Then you can add another layer still if you want in the removed area.

- Add the title and author name by going to "Insert", clicking on "Shapes" and selecting the rectangle. You can resize the rectangle by dragging on a corner, or move it around to where you want it to be by dragging it across the page. Go to "Shape Outline" and hit "No Outline" to remove the black line around it and go up to "Shape Fill" to select whether you want a block colour as its background, or maybe even "No Fill" to allow the imagery underneath to show through.

- Add text by hitting "Insert" and "Text Box," choosing "Draw Text Box" and then typing inside it. You can leave out the step above and simply go straight to the text box if you don't want any background to it, or you can build up layers by overlaying one shape over another and choosing a different colour for each, adding the text box onto the top so it eventually looks like this:

- The text you use should always match your genre too. Don't use anything that comes with Windows such as Comic Sans, Times New Roman or Mistral, they scream amateur. Try to use two fonts – one for the title and something else for the author name. If you are trying to create an author brand, choose something striking and memorable for the author name. You can use more than two fonts if, for example, you have a subtitle or tagline in addition to the title but don't use more than one unusual font overall. There are links to some font sites in the Appendix. MS Word's maximum font size is 72pt, but you can overtype a different number in the point box and Word will apply it to any text you've highlighted.

- Letters can also be spaced differently too. Go to the "Home" tab, and underneath the "Font" box click on that tiny little diagonal arrow here:

That will bring up a new "Font" window. Click on the "Advanced" tab to see the "Spacing" option where you can set the text spacing to "Expanded", "Normal" or "Condensed" and by how many points.

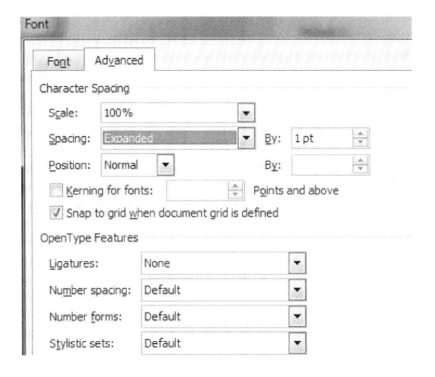

If you want to centre text, drag the walls of your text box to the edges of the cover, then click the centre text icon. In the "Paragraph" section, hit the tiny diagonal arrow, and make sure the Indentation is set at zero to ensure the text centres correctly.

- To add the author name under the title the best option is to copy the text box you've already created and paste it to form a duplicate text layer. Set the font, point size and text width to suit and add the author name.
- Finally, if you want to make the text stand out more, use the same type of enhancements you used in the PowerPoint option: bevel, glow, outline, shadow etc by clicking the "Format" option and selecting which

special effect you want to apply. You can play around with colours, gradient, transparency or even add more than one effect at a time.

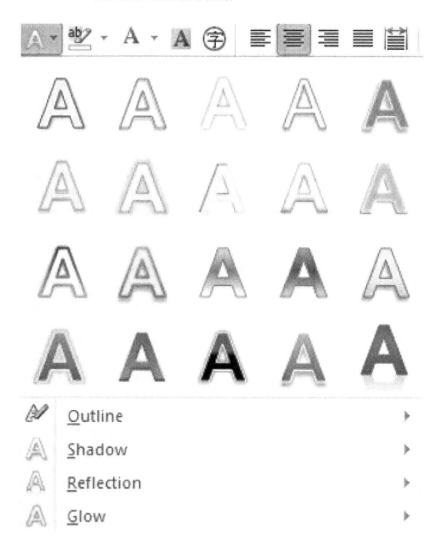

- You can also texture or add special effects to the image itself by selecting the layer behind the text and again choosing "Format". Use the "Selection Pane" which will still be on the right-hand side of your screen. There you can select the layer or hide the two text layers if you are having difficulty isolating the layers.

- You can also format the overall shape by clicking once on the background rectangle to bring it up, right click and choose the last option: "Format Shape". Here you can access other formatting options such as the "Glow and Soft Edges" tab which you can use to make soft edges big enough for images to transition seamlessly into each other.
- You can continue to add layers and other images until you are happy with the overall result but be careful not to cram too much in and make the whole cover seem crowded. Maybe adding gradient to the cover might have more effect than adding more imagery – hit "Page Colour" and then "Fill Effects" to add a gradient.
- Normal pictures don't have a transparency option, only shapes, so make sure the shapes are in front of the images in order to apply gradients.
- Last of all, if you add another effect and decide you don't like it, all isn't lost. Just hit the little blue arrow facing away from the screen in the top left-hand corner (the "Undo" arrow) and you will remove the last revision you just made. Save as a jpeg and then resize to meet Kindle pixel requirements and you have a cover.

NOW FOR THE BLURB!

The words you put on the back cover of your book are potentially the most important words you write about your book. Why? Because after the book title and front cover, the back cover is the next thing a reader looks at when deciding whether or not to buy it. If your book is only in ebook format then this will apply to the book description you put on Amazon or any of the other sales platforms you use – equally so for a print book, by the way because a potential purchaser will read the book description online, not the back cover. It is therefore the main initial promotion for your book. One hundred-and-fifty words to sell it – a tough call!

So what do you include? Here are some tips:

- First have a look at other books in your genre to see what they have to say for themselves.

- If you are a novelist, your description/back cover should be a summary of what your book is about. Include the hooks – you could use the ones from your query letter if you submitted to agents and publishers. Perhaps end the description with an intriguing question or a point of conflict, something that highlights the central character's dilemma, but keep to the bigger picture, not the intricate detail.

- Non-fiction authors should list the book's main features in bullet points and include that list on the back cover. Three to five will do it (apparently odd numbers work best according to market research). Within the bullet points, tell the reader what the book is going to do for them and keep the style consistent – i.e. if you start with participles, stay with them, or if you start with clauses, stick to them. For example I didn't say in the blurb about this book:

"In PUBLISH find out how to get your work published:

- *Writing a synopsis, pitch letters and submitting to agents and independent publishers.*
- *A review of the possible self-publishing platforms to consider.*
- *How to format for print and ebooks – a step-by-step guide, plus cover designs, cover blurbs and pricing."*

I said:

"In PUBLISH find out how to get your work published, including,

- *Writing a synopsis, pitch letters and submitting to agents and independent publishers.*
- *If self-publishing, a review of the possible self-publishing platforms to consider.*
- *Formatting for print and ebooks – a step-by-step guide, plus cover designs, cover blurbs and pricing."*

- Your back cover also needs a professional-looking photograph of you, the author; a good close-up photo of your face, with no one else in the picture, and current so that you could be recognised from it. Accompanying this should be a brief bio about you. You can include a more formal and complete author bio in your book, on your website and on your Amazon Author Central pages (more about these later).
- DON'T repeat anything you've already said elsewhere – you've only got a small space so why do it, and it will only put a potential reader off. Also, make sure you go for 'understated'. If you tell people how awesome this book is you will not only look amateurish, you will be inviting challenge.
- Endorsements and reviewers/critics quotes: if you have them – short pithy comments from people either relevant in your field, well known in your genre or relevant to the book – include them in the description. Want to get some endorsements? Cultivate connections with well-established writers in your genre at writers' conferences, networking events, author talks, or even initially via social media. Establish sufficient of a working relationship with that writer for them to know and respect your work and then simply *ask*, very politely.
- Metadata: is the secret sales machine I go into in more detail in PROMOTE, but for now be aware when writing your blurb/book description that there are certain key words and phrases that you want to incorporate. These are the words and phrases that will get your book 'found' online. They are the words and phrases that readers who are looking for books like yours will be using in their searches. You can target them in a variety of ways, using things like Google Adwords or even starting to type words into Amazon's search bar and taking note of what Amazon so helpfully provides for you. There is also software that can make such search term identification even easier for you, like Kindle Spy and Kindle Samurai. I would suggest reading Chapter 16 first (crazy though that sounds) and then writing your blurb/book description.

So now you have file, cover and blurb – you're ready to roll the presses (or open the browser)!

To publish and distribute through Amazon:

- For CreateSpace (print books) you want to go to: https://www.createspace.com/
- And for Kindle you want to go to: http://kdp.amazon.com/

Chapter 15: Uploading to Amazon

For both KDP and CreateSpace, you will need to create an account – an account for each, that is. It's very easy to upload your book – I am going to call your book a project in this chapter because it is, as it now contains a number of elements that make up your book, and each of them need to be ready before you start so this is now a project. I am not going to go through each screen in the uploading process as it is quite straightforward if you simply follow the process through as guided by KDP or CreateSpace, but I will cover specific points you need to deal with along the way.

ACCOUNT AND PAYMENT CONCERNS

- **Tax:** To set up an account you will need to also be able to enter tax information and bank account information for payment of royalties. If you are a US citizen, you will already have a TIN (Tax Identification Number made up of a Social Security Number – SSN, or an Individual Taxpayer Identification Number – ITIN). If you aren't a US citizen, then you need to obtain a TIN if your country has a double taxation treaty agreement with the US which will allow you to receive your royalty payments without the deduction of withholding tax (usually 30%) at source. In order to do this you will need to fill in a number of forms, including an IRS Form W-7 to obtain a US ITIN, which requires you to provide an amount of documentation to the US or one of its embassies. You will have to fill in W-8 forms relating to tax and income receipts even if you don't. You will find all of the guidance here: https://www.createspace.com/tax-interview/help?nodeId=201447640&locale=en_US
- **Receipt of royalties:** both CreateSpace and KDP will

require specific bank account details from you to remit royalties and they will require international banking information to do so – remember they have to comply with money laundering legislation as well as ensure your remittances get to you without mishap. For payments to be made directly into your bank account (recommended as there is no bottom line figure required before payments are made as there are with other payment options) you will need to provide both the IBAN and SWIFT codes which are used in international/online banking. You can find these on the top of your paper bank statements or online in the account information generally displayed at the top of the statement screen.

DISTRIBUTION CHOICES:

On KDP, there is no choice – it's all simply set up for you. On CreateSpace there are a number of options. What is available to you is limited in one instance by whether you have chosen to take up CreateSpace's offer of a free ISBN. If you have, you can also opt for your books to be distributed to libraries and academic outlets, but if you haven't there are other ways of making your books available to libraries and recouping lending fees via ALCS, so look carefully at Chapter 20 in PROMOTE for information about this. How your ISBNs are registered and what ISBN you use is also very relevant to where your books will be distributed. Basically distribution choices are this:

> **CreateSpace:**   Amazon.com
> Amazon Europe (.co.uk etc)
> CreateSpace eStore
> Bookstores and Online Retailers (Barnes & Noble, Ingram and NACSCORP)
> Create Space Direct (certified resellers such as independent bookstores)
> Academic Institutes and Libraries (only with a CreateSpace ISBN)
> **KDP:** Amazon.com
> Amazon Europe (.co.uk etc)

162

If you move away from Amazon, there are a number of other outlets as already outlined in Chapter 11, Ingram being the major rival to CreateSpace.

FEATURES	CREATESPACE	INGRAM SPARK
Cost Per Copy B&W	4.45	4.86
Cost of Setup	$0	$49**
Discount	40/60%*	40/55%*
Distribution	Amazon/Extended	Worldwide
ISBN	Yes	Yes
Quality	Very Good	Excellent
Shipping	Exc. US/Int'l okay	Very Good US/Int'l excellent

Return on investment (ROI)
Based on 300 page B&W book 6 inches x 9 inches

BASED ON RETAIL PRICE OF $15	PROFIT IF SOLD ON AMAZON	PROFIT IF SOLD ANYWHERE ELSE
CreateSpace	4.55	1.55
Ingram Spark	4.14	4.14

Suggestions: Use both CS and Ingram.

Use CS for:
- Fast and good distribution to Amazon.
- Fast and affordable shipping to US customers.

Shipping "review copies" to bloggers and/or for giveaways like on Goodreads.

Use Ingram for:
- Distribution to all stores except Amazon.
- Fast and affordable shipping to international customers.

Shipping high-quality copies as samples to bookstores, autographed copies, etc.

You may find you can partner with a local independent bookstore for a small supply, especially if your book is of local interest. Bookstores do tend to work on a sales or return basis though – i.e. if it doesn't sell they hand it back to you, and they won't pay you until a sale has been made. They also generally prefer to obtain books through a wholesale distributor and usually at a discount of between 45% and 65% on retail price, which doesn't leave much profit margin for you. They also are wary about taking POD (print on demand) books, preferring wholesalers as suppliers. You can sell directly from your own website if you have enough existing visibility or audience following to be able to do so – perhaps you are publishing books that are no longer available via mainstream publication from a back catalogue. Most debut authors are not likely to be able to do much this way though.

You can also become your own distributor on Amazon by becoming an Amazon vendor and if you look at the box alongside the CreateSpace eStore in the distribution screen, there is an option there to set up your eStore if you want to – most suited to those already versed in marketing. If you run your own eStore you are also responsible for filling your own orders (back to that booklog…).

ISBN issues:

- If you use a CreateSpace ISBN or an ISBN provided by any other distributor you will be tied to their distribution platform. If you later decide you'd like to distribute through other channels, you will have to provide another ISBN for the new distributor.
- You don't need an ISBN for Kindle books at all as Amazon allocates you its own product identifier in the form of an ASIN (Amazon Standard Item Number), but again if you want to sell ebooks other than through Amazon, you will run across the same tie-in issues as with print books, so you may want to allocate your own ISBN to your ebook version as well as your print version.

SOME TECHNICAL ISSUES AND TRICKS:

KDP:

On the first screen you see when uploading your book:

- Upload the book title and subtitle information, and this is where your book description is the online advert for your book. The text box only allows you to type in or copy and paste and if you do that, you will simply get a solid block of text. You can, however, use limited HTML to pretty it all up and it's well worth doing so. There are two ways of doing this – on your own or with some assistance. First, with assistance:

    - Using the Author Marketing Club (http://authormarketingclub.com/), which you have to join and subscribe to, then you can use their Book Description HTML tool in the premium members area. Put your description into the appropriate boxes on the screen and the tool will automatically add the correct HTML tags for you. The Author Marketing Club also has some other useful tools and tips on offer to premium members but it will cost you $149 (about £100) a year for the privilege.
    - Using a limited knowledge of HTML and a great deal of patience, you can create the same pretty formatting yourself and check it out here: http://ablurb.github.io before uploading it to KDP or CreateSpace. The relevant tags to use are shown opposite:

And after using each tag always repeat the tag with a / to signify that the piece of coding is now complete, for instance: **<h1> word</h1>**

What do they mean or do?

Well basically, if you do nothing more than use these:

- Bold: The text you want bolded

<h1>	<p>	<b>	<hr>
 	<i>	<em>	<li>
<font>	<ol>	<h2>	<pre>
<h3>	<s>	<h4>	<strike>
<h5>	<strong>	<h6>	<u>
<sub>	<sup>	<ul>	

- Italics: <i>The text you want italicised</i>
- Headline: <h1>The text you want for a headline</h1>
- Amazon Orange Headline: <h2>The text you want in bold</h2>

Your description will stand out better if you use html so it's worth mastering.

You can add in quite a bit more, if you want to, including numbered lists and bullet points. Below is an example of how a variety of html tags translate into print.

<b>help</b>
sell</br>your</br><em>book</em><font>by</font><h1>using</h1><h2>HTML</h2><h3>to</h3><h4>make</h4><h5>the</h5><h6>text<h6><h2>stand</h2><h3>out</h3><h4>more</h4><h5>and</h5><h6>surprise</h6><hr>readers</hr><i>with</i><li>what</li><ol>they</ol><p>find<p><pre>in</pre><s>your</s><strike>description</strike><strong>on</strong>_{Amazon}^{or}<u>CreateSpace</u><ul>now.</ul>

Translates to this:

help
sell
your
*book*by

using

HTML

to

make

the

text

stand

out more

and

surprise

readers*with*
- what

they

find

in

~~your description on~~ Amazon or CreateSpace

now.

And this:

<h2>Winner of a BRAG Medallion for excellence: </h2><h3><i>Patchwork Man is a dark, fast-paced British legal mystery and crime thriller where a lawman must turn vigilante to

survive. </i></h3><p></p><p>British barrister Lawrence Juste is a man with a past, a patchwork past – but so cleverly stitched up he thought it could never come unravelled; not until he's forced to play detective with the family and people he's spent years running away from.</p><p></p> <p></p><p></p><p>Then he was an abandoned boy, steeped in organized crime and operating outside the law. Now he's a wealthy and respected barrister, tipped for High Court Judge.</p><p>Now he's faced with the blackmail note his dead wife has left him. Then he was running from the enemy; the one who has just found him again.</p><p>Then he forced himself into an emotionless existence, shutting out any risk of vulnerability. Now he's discovered the passion his past has always lacked. But that passion and that past could kill him.</p><p></p><p></p><p><i><b><i><b>Patchwork Man is the first in the Patchwork People psychological mystery and suspense thriller series.<i></i><b></b>

Translates to this:

Winner of a BRAG Medallion for excellence:

Patchwork Man is a dark, fast-paced British legal mystery and crime thriller where a lawn

British barrister Lawrence Juste is a man with a past, a patchwork past – but so cleverly stitched up he thought it
the family and people he's spent years running away from.

Then he was an abandoned boy, steeped in organized crime and operating outside the law. Now he's a wealthy and

Now he's faced with the blackmail note his dead wife has left him. Then he was running from the enemy; the one

Then he forced himself into an emotionless existence, shutting out any risk of vulnerability. Now he's discovered th
could kill him.

Patchwork Man is the first in the Patchwork People psychological mystery and suspense thriller series.

- Check the box to claim worldwide publishing rights (*This is not a public domain work and I hold the necessary publishing rights*).
- **DO** enable DRM (digital rights management). This protects

your book from being pirated.

- If your book is for children you will need to check the appropriate age range – see Chapter 2 in WRITE, but here are the age ranges again:

    - **Preschool** = Picture books (ages 0 to 4).
    - **Kindergarten–2nd grade** = Early, levelled readers; first chapter books (ages 5 to 7).
    - **3rd grade–6th grade** = Middle-grade chapter books (ages 8 to 11).
    - **7th grade–12th grade** = Teen and young adult chapter books (ages 12 to 17).
    - **Young Adult fiction** generally covers the age range 14 to 18 and includes the themes of love and some sex – diplomatically alluded to.
    - **New Adult** generally covers the age range 18 to 22 and may include quite explicit sexual themes in the context of young people finding out about themselves, their world and their emotions.

- Be careful to note the date by which your final document must be uploaded if putting your book on pre-order release. KDP will block your right to do this for a year if you miss the deadline.
- Always proof the book thoroughly using the online or downloadable viewers in case what you thought was formatted perfectly appears quite different on Kindle.

On the second screen you see when uploading your book:

- Choose worldwide distribution rights (unless you don't have these – for instance if you are following a hybrid publishing model and have already sold some rights.
- Select the royalty you require – 70% or 35%, noting that the price you can charge is regulated by the royalty being paid. Also note that you can set specific prices in specific countries if you wish by unchecking the "Set price automatically based on US price" box.
- Enrol in Kindle Matchbook – i.e give those readers who

have already bought your book in print form the option to buy the book in digital form for less than half the price of the ebook; worth doing as some will take it up and any option for a sale is worth having.

- Kindle Book Lending Programme – the last option for you to consider – allows readers who have bought your book to lend it to someone else for up to 14 days with no charge to them or the new reader. Do you want to allow this? It is an option you can take your book out of if you are in the 35% royalty, but not in the 70% royalty. Let's face it, if your book is in the 35% royalty category you can charge anything between $0.99 and $200 so it will depend on the price you've set for the book. If it's a mere $0.99 why would you let someone read it for free when it's only going to cost the new reader $0.99 to buy it themselves? On the other hand if it's the first in a series and reading the first book might get them hooked and buy the rest in the series, why not? Simply make sure the other books in the series aren't in Kindle Book Lending Programme.
- Finally, only "Save and Publish/Submit for Pre-order" when you're absolutely sure everything is exactly the way you want it to be. If in doubt 'Save as Draft" until you are.

CreateSpace:

- **Title Information**: be very careful what you enter here as once entered and saved, it cannot be changed.
- **ISBN**: read through the information I've given about ISBNs in this chapter and in Chapter 11 and decide now what you will be doing with this book in the future as that will greatly affect your decision about ISBNs. You can, however, change the ISBN details at a later stage *before* you publish.
- **Interior**: this relates to book size and the interior contents (a PDF file) and this has been discussed in Chapter 11 as well. The industry standard for fiction books is a colour cover and cream paper. Non-fiction may have white paper, if preferred. Do always thoroughly review the interior online as a minimum, but preferably order a proof copy to

check too.

- **The Cover** is a choice between matte and glossy – most choose matte – and of uploading your book cover, which will be a PDF file, unless you are using the CreateSpace cover creator option.
- **Complete Setup** gives you another chance to review what you have uploaded before setting up the distribution channels and releasing the book.
- **The Description** is where your book blurb/ description becomes important. Use HTML as with the KDP instructions above.

You may have noticed I haven't said anything about BISAC Categories or Keywords yet and I will do at length below, so save your work as a draft and read on.

Chapter 16:
Keywords, Categories and SEO

So your book and at least 12 million others are swilling around on Amazon. You check your KDP dashboard and find you have no sales – not even a sniff of one, in fact; why? You need to be found, and there are a number of things you need to do to achieve this. Amazon, Smashwords, Lulu and all of the sales platforms are really just giant search engines. You look online, type in the sort of thing you're looking for and the site offers you a selection of things matching your preferences – thousands of them! If it's a potato peeler, there'll be all manner and make of them. If it's a book there are all kinds of categories and genres, so you need to establish the words, phrases and lists readers might look in to find a book like yours; in other words, keywords and categories. This is what KDP and CreateSpace give you the opportunity to do in the Keywords and Categories boxes when uploading your file.

CATEGORIES – these are the genres your book falls into. For example, let's look at Amazon. On the left-hand side of the Amazon page there are lists of categories – in Kindle books there are thrillers, literary, romance etc. Click on one of them – say mystery – and you'll find more options.

As of today I found these possible mystery categories:

Women Sleuths (14751)
Police Procedurals (8564)
Hard Boiled (6979)
Private Investigators (5594)
Collections & Anthologies (4793)
Cozy (6446)
Mystery (10185)

Historical (6779)
International Mystery & Crime (3731)
Cozy Animal Mystery (2,828)

The numbers after the description are the number of books currently on sale in that sub-category of mystery. Drill down further and you'll find yet more sub-categories. Your mission is to find the sub-category that best fits your book, but with the least competition in it. That way, when a potential reader looks in the category, hey presto! They find your book high up on the list. Discoverability!

Amazon will allow you two of these category descriptions per book. They are referred to as BISAC codes and the most up-to-date list of current BISAC codes can be found here https://www.bisg.org/bisac-subject-codes. Here's a useful tip: if you can't find the right category in the BISAC lists on your KDP dashboard when you're entering the data for your book prior to, or after updating it post-publication, choose 'non-classifiable' and then email KDP with the category you think your book falls into (as long as you've seen it elsewhere). KDP will very helpfully add it for you.

Why are categories so important? It's all to do with achieving the highest ranking you can in that category because when a potential reader searches for a book, you want to be one of the first books they find.

KEYWORDS… are the words people use to further define what they're looking for within categories. They need to relate specifically to your book as well. They're trickier than finding the right category because there are infinite possibilities. How do you decide? There are two answers to this, the long one and the short one:

The long answer requires you to research what other books similar to yours have used for keywords. You can do this by typing in various suitable words and phrases in the search bar on Amazon and reviewing the results. Amazon itself can be quite helpful here, automatically prompting you with alternate versions of the phrase, which you can also try. It's a time- consuming process, but done logically and patiently, will produce some solid keywords – and keywords work best as a two or three word phrase, such as *thriller series* or *serial killer mystery*. You are ultimately looking for keywords that are popularly searched for, but do not simply pitch you up against major competition. The idea is *to be found* and you won't be found if there are hundreds of other books popping up in the search results before yours does.

The short answer is make use of some of the tools available to help, like Google Adwords (https://adwords.google.com/KeywordPlanner https://adwords.google.com/KeywordPlanner), or better still, some smart software you can buy which will draw off popular keyword phrases based on a sample you input, suggest other suitable variations and provide you with the statistics relevant to each keyword – popularity of use, average rankings of other books using the same keyword, average pricing and the average number of reviews those books have. From the statistics they provide you can determine the most helpful keywords and phrases to apply to your book to be able to compete. I use two pieces of software that can do this; Kindle Spy and Kindle Samurai. You will find details of where you can find them in the Appendix.

Tips on choosing keywords:

- Think like your potential customers. What would you search for if you were your customer? Ask others to suggest keywords they'd search for too.
- Focus on things that are unusual or specific to your story within your setting, character types (e.g. single parent), character roles (e.g. female sleuth), plot themes (e.g. coming of age), story tone (e.g. apocalyptic).
- To be included in certain categories on KDP your keywords must include some specified for that category. You can find the lists here: https://kdp.amazon.com/help?topicId=A200 PDGPEIQX41
- Also, bear in mind that keywords mean 'long tail keywords', i.e. not a single word, but a phrase that best describes your book, content, genre or subject matter.
- DON'T include:

  - Information already covered elsewhere in the book's metadata like title, author name etc.
  - Subjective claims like "the best…"
  - Statements that aren't permanently true like "newly released"
  - Information common to most items in the category, e.g. "book"

- Variants of the same, for example, "computer" and "computers"
- Anything potentially misrepresentative, like "bestseller".

- On CreateSpace, the number of keywords is 5, and with a maximum of 25 characters including spaces per keyword. You can enter 7 keywords on KDP and the number of characters per keyword is much larger. Always separate keywords with a comma and leave out spaces wherever you can to maximise use – especially on CreateSpace, so, for example, leave out spaces between words and commas.
- A little-known tip with keywords if you have difficulty in finding the right category or your book is wide-ranging in subject matter – it's called keyword stuffing. For the first 6 keywords, input as normal and for the 7th keyword slot, type in whatever comes to mind about your book *without* commas separating the words (or each will be regarded as a separate keyword and KDP will reject all but the first word you enter). The KDP keyword box has quite a bit of room, so you can write a few dozen words usually. Use them wisely. It's not as good as specifically targeted keyword phrases separated by commas, but it can help a little in getting wider exposure.

LOOK INSIDE:

If you upload your book to KDP and CreateSpace yourself, the 'Look Inside' feature – which allows potential readers to look at a small percentage of the book for free; a taster, is automatically activated after about a week for books on Kindle. For print books you will need to sign up and enrol your book in the programme via your 'Author Central' page on Amazon. Not only does it enable book sampling, it also facilitates 1-click purchasing – making it as easy as possible for a buyer to buy – and improve search results by actually employing words from within the book itself as well as the keywords you've entered for the book, so if someone is searching for a book on cleaning using natural or organic products, if your book says so using these words within it, Amazon will show it in the search results. Well worth doing, therefore.

And finally SEO: not just for your website…

SEO stands for Search Engine Optimisation, and when you consider that Amazon and the other distributors like Apple etc are really just gigantic search engines designed for customers to find the product they are looking for and then to sell it to them, you'll see why being found is the most important aspect of getting sold. Effective SEO helps you be found. The periphery – the other forms of promotion and marketing – are merely funnels into the search engine so when your potential readers get there, by whatever means, you need to be discoverable by using the kind of terms, words and phrases they're likely to use when they start searching. Keywords and categories are what work inside Amazon. Search Engine Optimised words and phrases are what work outside as well. Search Engine Optimisation (SEO) is simply a way of ensuring a website or other online content – a blog, or on Amazon, a book description – can be found in search engines for words and phrases relevant to what the site or the product is offering/about. It relies on 'free', 'organic', 'editorial' or 'natural' search results – that is, not something you have paid for through advertising but the kind of things people are searching online for all the time.

All the major search engines such as Google, Bing and Yahoo curate primary search results, where web pages and other content such as videos, blogs and local listings are ranked based on what the search engine considers most relevant to its users. If you can find content that the search engine thinks highly relevant your website or listing will be pushed up the rankings and shown more often to its searchers. What happens then? Well if you're seen more often, you're looked at more often and it's a self-perpetuating process that happens without you having to do anything except post online more of the same kind of thing. SEO is created through content, pure and simple, in the first instance – what you put on your website or in your book description. It's all about creating something potential customers are interested in reading and that is relevant to both what they are searching for and what you are marketing. Google's SEO guide is here http://static.googleusercontent.com/media/www.google .com/en//webmasters/docs/search-engine-optimization-starter-guide.pdf and is worth having a look at to explain some of the finer points in a basic way to help you get started.

How does SEO translate into practice? Well, on Amazon I structure my book descriptions around the keywords I have used and on my website I do the same and ensure the same keywords feature in the page headings/descriptions on my website or in the tags I attach to my blog posts.

Here's an example I used for *Patchwork Man* at one stage:

Keywords in KDP Dashboard: *family saga series, British legal thriller, organized crime, maverick detective, blackmail and murder mystery, conspiracy and suspense mystery, London barrister.*

Book Description: (keywords are underlined)
"Patchwork Man is a dark, fast-paced British legal thriller where a lawman must turn maverick detective to survive.

London barrister Lawrence Juste is a man with a past, a patchwork past – but so cleverly stitched up he thought it could never come unravelled; not until he's forced to play detective with the family and the crime he's spent years running away from: the mystery behind another mystery he's living right now.

Then he was an abandoned boy, steeped in organized crime and operating outside the law. Now he's a wealthy and respected barrister, tipped for High Court Judge.

Now he's faced with the blackmail note his dead wife has left him. Then he was running from the enemy; the one who has just found him again.

Then he forced himself into an emotionless existence, shutting out any risk of vulnerability. Now he's discovered the passion his past has always lacked. But that passion and that past are also part of a conspiracy that could kill him.

Patchwork Man is the first in the Patchwork People family saga involving blackmail and murder, conspiracy and suspense at the deepest level: leave behind all you thought justice entailed."

Categories it showed up in on KDP Dashboard:
Kindle Store > Kindle eBooks > Mystery, Thriller & Suspense > Mystery > **Series**
Kindle Store > Kindle eBooks > Mystery, Thriller & Suspense > Thrillers > **Conspiracies**
Kindle Store > Kindle eBooks > Mystery, Thriller & Suspense > Thrillers > **Legal**

If you look now, the description is different again – and so are the keywords – which is another tip worth mentioning; don't put your description and keywords out there and just forget about them. Monitor, amend, update; tweak to fit the current trends and your market because with more than 12 million books, and counting, things are always moving on…

Good SEO also comes from other sources such as return links from other sites that curate or offer content similar to yours, and other online sources such as book trailers (video is a prime mover in gaining visibility), podcasts and similar. More on book trailers in PROMOTE and the resources you can employ to do just that for your book.

Chapter 17:
Copyrights, Tax, More Distribution,
& all that Jazz

First of all, copyrights – and yes there is more than one sort...

COPYRIGHT is the law that gives you ownership over anything you have created, so if you've written a book, it's the copyright for your book. It could be a painting, a photograph, a poem or even an article. If you created it, you own it and if anyone else wants to use it, you have to grant them that right before they can do so. Copyright law grants come with a variety of rights exclusive to you, including:

- The right to reproduce the work you have created.
- The right to prepare derivative works based on it.
- The right to distribute copies of it.
- The right to perform it (a play, on TV, film, read aloud, etc).
- The right to publicly display it.

MORAL RIGHTS are a major element of European copyright law, although not recognised in the US. These are separate from the author's copyright on a piece, but are considered inalienable, so they cannot be given away or sold. They continue to exist even if the copyright to a work is sold and are, according to the Berne Convention:

- The right to claim authorship of the work.
- The right to object to distortion, mutilation or modification of the work.
- The right to object to any derogatory action that may

damage the author's honour or reputation.

So moral rights may still apply even where copyright is already sold or has been lost or given away (e.g. Creative Commons), so it remains the author's ongoing defence against plagiarism.

INTELLECTUAL PROPERTY RIGHTS (slightly different) are bound up in something unique that you physically create. An idea alone isn't intellectual property, but a description of it is. You own intellectual property if:

- You created it (and it meets the requirements for copyrights, patents or designs).
- You bought the intellectual property rights from the creator or previous owner.
- You have a brand that could be trademarked – for example, a well-known product name.

You can willingly give up your rights – for example via a Creative Commons Licence, but no one is allowed to violate them legally if you don't. This means that you have to formally agree for anyone to use or reproduce your work in any way.

It works in reverse too, of course. If you want to use a piece of work you've found, you must formally acquire permission to do so (covered in Chapter 8 of WRITE) or confirm that it is already in the public domain (check here: http://www.unc.edu/~unclng/public-d.htm). Of course you can also sell your rights, and not all in one hit either. Usually if you are signed by a traditional publisher, you will sell the publishing rights to your book(s). Traditional publishers usually contract with you for 'world rights' but you don't have to sell world rights. Small or independent publishers may take specific country rights or even rights for just one form of reproduction. These are the rights a publisher could buy from you:

Print distribution
Digital distribution
1st serialisation
2nd serialisation and so on …
Film rights

TV rights
Digest (condensed version)
Radio and TV straight reading rights
Audio rights
Book club rights (some 'Classic' book clubs buy these)
Large print rights
Anthology and quotation rights

How do all these rights work for an author?
Answer: you can make money out of all of them. I've covered how in Chapter 24 of PROMOTE.

When you become a self-published author, you also become a self-marketer and that involves going back to Second World War attitudes; never waste any part of what you have fought so hard to win – in this case, your book in print or digital format. Talking of getting paid for your book, here's a little bit of information often overlooked in the hustle and bustle of getting a book out there…

WHAT DO YOU DO WHEN IT IS OUT THERE AND YOU'RE ABOUT TO GET PAID FOR IT?

Well, first of all, KDP, CreateSpace, Smashwords, Lulu and any other potential publisher/distributor of your book will have already required you to set up an account with them and because this involves (you hope) them paying you royalties at some stage, they have a number of hoops both you and they have to jump through. One is money laundering regulations – checking you are who you say you are, the second is how they're going to pay you, and the third is how you're going to account for it to the tax man.

Accounts and payments:

- **Tax:** To set up an account you will need to also be able to enter tax information and bank account information for payment of royalties. If you are a US citizen, you will already have a TIN (Tax Identification Number made up of a Social Security Number – SSN, or an Individual Taxpayer Identification Number – ITIN). If you aren't a US citizen, then you need to obtain a TIN if your country has a double taxation treaty agreement with the US which will allow you to receive your royalty payments without the deduction of withholding tax (usually 30%) at source. In order to do this you will need to fill in a number of forms, including an IRS Form W-7 to obtain a US ITIN, which requires you to provide an amount of documentation to the US or one of its embassies. You will have to fill in W-8 forms relating to tax and income receipts even if you don't. You will find all of the guidance here: https://www.createspace.com/tax-interview/help?nodeId=201447640&locale=en_US

- **Receipt of royalties:** both CreateSpace and KDP will require specific bank account details from you to remit royalties and they will require international banking information to do so – remember they have to comply with money laundering legislation as well as ensure your remittances get to you without mishap. For payments to be made directly into your bank account (recommended as there is no bottom line figure required before payments are made as there are with other payment options) you will need to provide both the IBAN and SWIFT codes which are used in international/online banking. You can find these on the top of your paper bank statements or online in the account information generally displayed at the top of the statement screen.

FINALLY, WHO MUST THE FIRST 'CUSTOMER' TO RECEIVE A COPY OF YOUR NEWLY PUBLISHED BOOK BE?

In the UK: The British Library.

In the US: the Library of Congress.

The Copyright Act 1911 established the principle of the legal deposit. This ensures that the British Library and five other libraries in the UK are entitled to receive a free copy of every item published or distributed in Britain. The other five libraries are:

The Bodleian Library in Oxford.
The University Library in Cambridge.

The Trinity College Library in Dublin.
The National Library of Scotland.
The National Library of Wales.

The British Library is the only one that must automatically receive its copy. The others are entitled to these items if they specifically request them, via the Agency for the legal Deposit Libraries. You can make a case for not supplying additional copies if it would be unduly onerous on you, the individual, to do so. If you are a self-publishing Indie, selling only a handful of copies, you have a case to make.

Under the terms of Irish copyright law (most recently the Copyright and Related Rights Act 2000), the British Library is also entitled to automatically receive a free copy of every book published in Ireland, The national Library of Ireland, the Trinity College Library at Dublin, the library of the University of Limerick, the library of Dublin City University and the libraries of the four constituent universities of the National University of Ireland are also entitled to request copies on the same basis as the five English libraries above.

In the US, for any copyrighted work that is *published,* two copies should be submitted to the United States Copyright Office at the Library of Congress. In theory, in the US, copyright is assigned to your work as soon as it appears in a physical form – on paper or on your laptop. Of course, I'd hate to argue that in court and expect to win if a challenger was more organised than you...

Congratulations! You've written and published your book; now on to the mammoth task of promoting and selling it.

Part 3: PROMOTE

Chapter 18:
The Online Soapbox:
your Author Platform

There are four key areas to marketing: the product, the place, the price and the promotion.
In summary it looks a little like this:

Product:

- Produce a professional product; edit, proof, copyright, format, catalogue (ISBN).

- Give it a professional outer finish: cover, title, blurb, and remember to think about what it looks like in a thumbnail.

- Think of your book as a product, not your 'baby' it's taken years to write.

Place:

- 95% sales of self-published books are generally in ebook format so online is essential.

- Amazon is estimated to have 80% of the UK book sales market, and similar in the US.

- Regularly look to see what is selling, at what price and in what genre. Find the right sales niche for your book.

Your book

Promotion:

- Use common sense and don't spend beyond your promotional budget.

- Establish your target audience.

- Work on only one promotional strategy per book at a time.

- Use your assets well - e.g. use the first book in a series to sell the rest.

- Think like a consumer.

Price:

-Study the pricing strategy of other successful authors in your genre.

- Read the terms and conditions carefully of each distributor you use.

- Exclusivity with Amazon gives some advantages but still weigh them up carefully against other promotional strategies.

The product is all about creating a product people want to buy – or in this case, a book readers want to read. The place is all about determining where you intend selling your book and taking the appropriate action to do so. The price is about finding that sweet spot that creates some profit for your hard work in creating your book whilst ensuring there is no barrier to anyone buying it, and the promotion is all about finding the way that works for you and your book – and that will be different for every author and every book.

How do I sell my books on the internet? I'm radical. No – not politically, or even behaviourally (unless it's after a glass or two). It's a mnemonic for how I approach selling my books, and is based on:

READABILITY
ACCESSIBILITY
DISCOVERABILITY
INTERESTING THE RIGHT PEOPLE
CREDIBILITY
ADDING VALUE
LETTING IT FLOW...

When setting off on the road to self-publishing, remember that books are written for one thing, and one thing alone: to be read. A book that isn't well-written, informative, authoritative, credible, interesting and well-produced won't be – especially important now Amazon is about to cap royalty payments based on the number of pages that have been read if a book is self-published. The second is that your book is just one amongst millions out there. Just imagine, millions of needles all in one giant haystack – and yours is at the bottom of the pile. How will anyone find it? Selling books is all about writing something readers will want to read, and finding a way of making them aware of that fact, i.e. aware of you, and your book. That's where the mnemonic comes in. I'll address them all in the following chapters.

READABILITY

Your book needs to be well-written, interesting and well-produced. It also needs to satisfy the needs of a reader demographic. Do you know what or who your readership is likely to be? If you don't it's time to figure it out fast because you're going to need that in order to be noticed.

For a book to be well-written, it needs to be

- Written from a solid knowledge base derived from sound research.
- Articulate, grammatically sound, and with inspiring narrative, a strong voice, credible dialogue and an intriguing plot. Join a writers' group, attend creative writing classes and workshops, and get professional and peer feedback before you go public!
- The finished article then needs to be professionally edited, proofed and formatted. If it's not, readers will soon become disillusioned by typos and poor presentation – and you're a professional, right?
- And of course it needs to be something your readers will actively want to read...

All of this has been covered in great detail elsewhere in this book, so I won't go into the hows and wheres here; other than to reiterate all that good advice. So now you have the finished product, with a stunning cover and it's time to sell it. On to the rest of my mnemonic.

ACCESSIBILITY

Some people like paperbacks, some like digital books, some like audio books. Some people use Kindles, some Nook or Kobo formats, some even read on their phone. When you're considering your readers, also consider where and how they're likely to both read and buy your book. Amazon isn't the only self-publishing platform. By no means definitive, the list of publishing options is covered in Chapter 11 in PUBLISH and repeated again in the Appendix.

Each have their pros and cons, with Amazon being probably the most go-to service out there as it can – and will – do everything for you, including promote your book; as long as you play it Amazon's way. However, bear in mind the fact that the other platforms have their own unique selling points, and it isn't necessarily a good thing to be exclusive to just one. Lulu, for example, allows your book to be available via Barnes and Noble http://www.barnesandnoble.com/ which potentially puts your ebook in front of a huge audience, alongside 30 million other products. Or do you cherish dreams of being on the big screen?

BookTango allows you (for a price) to have your book formatted so it is available for Hollywood producers and agents: http://www. booktango.com/Services/ServiceDetail.aspx?ServiceId=BS-3087 . Alternatively, publishing through both Smashwords or Draft2Digital and Amazon allows you to have a perma-free book (see below) – potentially a very powerful marketing aid. Consider your options carefully before tying yourself in – especially where any pre-publication cost is involved.

DISCOVERABILITY

This is all about how your book will be found. It starts with choosing the right keywords, categories and using SEO in your book descriptions, and continues with your online presence – your author platform – and how you are presented via third parties – bloggers, reviewers, promotions, readers' sites, forums, personal representation and appearances and social media. If you're unsure what I mean about keywords, categories and SEO, reread Chapter 16 in PUBLISH.

- Make sure you have an author platform – your shop window, if you like. It should include a website, a social media presence and,
- An Author's page on both Amazon.com and Amazon.co.uk if you are selling your books through Amazon (generally a good idea given Amazon's reach). Here's a snippet of my Author's page on Amazon:

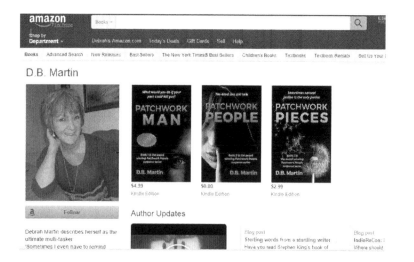

- Be active on active on social media – maybe start with Twitter and Facebook and stay with just them if this is all you feel comfortable with, but do have a presence so you can easily be found, and potential readers have somewhere to easily find out about you and your books.

Go to **Author Central** on both Amazon.com and .co.uk and set up your author page as the very next step you take after releasing your first book. Click on your author name and you will go to a blank page set up for you and follow the instructions to join Author Central. Amazon will allow you to have up to three pen names all linked in to the same account. They will display separately and the books penned under that specific name will appear on that pen name page, but it provides a go-to place for readers interested in reading other books you have written, so it's as important as your author website. It's your little piece of Amazon; use it well – integrate:

- A good author bio, making sure this doesn't extend below 'the fold' – i.e. the place onscreen that disappears off screen unless you scroll down the page to see more.
- A good head shot photo of you to accompany the bio – readers like to know who they're reading.
- Social media in the form of blogs and Twitter feeds.
- Book trailers.
- Your website link.
- Reviewers and editorial quotes and testimonials (you can't put these in the buyers' review area but you can add them yourself as testimonials on the book's own page in Author Central under 'editorial reviews').
- This is also where you can set up 'Look Inside' for your books.

YOUR AUTHOR WEBSITE

This is a must. Why? Because once you have a book on sale, you need to start building a relationship with your readers. First stop for them will be your author website where they can find out more about you, your books, your mailing list, your special offers...it's an extension of your book on its sales platform, in fact.

There are many cheap and easy to build options available now so having no technical knowledge is no longer an excuse. Many sites employ 'drag and drop', i.e. having chosen the overall design you want for your website – the 'template' – you drag the elements you want to appear within the template, type in or copy and paste the content, add images and links and you have a website without even knowing the tiniest piece of code. Many authors use Wordpress (https://wordpress.com/) because it has a variety of useful 'plug-ins', add-ons that enable you to do clever things like feature a pop-up mailing list sign-up and you can create an online presence for yourself virtually for free by adapting the template for your blog so it has the look and feel of a website. Opt to buy a domain name and the effect is complete (but not free so make sure you are aware of the costs of maintaining ownership of the domain name and hosting charges). Alternatively, investigate some of the other paid website builders. There are a number of other popular alternatives, some are free or almost free, some are paid. Here's a list current as I write:

Sitebuilder.com
Websitebuilder.com
Sitey.com
eHost.com
Godaddy.com
1&1.com
Squarespace.com
Webs.com
Wix.com
Weebly.com
Sitelio.com
Ideahost.com

Some hints when building a website:

1. KISS – "keep it simple, stupid" is always worth remembering. Yes, your readers – or would-be readers have come there to find out about you and your books but they will soon leave if your website is complicated to navigate and doesn't contain interesting content. Regard it essentially as your shop window, and what do you have in your shop? You, as an author brand, and your books.

Keep it to that. A page about you, where a reader might come across you next, a means to contact you, information about your books and a way to sign up to your mailing list – generally via a charming bribe, like a free book, technically referred to as a 'reader magnet', and a page or section about each of your books.

2. Brand it. This is about you and your books. Create a sense of what your books are about in the feel of your website.

3. Make sure each book has its own page or special area. Link books in a series together and if you write in different genres, delineate between them so a visitor to your site comes away with a clear idea of what you write and under which pen name if appropriate.

4. Ensure you always have fresh content feeding onto the site – and the easiest way to do this at a most basic level is to link your Twitter feed to it. There's always a fresh tweet coming out from you on your Twitter handle, right? Or there should be. This helps to keep the site in the Google rankings – Google loves fresh content – but you will also have to keep it updated. There's nothing worse than a website that was last added to a year ago – how interesting is it if all that's on there is old news?

5. Make sure you also publicise and regularly update any events you are involved in.

6. Use SEO – see Chapter 17 of PUBLISH and make use of Google's guide I have given the link to. The idea of a website is to be informative and unless it can be found, it can't inform.

7. Use good clear images of you and your books. Keep your website crisp and interesting.

So now your face as well as your books is online. What have you got to say for yourself and how are you going to say it? The author on their soapbox needs a microphone and social media is it.

Chapter 19:
Social Media Strategy

Other elements of your online soap box include the social media you use. Twitter, Facebook, Google+, LinkedIn, YouTube, Pinterest, Reddit, Tumblr, Instagram, Wattpad, Goodreads, Vine, Snapchat, Flickr, Swarm (by FourSquare), Pheed – and of course, your blog… There are more, but surely that's enough to be going on with? And also probably to despair of ever doing anything other than social media; agreed! There are really just two tricks to mastering social media:

- Pick one or two that you will do well and be consistent doing, and stick with them and them alone. ENJOY using social media – that is what it's for, after all; being sociable online.
- Use them as a **social network,** employing the 80:20 rule – 80% of your posts will be social – about you, your life, your passions, your frustrations, the things that make you laugh, the things that make you cry, the interesting thing you're doing on Saturday night, the boring thing you're doing on Saturday night. The other 20% is about your books and your writing. The worst thing you can do is repeatedly say 'buy my book, buy my book' – even if in a variety of different ways. Social media is your opportunity to build a relationship with potential readers and interest them in your books through being interested in what you have to say *without* trying to sell them your books.

I would also add this:

- Make sure the audience for your tweets or your posts is the potential audience for your books – not a whole mountain of other authors and promoters/marketers who'll all be doing the same thing as you and hoping to interest a potential reader in their books through 'chatting' to them on social media.

The rules are different for each form of social media. Let's look at some of the most used forms.

FACEBOOK

By the end of 2014 it was claimed that over 70% of all adults online used Facebook (source: Pew Research http://www.pewinternet.org/fact-sheets/social-networking-fact-sheet/). This figure has no doubt grown even higher since then. Clearly Facebook is where you should be too. Add to this that in the US, women are most likely to use Facebook approximately 10% more than men and it is the favoured social network for teens and it clearly beats all other social media formats hands down. However, Facebook intends you to be personal, especially on your personal profile, so posting about your writing or your book on your personal profile can seem rather spammy. This is where your author page comes in. This is your public, business page whereas your profile is your personal social interaction space. Set up an author page by going here off your personal account: https://www.facebook.com/pages/create and choosing 'artist, band or public figure' and then 'author' from the drop-down box. Simply follow the instructions from here. You will need to collect likes for your posts to be shared with your audience – start with friends and fellow authors and then build a campaign to encourage people onto your page, but one word of warning: Facebook has now reduced the amount of coverage for your posts – even to those who have liked your page – mainly no doubt to encourage professionals and public figures to use Facebook advertising instead, so don't spend a lot of time, effort or cash on obtaining 'likes'. I'll cover using Facebook to advertise in Chapter 22. Use Facebook to:

- **Brainstorm** with for inspiration – run polls and discussions to encourage engagement and feedback.
- **Post updates** on newly released books, blog posts and any content you think fans might enjoy, using images and video

as much as possible as it is a proven fact that people interact with visual content better than with pure text.

- **Run targeted ads** – you can narrow down your ad audience to age group, region, gender, and interests amongst other things; extremely effective if you get it right.
- **Run competitions and offers** to encourage people to 'like' your page – not that likes are as important now but a fan is more likely to engage than a non-fan and fans may also bring friends to your page too, to become new fans.
- **Create events** – like a book launch. By sending out invites you can gauge likely attendance better. Your event needn't be an actual event in an actual location, however. It could be online where you host a day of offering competitions, prizes, giveaways etc from your page.
- **Get involved in** groups, discussions and get feedback from other writers/readers. Groups can be a great way to promote sales and ask for reviews too; more on groups below.

Facebook groups: there are hundreds of thousands of groups within Facebook, for hundreds of thousands of interests, including books, ebooks, Kindle, review sharing, bargain book sharing and so on. Use the search tool to find groups you might be interested in – for instance 'Kindle books' will bring up a public group with nearly 20,000 members called Free Kindle Books, so if you were intending promoting a free book offer you have, here's a place to mention it. Join as many groups as you can specific to your genres and be active in them. I've included the list of Facebook groups I'm part of in downloadable material referred to in the Appendix. Post and interact within their guidelines please.

TWITTER

Apparently, approximately 23% of all online adults use Twitter. Most live in urban areas, more are male than female and the audience is quite young; generally between 18 and 49. What does this mean for you, the author? It means that there is a relatively young and potentially upwardly mobile (town and city dwellers) audience for your tweets. Twitter is also one of the easiest social media platforms to find an appropriate audience on. Use it to:

- **Announce book launches,** especially if you can get high influencers (those with thousands of followers) to retweet you – the reach this way is massive.
- **Exchange views** about topics in your subject matter. Other Twitter users' followers will see the conversation and may be interested in following you.
- **Share interesting content** about the subject matter of your book – this is like adding value to what you've written and also positions you as an 'expert' in your field. Your audience may then interact with you and enable you to guide them towards your book without you openly saying 'buy my book'.
- **Retweet other people's posts.** They may then return the favour and interest some of their followers in you by doing so.
- **Use hashtags** (#). Using hashtags enables people to see what is beingposted within specific subject areas. With only 140 characters to make your point, hashtags are a means of flagging up specifics, so someone may search, for instance on #amwriting if they are interested in comments from the latest in the writers' world. Hashtags come in all shapes and sizes and will also tell you what's trending. Everyone always hopes something they say will go viral and make them a household name.
- Unlikely for most of us, but using a hashtag may help just the minutest fraction. Don't over use them – and never more than three hashtags per tweet. Here's a list of a few of the hashtags writers should use:

  - #amreading
  - #amwriting
  - #MustRead
  - #IndieAuthor
  - #99c (to offer or pick up an ebook bargain)
  - #BookGiveaway
  - #BookMarketing
  - #FollowFriday
  - #FreeReads
  - #Novelines (to quote your own work)

Hashtags allow you to find new readers and connect with other writers, but they also allow you and others to find out about opportunities such as writing competitions or to attract interest from publishers, agents and editors, for example Pitmad which is a pitch party on Twitter where writers tweet a 140-character pitch of their book. Pitmad rules can be found here: http://www.brenda-drake.com /pitmad/ There are others along a similar vein, for instance #PitchMas and #WFpitch. I've included a list of hashtags as one of the downloadable files referred to in the Appendix, so get tweeting, get pitching and get selling yourself (in 140 characters or less…).

Also look for hashtags that are trending in your genre using sites like Hashtagify.me and Hashtags.org.

LINKEDIN

According to Pew statistics, 28% of all online users are on LinkedIn, meaning there are actually more people on LinkedIn than on Twitter. LinkedIn is generally thought of as where white-collar professionals network and the Pew survey further adds that these networkers tend to be high-income, well-educated people between 30 and 49 years old, building to or at the peak of their careers – a perfect audience for well-written and informative books! But LinkedIn isn't just for business networking. It can work for authors too. Use it to:

- **Increase your visibility as an author** because your LinkedIn profile shows up in Google searches. Treat your LinkedIn profile as an online CV or résumé, perfect for building your credibility as an author and for networking with the publishing industry.
- **Create a call to review** for your books.
- **Connect and network** with editors, publishers, other authors and potential fans.
- **Research** agents, editors and publishers to see which ones might be of interest to you, and interested in you.
- **Create links** to your website and other online content, such as your blog. The Google search algorithm counts links

from LinkedIn even though it doesn't count links from Facebook, so an active LinkedIn account can increase your page ranking.

- **Exchange knowledge** and discuss issues with other authors in one of the many writer groups. Groups on LinkedIn of potential interest to authors include:

- **Ebooks, Ebook Readers, Digital Books and Digital Content Publishing:** https://www.linkedin.com/groups/ 1515307/profile with over 85,000 members, it provides a variety of resources to do with ebook publishing.
- **Books and Writers**: https://www.linkedin.com/ groups/1697027 considers marketing strategy as well as interacting with other authors and publishers. It has more than 96,000 members and growing.
- **LinkEds & Writers:** https://www.linkedin.com/groups/ 37917/profile one of the largest groups for proofreaders, editors and authors, with over 73,000 members. It is split into a number of speciality-based subgroups, so choose the group(s) most relevant to your work to network with their members.
- **Writers Hangout**: https://www.linkedin.com/groups/ 1927932 where you can share techniques, tips and ideas about self-editing and self-publishing. Over 23,000 members currently.
- **The Writers Network**: https://www.linkedin.com/groups/ 2033716 also connects writers at all stages in their careers, together with publishers, editors and agents. Over 24,000 members currently.
- **Writers and Authors**: https://www.linkedin.com/groups/ 2277497/profile aims to help writers refine and polish their writing skills.

PINTEREST

Pinterest is a visual platform so it could therefore be a very interesting forum given that books rely on their covers for immediate eye appeal. It has a very mobile audience and according to Business Insider (have a look here for more fascinating data on social media usage

http://www.businessinsider.com/demographic-data-and-social-media2014
-2?IR=T), over 48% of social media shares on iPads are via Pinterest.
There's a lot on parenting, family, food and drink related, but according
to Pew (again), 42% of all women online use Pinterest, so how about
those romance novels? Use it to:

- **Create topic boards** to attract readers in your genre. Use
  classic books in your genre, book reviews, book covers,
  writing quotes, behind-the-scenes looks at an author's life,
  or paintings and images relating to the era or issue in your
  book. Re-pinned pins retain the original link – i.e. you.
- **For inspiration** whilst writing. Have you ever got stuck?
  With its wealth of images Pinterest provides a massive
  resource to get a kick-start via vibrant images. Use the
  search tool at the top and type in your keywords.
- **Get feedback** on ideas, images, book covers, characters or
  topics you could write around.
- **Hold competitions and book giveaways.** Do a search on
  Pinterest for 'book giveaways' or 'pin it to win it' to see
  how others have done it.
- **Do market research** via its analytics. Finding out who re-
  pins your content will give you an idea what your audience
  is interested in.
- **Search for the boards that interest you** and utilise them
  for your own pins/ re-pins. Here are a couple of boards you
  might find interesting as an author:

  - **Book Community Board:** (https://www.pinterest.com/
    jellybooks/book-community-board/) with over 52,000
    plus followers it's anything book related, but not for
    promotion.
  - **Writing   Tips:**   (https://www.pinterest.com/writers
    museblog/ writing-tips-group-board/) with over 2.3
    million followers, there has to be something there to
    inspire you!

There are of course plenty of others. Have a strong presence on one or
two rather than spreading yourself thin and not achieving much on any,
but it pays to be familiar with all of them because you may find one that

suits you perfectly, or you may find the one that is going to be the next big thing.

REDDIT

Reddit is known as the 'front page of the Internet' as many things that start trending online start out here. Pew reckons that 6% of adult online users are regularly on Reddit, mainly the younger age group. It's 'hip', but Reddit can also improve your writing, get feedback and create a buzz, but it won't stand for pure self-promotion, so what you post has to have intrinsic value for it to make the front page here, although it's certainly a place where you could go viral from. The subreddits are the really interesting places for authors:

- Try /r/books for hosting an author "ask me anything".
- /r/writing is an active writer's community offering sometimes brutally honest critiquing. This subreddit does have a thread for self-promotion.
- /r/writersgroup is another subreddit group that focuses on creative writing.
- If you are a freelancer, /r/freelance is worth looking at.
- And if you simply want to hone writing skills, have a look at subreddits like /r/promptoftheday, /r/wordplay, /r/oneparagraph and /r/roundrobin.

GOOGLE+

The Google+ audience is more predominantly male and doesn't spend as much time on it as on Facebook but it still has some large book communities to interact with, such as:

- The Google+ Book Club: https://plus.google.com/communities/115163419704378077670 has over 36,000 members.
- The Writer's Discussion Group https://plus.google.com/communities/106134988944933826164 has over 31,000 members.
- Writers, Authors, Bloggers

https://plus.google.com/communities/10722061149561390
2403 has over 33,000 members.

TUMBLR

Tumblr is perfect for young adults and/or content involving intense self-expression. According to a recent survey by Pew, about 14% of teens use Tumblr, predominantly girls and the age range tends to be between 13 to 17 years old. It is clearly a good place to be talking about YA and New Adult fiction.

YOUTUBE

YouTube is the go-to place for video. According to Nielsen it reaches more people under 34 years old than TV networks. Some authors – for instance, John Green (*The Fault in Our Stars*) have had amazing success on YouTube, growing his fans into the millions. You need bursting personality and a lot of time to host your own channel, but it's still a good way to promote interviews of yourself and book trailers online to gain exposure.

INSTAGRAM

Instagram is also a young adult market place. According to data from Business Insider (see link above in the paragraph on Pinterest), over 90% of Instagram users are under the age of 35. Instagram is very visual, like Pinterest, and has a lot of traction with teens. Perhaps it is worth remembering this when considering what appeals to your audience depending on age – the fact that teens work in a visual way on social media? Use it to post book covers, quotes, sneaky peeks and insider author lifestyle images whilst combining it with hashtags for discoverability – and hopefully also – hype.

OTHER PLACES YOU MAY LIKE TO HANG OUT …

Some sites are more like a cross between social media and social reader. Facebook Groups are part way to this, but you'll find the following are major contenders for finding and connecting with readers, as well as offering other promotional opportunities:

GOODREADS

Goodreads claims to have a community of 40 million people and this is where all the hype for E L James' *Fifty Shades of Grey* originated – although it started its life on Fanfiction.net, an online forum where fans write stories based on the settings and characters of their favourite novels. You can see the possibilities though: 40 million potential readers? Goodreads is therefore a must for any author, targeting readers in your genre as well as generally.

- **List books and share** your own alongside favourite reads via 'Listopia'.
- **Do targeted advertising, if you have a budget to pay for it.** Target readers who like authors similar to you.
- **Hold book giveaways** to get exposure and (potentially) reviews. In the giveaways I've run, I've had between 300 and 1000+ enter for the chance to win. A percentage of them will inevitably put the book on their 'to read' list, and some will actually get round to both reading and reviewing in time.
- **Start discussions** about your books, giving you the chance to directly interact with your readers and obtain feedback.
- **Integrate your blog** with Goodreads. Readers automatically receive email updates weekly if you do this.
- **Share book excerpts** and teasers to tempt interest.
- **Compile a quiz** to encourage interaction.
- **Show off Goodreads reviews** on your own website using their author widget.
- Goodreads is the perfect place to give away Advance Release Copies (ARCs); it has a giveaway programme called First Reads https://www.goodreads.com/giveaway where most authors can list their galleys.
- Another Goodreads feature to consider are events: https://www.goodreads.com/search?q=ARCs&search%3Cp re%3E%5bsource%5d%5b/source%5d%3C/pre%3E=goodr eads&search_type=events&tab=events where you can list events you are involved in and invite participation. List your pre-release giveaway (for review, of course).
- Goodreads also has a feature called 'groups', where you

can offer ARCs and invite reviews from interested groups. https://www.goodreads.com/search?q=ARCs&search<pre> %5bsource%5d%5b/source%5d</pre>=goodreads&search_ type=groups&tab=group

WATTPAD

Wattpad has over 30 million users but only about 10% are writers, which means the rest are hungry readers! It's an interesting forum for short stories, but some authors have published their books there chapter by chapter to obtain exposure and feedback. For some it's also built buzz sufficient for self-publishing success to kick in immediately when they eventually release the whole book. One author's success story can be read here (http://www.publishingtalk.eu/case-studies/emily-benet-wattpad-suc cess-story/), together with her tips for using Wattpad successfully – worth a try, if only once, I think…

LOVEWRITING AND LOVEREADING (UK BASED)

Lovereading (http://www.lovereading.co.uk/) is purely for mainstream works, and Lovewriting (http://www.lovewriting.co.uk/) for self-published authors. Both are dedicated to books and reading, and are also frequented by publishers to promote their books but be aware that Lovereading does so at a cost and your book must be stocked by Gardners or similar. Lovewriting offers a similar service – but again for a significant fee (currently around £199 per book per annum) – specifically for independent authors although Lovereading does feature some Indies. Make use of free opportunities first – social media, Goodreads and Wattpad – but don't overlook the power of well-targeted paid advertising as your writing career unfolds.

YOUR BLOG

I have mentioned your blog several times in this section, but not in detail. Many authors believe they must have a blog. Many authors don't see the point in having a blog because they could spend the time they spend writing blog posts writing novels. I have a blog and am notoriously sporadic in posting on it. It depends what you are using your blog for. If it helps to share content, ideas and information – or to ruminate on how or what you're writing – do it. If it doesn't, don't. Like all social media, because a blog is precisely that, do it if and when you enjoy it. Otherwise, yes, do spend that blogpost writing time writing something more productive.

You can also post content from other blogs on your blog, as long as you provide a link to the original source and give it credit. On this basis you might personally blog, say, once in a month and post something from another blog as well, so you will be blogging more or less every fortnight – not bad at all. Have a look at this article on Readers Writers Journal for ideas: http://readerswritersjournal.com/2015/05/19/writing-prompts-for-author-blogs/, or set up Google alerts https://support.google.com/alerts/answer/4815696?hl=en for things like 'self-publishing', 'book news' etc for new content to be sent directly to your inbox, or use feed sites like Alltop Literature http://literature.alltop.com/ and Bloglovin http://www.bloglovin.com/ for articles to use (remembering to credit the source).

There are many platforms you can use if you do blog: Blogger www.blogger.com, Wordpress http://www.creativebloq.com/tag/word press, Tumblr https://www.tumblr.com/, Medium https://medium .com/, Svbtle https://svbtle.com/, Weebly http://www.weebly.com/uk/, Postach.io http://postach.io/site, Pen.io http://pen.io/, Ghost https://ghost .org/ or LiveJournal http://www.livejournal.com/. Try each of them out and see what work best for you as they are all slightly different and you may find one is more intuitive to you than another.

How do you balance the time spent using social media with writing so that social media doesn't take over? Be organised; plan a certain amount of time per day on social media and don't go over it. Don't be tempted to go off at a tangent if on Facebook. Regard it as a series of targets you need to achieve and as soon as you have, sign off and switch off. Of course there may be times when you don't want to switch off – if you're in the middle of a launch or a campaign, for instance – but at these times social media and marketing are taking priority over writing so accept that is so. The secret of productivity is organisation, planning and execution.

- Plan the bulk of social media posts you will be making ahead of time, but allow for a smaller percentage that will be spontaneous.
- Schedule that time into your working day – or the time you have allocated out of spare or leisure time to write if you

aren't a full-time writer (not many of us are).
- Keep on top of it; do it regularly.
- Set up feeds and content searches for interesting content you can post on. For example, subscribe or follow blogs you are interested in and file relevant posts into a separate folder to look at when you are working on social media, or set up RSS feeds, create lists on Twitter and so on.
- Use a social media scheduler to take the pain out of bulk scheduling – Hootsuite https://hootsuite.com/ is excellent for simultaneously covering a range of social media platforms, as is Buffer https://buffer.com/, IFTTT https://ifttt.com/, and Socialoomph https://www.socialoomph.com/ and Tweetdeck https://tweetdeck.twitter.com/ work well for just Twitter.

So now your author platform is up and running, get on your soapbox and start promoting your first book both online, and off – which is what the next chapter is all about.

Chapter 20:
Release and Pre-Release –
Getting it Out There

So your book is finished, formatted, bound and just awaiting release day. Now you can think about marketing it, right?

Wrong.

Marketing of your book starts whilst you're still writing it.

- First of all, you want potential readers to be eagerly anticipating it so they buy it as soon as it's available to give it that 'first day' launch.
- Secondly, you want a whole host of reviews to mushroom around it as soon as it is available – and if you're part of any of Amazon's publishing programmes – White Glove and its other imprints – you'll notice that their publications have been gathering reviews even before the books are released via Amazon's clever little trick of putting some carefully selected books on special promotion even before they're on sale! Of course, being part of this kind of promotional boost is very much down to the support you have, and for that reason alone White Glove is worth considering. After all, with arguably the world's largest promotion machine behind you, your chances of selling skyrocket!
- Thirdly, the first 90 days of a book's life on Amazon are the most important to get it off to a good start because Amazon will actively promote your book (once you've gained a little

traction from independent purchases and reviews) during this period more than at any time – unless you've hit the winning formula of continually increasing sales.

Running up to a launch you have to have arrangements already in hand, so:

- Put your book up on pre-order and encourage fans to order it before release with bonus offers and incentives.
- Contact bloggers and reviewers and offer an ARC (Advance Release Copy), which is a copy of your book ready for publication, explaining if there are any last minute tweaks still to make that they should take account of.
- Contact local independent retailers and book shops and ask if they'd like to stock it when it's available on a trial sales basis.
- Plan your launch, be it virtually (online), or actually – in a book shop or other venue.

Use your mailing list to:

- Work on growing your general mailing list months beforehand in preparation for the launch.
- Draw up a team of ARC reviewers from it.
- Set up a band of willing first day purchasers from your mailing list, and also from friends, family and writing contacts.
- Set up a series of newsletters counting down to the launch, encouraging fans to buy the book – offer it at an incentive price.

Obtain pre-release reviews:

- Reviews that are not the direct result of a third-party purchase of your book should not be posted under the general reviews section on Amazon, but you can post any number of 'editorials' from your author page so all reviews you can gather before a new book is released will all help provide social proof for its worth directly beneath its description.

- On the lists available via the sign-up list and Appendix there are hundreds of bloggers and reviewers, including well over 200 on Pinterest. Pick those reviewing your genre and check the submission criteria, if there aren't details on the spreadsheet you can download. Before submitting anywhere, ALWAYS check the submission criteria on the site, please. These may change from time to time, or a blogger/reviewer may need to take time out because they are inundated. Always thank a reviewer for their review as well. Many do it entirely voluntarily for the sheer love of reading.

- Use an ARC interface with serious reviewers, like Net Galley https://www.netgalley.com/ to get your pre-release book into the hands of potentially influential reviewers. Net Galley is used by traditional publishers for precisely that purpose so you will be battling against books being pushed by the big boys of publishing as well as other indies, and it is a paid service too – an expensive paid service, running between $399 and $599 for a six-month listing for one title alone. You can test it out via some bloggers who will offer you a one month or more spot for much less – such as Xpresso Blog tours (a list of book tour providers can be found amongst the downloadable material listed in the Appendix), with one month costing in the region of $60 as I write, and options to extend the listing up to six months. There are always options out there if you look for them…

- Do be aware that when being offered anything for free you shouldn't expect too much. The average response rate is 50% or below.

Circulate the good news:

- Send out a press release. Press releases can also be targeted towards reviewers as well as the media in general. There are a number of press-release writing and distribution services you can use but make sure they will be targeting the right media (and/or reviewers). Ask them for some information about their distribution list before you pay over any hard cash. I have used Bostick Communications (www.bostickcommunications.com) with some success but I have also had to supply them with my own press release. Never written a press release? Here's how:

PRESS RELEASE FOR IMMEDIATE RELEASE:

Include an image of your book.

Start with a catchy headline in bold type that states the reason or purpose of the press release.

Your first sentence should tell readers exactly what your release is about. Cover who, what, when and where by the end of the first paragraph.

Keep paragraphs to approximately four sentences each. Your next paragraph could elaborate on your news. Include editorial praise. Include first reviews, comments or other media comments.

Have a boilerplate at the end. This is the 'About [You]' section you see at the end of a press release. It's basically a short, one-paragraph description of you – your bio – and where readers should look for more information.
Include:
Your website.
Your social media links.
Your phone number.
Your email address (and/or your agent's).

Some other points to address are:

- Only capitalise the first word in your title.
- Include the product name, cost and where it can be obtained from – in this case; your book!
- Make it easy for a journalist to copy and paste chunks. They're working to a deadline, so if you write your press release like an article, they can lift and run with it – precisely what you want.
- Include quotes from reviewers, not you. A third-party endorsement is of interest to a journalist. What you think isn't.
- Use bullet points if there's a lot of information to scan – they're easier to take in.
- Preferably keep it to one page. A busy journalist or reviewer isn't going to turn the page for yet more...
- Check your grammar, punctuation and spelling before release.
- Use a clear legible font, single spaced and definitely not more than a page and a half in length over all.
- The three most effective words to use in writing a press release are *free*, *best*, and *new*. Use them to good effect (if appropriate).
- Note that reporters and their copy editors religiously follow guides like the Associated Press Stylebook and/or the Chicago Manual of Style; check out the AP Stylebook Twitter feed for hints and tips https://twitter.com/ APStylebook. So, for example, don't ever use "you", "we" or "I" – except in the quote. A press release should be written in the third person like news stories are.
- Use the keywords that you are using to sell your book if possible.

And some don'ts:

- Don't use industry jargon. The people you're targeting aren't necessarily in the know.
- Don't use hype and hyperbole. It will be ignored.
- Use clear language that won't be misconstrued.

- Don't 'advertise'. Stick to facts.
- Don't use exclamation marks. A press release is a formal announcement and you won't find exclamation marks in news articles.

Apart from a press release, some other pre-release information you can circulate is:

- **The Advance Information Sheet (AI):** this is a one-page sheet of all the information a potential rep, distributor, stockist and retailer might need. It will include comprehensive ordering data, the book cover image, a concise paragraph describing the book's content, the targeted audience, the author's contact details and any online platform (website, for example). If you're being published by a main stream publisher they should do this for you automatically, and include it in their catalogue. If you're self-publishing via a paid do-it-for-you service, they should similarly do it for you as you cannot realistically distribute an AI to the trade yourself. An AI is only of use if sent out pre-release and to those interested in selling your book.
- **A reviewer's information sheet:** similar in a way to the AI but aimed purely at reading and quality statistics. I've put one together for several of my books if contacting a number of reviewers simultaneously. You can find an example of one I created a while ago in the downloadable material in the Appendix. Again it should include the book cover, a description of the book content, the length in pages (very relevant for a reviewer allocating precious time to reading it), audience, any previous editorial review comments, reader stats, star rating if already released or rated. It doesn't replace a nice email directed personally to a reviewer but it's a useful quick-scan summary sheet for them to refer to.
- **General promotional materials:** that you can also continue to circulate after release too, such as flyers, postcards, business cards, promotional goodies (pens, bookmarks etc), pop-up display stands if you are doing any

book signings or a formal launch. However, be aware that of these, only the business card is of really lasting value, and here's a tip: print on both sides of a business card – your name and contact details on the front and all your book covers on the flip side. Don't print too many at a time – probably 100 maximum, so you can update it regularly as you have more books released.

And so comes the actual day of release. You may have decided to go for a hard launch – a big launch party, a series of book signings you've arranged with co-operative book stores, flyers, adverts and media interest. Of course we'd all love to be able to be the star of the day, but it takes a lot of organising to do a hard launch successfully – and money! You may instead decide to play it safer and schedule a soft launch with blog tours online, a press release, and a Facebook 'launch party'. Always keep in mind that you're not really marketing your book, overall you're marketing you; the author. YOU are the brand and your books are your products. Big businesses use branding to sell their image and create relationships with customers. By marketing yourself as an author, you are aiming to establish a fan base that will buy your books, whatever book you are currently launching or promoting. Whether you choose a hard or soft launch, here are some points to think about when planning how you grab the media's and the general public's attention:

- **Trying to promote your book with *"Look, I wrote a book"* is a definitely a 'no'.** Once upon a time, writing a book was newsworthy. Now – with millions of books already on Amazon, and thousands of new ones appearing every day – it's not. What is newsworthy is whatever is unique about your book. Find the newsworthy content of your book and focus on that. Look for trends and issues in the news that your book links to, or talk about the reason you wrote the book if that is unusual or topical. I re-released *Chained Melodies* at (coincidentally) the same time the transgender issue was being thrust into the limelight by activists and the film *The Danish Girl* was about to go on release. It got me some airtime, I might not have got otherwise, simply because it was on-trend since it is fictional story about a transgender and their transition, but based on real-life research and people.

- **Present the person you are querying with ready-made topics** to base media focus around, for example, for *Chained Melodies* I could suggest:

   - *Can transgender men and women really live as who they were meant to be?*
   - *Can transgender men and women really develop normal relationships with non-transgender (cisgender) men and women?*
   - *How have attitudes to transgenders changed since Lili Elbe's era? (Or April Ashley's?)*

   And make the book secondary to the issue by winding up with something like:
   "Please let me know if you are interested in receiving a complimentary copy of [your book title] for review, or would like further background information from [your author name] for features or profile interviews."

- **Don't target too widely.** For example, your book may be a mystery/thriller and therefore of interest to a large reader pool, but think about the precise mechanics of your plot. Will it appeal to all ages, male and female alike? Or is it really more suitable for a more highly defined niche? Look at the 'themes' and categories under 'Mysteries and Thrillers' on Amazon and target accordingly, including cross-genre themes such as the fact that it's part of a series, or it's a historical mystery. If you mis-target, you may get a bite the first time round but if they feel misled or disappointed, they won't remain on board and then your reviews or the media reaction may not be as positive as you would wish.

- **Over-the-top doesn't sell.** Slick, to the point, intriguing and professional does.

Focusing on some specific events you may run:

1. **Book signings** can be awesome or awful. If you persuade

a local bookstore to let you do a book signing there, make sure you've done your homework and your promotion first. People don't just happen into bookstores in their hundreds and there is a lot of administrative work to attend to beforehand too:

- You will need to publicise the event – and with a lure like the chance to win something, or meet someone/experience something unusual.
- You will also need to supply the books yourself if you are self-published, and be prepared for the swingeing discounts bookshops expect on trade price to them. If the bookshop buys through wholesale – only if you are self-published through a service provider generally, or traditionally published – be aware that they will also have a SOR (sale or return) policy if they stock the book for you, and the cost of the books will ultimately fall on you if unsold and publishing through a self-publishing print provider.
- Have some promotional items to remind passers-by who you were and what your book was about, and be prepared to give a talk as a lot of bookshops don't like signings unless they're part of a package now.
- To find bookshops near you in the UK, have a look on here: www.localbookshops.co.uk and use your AI sheet, plus a friendly email to approach them, and suggest an angle whereby they will benefit from hosting the event for you if you can. Independent bookshops are a beleaguered race and they need to know you are going to be a boon not a liability in an already cut-throat commercial world.
- Be prepared for a long, tiring and tedious day – without many sales. You will be most likely to meet with success if you approach independent book stores, although I've always found Waterstones very responsive too.

2.   **New release parties** can also be a bonus or a beast, again based on the amount of publicity you arrange beforehand. Bear in mind that you will have to provide the books for sale, the refreshments and promotional items as well as the cost of publicity beforehand.   Unless you are

upselling – selling something else that will draw interest as well as your new book, such as an author talk on a popular subject – they generally tip the scales on the expensive side and you will rarely sell enough books to cover the costs overall, unless you are the NEXT BIG THING (which I hope you are).

3. **Promotional talks and literary festival events** are all good to be invited to/arrange – some are even paid! However, don't assume that you will sell hundreds of books at them. Look on the internet for events you might be a good fit for. In the UK, http://www.literaryfestivals .co.uk/list_of_literary_festivals.html has an alphabetical list of those in the UK and I'm delighted to see the one I chaired in 2014 on there – the Wantage (not just Betjeman) literary festival, so it seems a pretty comprehensive list overall. Internationally, have a look here: https://en.wikipedia.org/wiki/Category:Literary_fes tivals_in_the_ United_States Good old Wikipedia! Also look in local and national press and search for writers' conventions. Generally there is an opportunity to book sign after the talk, and of course the festival will be promoting you – although you should also be promoting the festival too for best effect.

4. **Radio and TV interviews** are best arranged by direct personal contact. Look for local channels first. Most local radio and TV stations are delighted to be told of a newsworthy story they can run because they have to fill airtime day in, day out. Most interviews will be short – less than ten minutes – and live on air. A skilful presenter will 'lead' you into talking about the book, you, the topic and so on, but they will also be cueing music, taking calls, answering tweets and emails too so have some of your own copy ready to launch into. Remember to state the book's name, the price and where it can be found before the interview winds up and a good promotional twist is to have a competition or giveaway running at the same time – either via the radio station, or independently, which you publicise; perhaps a signed copy of the book or a set of your books.

5. **Newspapers and magazines** are a competitive field to get into. Your press release will of course target the media, but the best shots initially are likely to be local press.

- Provide a good local news link when approaching newspapers.
- For features editors find a reason why the spotlight should shine on you as much as your book – you're the brand, remember, and a feature focuses on you rather than your products.
- Exploit local or personal connections to a geographical area if this features in your book too. Look for connections between your book and what the journalist you are approaching reports on. They're far more likely to react if it's within their remit.
- Make the approach personal – often a phone call will work better than an email as a first approach. You can send more detail via email as a follow-up.
- Don't forget freelancers who might be interesting in taking on your article and submitting it to nationals. Have a headline ready in case this happens.
- Book reviews in magazines are extremely difficult to get now, particularly since the major traditional publishers will have already elbowed most of the little guys out of the way in favour of publicity for their own books, now under siege from the many excellent self-published ones mounting an attack on the established domain of traditional publishing. If you can pay enough, you may find yourself a niche, but be prepared for a lot of cold-calling.
- If you're self-published there is a magazine that reviews only self-published books – *The Self-Publishing Magazine* www.selfpublishingmagazine.co.uk.
- Also try magazines that are there mainly to encourage writers, such as *The Writer*, *Mslexia*, Writers Online and Writers Forum – not so much for publicity (although, again paid advertising may be possible with some) but for ideas.
- Be organised, because if you are going to seek exposure via newspapers and magazines, you will be approaching *a lot*.

Create a spreadsheet of your enquiries, like you did for querying agents, and record the response as you receive it. Leave it a month before sending a polite reminder and if you don't get a response then philosophically move on.

6. **Libraries** – generally only stock from specialist library supplier catalogues.

- In the UK that's Askews/Holt Jackson (now part of Gardners) and BDS.
- In the US libraries purchase physical books through the distributors like Baker & Taylor, Ingram Library Services, Emery-Pratt Company, and a variety of other, with the remaining balance directly from publishers. For digital books, it's Baker & Taylor with their Axis program for digital books http://www.btol.com/axis360.cfm, Ingram http://www.ingramcontent.com/publishers/publisher-services and ProQuest http://www.proquest.com/products-services/ebooks/ebooks-main.html teamed with MyiLibrary http://www.proquest.com/products-services/ebooks/MyiLibrary.html.
- First and foremost make sure your book has the look of a professionally published title. Purchase an ISBN, use an experienced editor, copyeditor, and cover designer, create a polished website and promote your book.
- Positive reviews from the big reviewers like *Library Journal*, *Kirkus*, and *Publishers Weekly* – or awards – are important to the selection process. Try for reviews from *Library Journal*, CHOICE, Booklist, Publishers Weekly, or Kirkus Reviews (expensive).
- There are also programmes that will send flyers about your book to local libraries for a fee, for instance Librarybub http://librarybub.com/authors/.
- Another way is to work with a self-publishing platform like Smashwords which helps its authors get their titles into libraries through library aggregator partners OverDrive and Baker & Taylor. There is also SELF-e http://self-e.libraryjournal.com/, a new collaboration between *Library Journal* and the e-publishing platform BiblioBoard. Add to

this eBooksAreForever http://ebooksareforever.com/ the brainchild of indie author J.A. Konrath, so the doors are slowly opening.

- Apart from going online, visit local libraries personally, explain the book's significance and pedigree (editing, reviews etc) and *donate* your book.
- Continue marketing and selling your book because library shelves are like bookshop shelves. If it's not turning over, it's turfed out.
- Make sure you have registered for Public Lending Rights (PLR). Go to their website: www.plr.uk.com . Twenty-eight countries have a PLR programme, and others are considering adopting one. Canada, UK, Scandinavia, Germany, Austria, Belgium, Netherlands, Israel, Australia and New Zealand have one and France is considering one. If your country participates, register yourself and your books. In the UK, the PLR fee is currently 7.67 pence in 2016 every time a book is borrowed from a 'sample library'. Not every borrowing is recorded across the country – the undertaking would be enormous to do that – but you are paid on what your average borrowing would be. It may be not a lot, but it's still worth having. The location of the sample library changes every year so try to get your books into as many libraries as possible, cross your fingers and hope.

7. **Book blasts /tours** are a great way of sounding the new release fanfare, especially if combined with a competition or giveaway of some kind. I've included a list of blog tour operators in the downloadable material on my website. All the information about how to access this is in the Appendix. Do make sure you sign up and download all the information I've stored for you there. It may not all be suitable for you, but the possibilities are enormous. The aim of a book blast or a blog tour is to shout about your book pre-release and offer an ARC to gather reviews, or to trumpet blast its actual release and encourage sales. Both can be used to promote mailing list sign-ups via a competition or giveaway too. Prices and

blog stops vary. Do your homework to make sure the kind of blogs your book will be featured on will suit your genre, and the number of followers they have before choosing the most appropriate blog tour operator for yourself.

To round off this chapter, I'm going to mention rights again, because releasing a new book is precisely the time you should be covering all bases for potential sales. I've referred to outright sales and library loans/sales above, but the book you've written has a variety of rights attached to it and they are all saleable. Putting your books into libraries is a way of capitalising on lending rights. IPR License http://www.iprlicense.com/ can help you find buyers for many other kinds of rights – see Chapter 17 of PUBLISH and capitalise on rights you could be selling, but to recap, they include:

Print distribution
Digital distribution
1st serialisation
2nd serialisation and so on…
Film rights
TV rights
Digest (condensed version)
Radio and TV straight reading rights
Audio rights
Book club rights (some 'Classic' book clubs buy these)
Large print rights
Anthology and quotation rights

You may also want to join ALCS http://www.alcs.co.uk/ if you're in the UK. For a one-off fee of (currently) £36 you can join a community devoted to protecting writers' rights. I've repeated the name and the link in the final chapter of this book under useful support organisations.

Chapter 21:
Using Amazon to Promote Your Book

Did you know you can make use of Amazon's promotion machine to sell your book? And not via its paid advertising option. Amazon KDP has a number of promotional strategies you can make use of for free, but there is a catch… You have to sign up to sell your book(s) exclusively through Amazon for ninety days in order to avail yourself of them, so they may be something you try and opt out of in the long run if you decide it works better for you to be able to sell your books through a variety of distribution platforms and thereby make them available to read on a variety of different digital readers.

KDP Select – the programme you sign up to – offers:

- **Kindle countdowns**, a strategy involving scheduling a time-based promotional discount for your book. Potential customers will see the discount and the time remaining at that price level. It will gradually creep up over the period of time scheduled so the quicker a customer buys, the deeper the discount. Only one Kindle countdown can be scheduled per 90-day select period.
- **Kindle free days**, where you make your book free for between one and five days consecutively, or you can schedule blocks of days at different times across the 90-day period, but no more than five days in total.

Maybe you can see the reasoning behind the countdown deal – people generally respond positively to limited time offers – but why on earth would you want to give your book away for free? The short answer is visibility. The long answer is somewhat more complex and involves taking a look at Amazon's sales algorithms, and also looking at building other sales routes for your books outside of Amazon – for example, your mailing list.

Promoting a book on Amazon is like moving a mountain without Amazon's help. No matter how much you do to publicise it, the overall effect of sales will ultimately be controlled by Amazon's algorithms. Here are some examples of how they work:

Let's say you are running a Kindle Countdown Deal and after promoting it on a number of sites, you get 50 potential buyers. Let's assume of the 50 who look at your book by clicking the link on the promotion, 30 actually buy. Amazon's algorithms will notice that your book has suddenly had a spurt in sales and will calculate there may be some mileage in showing it to other customers too if it's on a roll. Out of that – from sheer extra visibility – you may get another 30 sales. If the sales fizzle out there then Amazon's algorithms will lose interest in your book and your increased sales ranking will gradually drop back to what it was before the sales burst by about 50% every 24 hours. If, on the other hand, you have continued to promote your book and can manage to send another 30 to 50 customers to buy it the next day, Amazon's algorithms notice the maintained upward trend and will recommend it to even more customers, independent of any promotional activity you have initiated. Say the next day you achieve 40 sales. Amazon's algorithms promote your book a little more, and so on.

No one actually knows (apart from Amazon, of course) exactly how the algorithms work, but whatever they are, ultimately one principle seems to hold good; they aim to maximise the number of books sold and therefore they basically boil down to that old saying about jumping on the bandwagon. If your book appears to be trending by reference to increased sales volume, then Amazon is going to help by recommending it to any potential customer that might be persuaded to buy it. Some enterprising authors have conducted experiments to try to work out the specifics (for example here: http://www.readersintheknow.com/blog/15/kindle-countdo wn-campaign-results), and although – again, of course – they have failed, they have managed to establish some givens:

1. External advertising need only drive above average sales over a short period of time to influence the algorithms, i.e. short burst advertising helps.

2. Sending above average sales over a sustained period (2–3

days) is better than one big hit.

3. Amazon's algorithms help upward trends but subdue sudden and non-sustained ones, so your one-day sales boost will deflate to original levels if it doesn't continue from day one until at least day three. Twenty sales each day for a week will raise your sales ranking more than a burst of 170 one day and none the rest of the week.

4. The higher and faster the climb, the more the algorithms assist in boosting results.

5. The higher the pre-promotion rank, the greater the boost and the longer it will last.

6. The more Amazon reviews you can muster, the more they seem to help.

7. Price itself doesn't seem to be influential where sales rank is concerned (so probably price at the most accessible level; 99c or 99p).

8. Being enrolled in KDP Select doesn't necessarily appear to affect algorithms, although I still wonder whether a KDP Select book being picked up by Amazon's algorithms would well perform better than one not enrolled – and in order to do a countdown promotion, of course the book *has* to be enrolled...

9. Kindle Unlimited borrows appear to influence sales rank immediately, so even if a borrower never reads your book you will still have a higher sales rank from it. I've already discussed the other ramifications in terms of payment and Kindle Unlimited in Chapter 11 of PUBLISH.

10. Using super URLs (URLs including the book's keywords or categories) certainly helps with positioning a book within its category as Amazon's algorithms also seem to take note of *how* a reader found your book. On a lot of promotional sites it's not possible to use tailored links – you supply the ASIN and the site finds the link for the book from that (or rather, probably creates an affiliate link from that so it garners a percentage commission on your sales as well as the fee you paid for the promotion in the first place). Some will allow you to provide your own links, in which case you can provide a super URL as a link so the effect of your potential sales/downloads will

influence your rise in rank in that specific category – very useful if you are aiming to hit #1 and have that nice little 'bestseller' badge against your book as a result. See below for how to work out your book's super URLS.

So how does having a book available for free help?

Free books are popular – for obvious reasons; it's free, right? What's not to like about that? Making your book free and telling everyone about it means – often – thousands of downloads. Thousands of downloads mean three things:

- Your book is now on the Kindle or compatible reading device (PCs are fine with Kindle's supporting and cloud software) of thousands of people. Your aim is for them to read and love what you've written and come back for more. If your book is the first in a series – wow! You potentially have a ready-made fan base looking for books two, three, four, and so on.
- Your book also has some carefully placed buy and sign-up links in it, such as super URL links for buying and a landing page (see Chapter 22 below) for your mailing list. You are about to start creating your own traffic and your own customer pool *outside* of Amazon.
- Your book has raced up the rankings in the 'Free' sections, now all you have to do is convert some of those last downloads to sales by following the steps below and your book can transfer from its now high ranking in the 'Free' section to an equally well-placed position in the 'Paid' store:

    - Make sure you've worked on getting reviews – at least ten 4 or 5*reviews are needed as social proof that this book might be worth reading – even free people don't want to waste their time. Tighten up your book description and author page too so they look as professional as possible.
    - Before your book is free, increase the price to between $4.99/ £3.99 and $9.99/£6.49. When your book is free,

Amazon will show the 'previous' price so now being free makes this book seem like a fantastic bargain. The psychological impact alone will drive downloads.

- Make sure all your buy links (super URLs) are included in front and back matter of your book.
- Make sure you have a link taking interested readers to your landing page to sign up to your mailing list using a 'reader magnet' – see Chapter 22 for this in detail.
- Run KDP 'Free' days in consecutive runs of two or three. One day won't get you very far, but two or three days – with promotion – will build up a head of steam, and remember, Amazon's algorithms work on a sustained increase in sales, not a one-day burst. You can have five 'Free' days per 90-day period. Spread them in groups of two and three with a suitable promotion planned for each – see Chapter 23 for tips on promotional strategy.
- Approximately twelve hours before you are going to end your 'Free' period, change the price down to 99c/99p.
- Physically end the promotion ahead of time yourself. You can do this by clicking on the 'Promote and Advertise' button on the bookshelf on your KDP dashboard. Amazon works on EST (Eastern Standard Time) so end your free promotion any time between 1pm and 3pm EST – between 6pm and 8pm GMT – as some potential customers will click the free link and still buy because the book is now high in the rankings but only 99c/99p so still a low risk if they don't like it. Use a converter like http://www.worldtimebuddy .com/est-to-gmt-converter to check on EST (Eastern Standard Time – US) /PST (Pacific Standard Time – N. America) / GMT (Greenwich Mean Time – UK).

What else helps Amazon make your book a bestseller?

KEYWORDS AND CATEGORIES: I talked about these in Chapter 16 of PUBLISH, but let's look at how you can manipulate them with Amazon's help to become a 'bestseller'. When Amazon gives your book that 'bestseller' badge, it gives you it for life. Your book may not stay at #1 but as long as it's hit it when Amazon changes the rankings (hourly), then it will grab the badge and the badge will help future sales. So how do you achieve it given the millions of books up on Amazon? You play the Kindle Categories game. When you were uploading your book to KDP you were asked to choose two categories and up to seven keywords (phrases). Now, have you noticed that a book with a 'bestseller' badge is not necessarily placed in one of those big categories you had available to choose from? It appears in a much smaller niche and this is derived from the keywords you used if you picked them cleverly. The 'category path' is how Amazon determines sales rankings. The main ranking you see is 'Paid in the Kindle Store', i.e. where your Kindle book is in the overall scheme of books on sale. This includes everything that relates in any way to Kindle – including accessories, hence why keywords are so important. The other rankings are for category paths and this is where you can use your clever edge with keywords.

For example, let's take the main categories and break them down piecemeal.

In 'All Departments' on Kindle there are these categories:

Kindle Store
Kindle eBooks
Mysteries
Romance
Thrillers
Teen & Young Adult eBooks
Christian Romance
Contemporary Romance
Contemporary Women's Fiction
Contemporary Literary Fiction
Suspense

Books
Mystery, Thriller & Suspense
Romance
Historical Romances
Suspense Thrillers
Literature & Fiction

Thrillers & Suspense
Mysteries
Contemporary Women Fiction
Cozy Mysteries
Romantic Suspense

If I choose to look at **Thrillers** in the Kindle Store, I will see that there are 83,693 (today's figure – it will be different when you look) books in the category – a lot of books to compete with. However, if I drill down and look at the sub-categories in Thrillers, I will find that there are these possibilities to choose from:

Legal (2,485)
Psychological (14,593)
Crime (11,079)
Political (3,140)
Espionage (8,073)
Assassinations (1,672)
Conspiracies (2,250)
Financial (482)
Historical (2,309)
Medical (1,355)
Military (1,777)
Pulp (947)
Technothrillers (3,508)
Terrorism (2,286)

The numbers in brackets are the numbers of books currently in that specific category. Now these categories aren't necessarily available to choose when choosing BISAC categories on your KDP dashboard but they *are* categories of books on sale on Amazon. So how do you get your book into them? Well, you can write to Amazon and ask nicely for your book to be included in that category and as long as the book fits into the niche, Amazon are very accommodating, but then you've opted to use one of your two categories up on it and wait – other books seem to be designated as falling within more than one category; how do they do that? They use their keywords to guide the book into the category because when potential readers find their book using those particular keywords, if they go on to buy the book, Amazon associates the keyword with the book and puts it in that category as well as the categories the author or publisher has chosen for it.

Finding the right niche category to aim for bestseller status in requires research. The most obvious choice may not be the best. You would think that Financial might be a good category to aim for with only 482 other contenders in it, but actually it isn't. Let's have a more detailed look at the Financial category:

In Financial, the bestseller's list (just look for the badge saying 'bestseller in...' for the appropriate list) shows that the current number one is a book called *The Dead Key* (as I write this) with 7,037 reviews – mainly 4 and 5* and as of today, ranking as follows:

Amazon Best Sellers Rank:

#474 Paid in Kindle Store
#1 in Kindle Store > Kindle sbooks > mystery, Thriller & Suspense > Thrillers > **Financial**
#1 in Books > Mystery, Thriller & Suspense > Thrillers & Suspense > **Financial**
#4 in Books > mystery, Thriller & Suspense > Mystery < **Amateur Sleuths**

That means that your book would have to reach #473 overall ranking in the Kindle Store to beat *The Dead Key* to #1 in the Thrillers > Financial category; a very tall order. A further look at numbers #2, #3 and #4 shows its contenders not far behind it with the #4 book having 156 reviews and standing at #2,536 overall in the Kindle Store. Not a good choice of category to try to rank in. By contrast, the Legal category (used for my Patchwork People series) subdivides further into potential bestseller categories of:

- 'Law media and the law' with its #1 in category riding at #3,960 overall in the Kindle Store.
- 'Criminal law evidence' with its #1 in category riding at #18,539 overall in the Kindle Store.
- 'Banking law' with its #1 in category riding at #13,506 overall in the Kindle Store.
- 'Child advocacy family law' with its #1 in category riding at #8,493 overall in the Kindle Store.

All are tough competitors because anything in any of the Mystery and Thriller categories are since Thrillers and Mysteries are one of the most popular genres, along with Romance. However, my thriller and mystery books would stand much more chance of ranking high in one of these categories than in some of the others. It's therefore worth looking at what the ranking overall of the #20 in the category is too and if you think – even in a very competitive category – you may be able to beat it, then adjust your keywords to edge your book into this category. Ranking – and therefore sales – are all about visibility. To be visible as #1 is best, of course, but to be visible as #20 still puts you in the front page of this category.

It's also worth checking category strings if you aren't ranking for a keyword category but can't understand why when you are outstripping others in the same category for your overall Kindle Store ranking. For example, *The Dead Key* is ranking #1 in Financial but look at the two strings. One is via the Kindle Store and one is via 'Books'. You may rank higher in one category string than another.

THEMES

Themes are what Amazon put together for fiction books because it was noticed that potential customers were searching for things like where the book was set, or the type of protagonist (amateur sleuth, gay protagonist etc). You can feed keywords that link with themes into both your keywords and your book's description to alert Amazon to the fact that your book fits in this niche too. So, for example if you've written a romance novel, you could use two theme words as keywords or maybe if you've written a mystery, you could replace more, dependent on how the themes fit with your book theme. Using themes as keywords is optional, but likely to be worth you doing if Amazon is. Also have a good look at the words Amazon recommends you use to get into particular categories as you won't make it into them without: https://kdp.amazon.com /help?topicId=A200PDGPEIQX41

SUPER URLS

I mentioned those earlier, didn't I? What are they? They're URLs leading to your book page on Amazon but incorporating the keywords of a specific category where you are ranking or working on ranking so that

Amazon associates sales with this traffic route and ranks you higher in the category as a result. How to get your super URL? A bit painstaking, but find your book in the list for the category you are trying to rank for and then click on your book. The URL that comes up in your browser when you reach your book page this way is the super URL for that category. Use it when providing third-party links to your book whenever you can, for instance in a blog post or in a press release. It won't make you rank – only sales will do that – but it will use SEO to tell Amazon the route customers took to go there and buy it, therefore triggering Amazon's algorithms to place you firmly in that category. You can also use software such as Amztracker https://www.amztracker.com/ – particularly useful if you are an affiliate marketer too. There's more on affiliate marketing in Chapter 23. To smooth the path for any customer in any country you can also use http://www.booklinker.net/ to create a universal link to send customers to the appropriate Amazon store for their geographical location. https://manage.smarturl.it/ does much the same thing.

The lessons to learn from this:

- Do your research well with keywords and categories.
- Promote them well – visibility is still all.
- Plan promotions to extend over a period of time.
- Plan promotions like a battle campaign – have a look in Chapter 23 for an example.

Chapter 22:
Reader Magnets: The Tender Trap

Have you ever watched iron filings stick to a magnet? Irresistible attraction! That's what you are aiming for with your promotion strategies. With a magnet it works particularly well with iron filings directly onto the magnet. It even works well with just a thin sheet of paper in between the two, but as the paper becomes thicker, the attraction begins to fail and the iron filings fall away. Let's substitute your books for the magnet, your potential readers/book buyers for the iron filings and sales platforms like Amazon for the ever thicker piece of paper between you. Yes, some stick with distance – and the bigger the surface area of the magnet (i.e. your book's visibility) the more are still attracted, but what if you could remove that piece of paper altogether? Well, you can. And you do it with a magnet; a reader magnet…

Do you have a mailing list so you can tell your avid readers when your next book is going to be released? Or when a book is on offer? If you haven't you should. Of course it's wonderful to see the graph of sales on your KDP dashboard rising, but not all of those purchasers will become readers, and if they do, not all of those readers will remember to look out for your next release. But your mailing list members will, because you will remind them…

So how do you generate a mailing list? By having an incentive for someone to sign up to it. A reader magnet. Reader magnets can come in all kinds of forms – free books, sample chapters, novellas or prizes. You can provide them through competitions and giveaways, such as via Twitter and sites that will specifically organise and run a competition or giveaway for you. You can promote it in one of your books, or you can use social media and an incentive to encourage sign-ups. You can even run a competition through Amazon itself – Amazon will run print book giveaways for you as long as you pay for the prizes and the shipping – or readers sites such as Goodreads, who will also run giveaways for you, again with you providing and paying for the shipping of the prizes. There are many kinds of giveaways and promotions you can do in this vein – with one end in mind: promoting discoverability and simultaneously creating a potential readership/fanbase to promote your work to via a mailing list. And a mailing list will not just enable you to promote your books directly to its members.

It paves the way to:

- Gaining reviews.
- Gaining more exposure.
- Promoting special offers.
- Helping launch new releases.
- Helping achieve bestseller status.

If you have a steady stream of people joining your mailing list all the time, when the time comes, you will also have a steady number of people keen to read what you've written next as a result.

HERE'S HOW TO SET UP A MAILING LIST

1. Subscribe to a newsletter provider; I would suggest Mailchimp http://mailchimp.com/ or Aweber http://www.aweber.com/ as the most popular mailing list services – and Mailchimp is free (with limited function-ality) until you hit over 2,000 subscribers.
2. Set up your list with an identifiable name which relates to the reader magnet you are using or target you are aiming at – say 'Free [your book title] subscribers.'
3. At the beginning and end of all of your books, have a link for readers to sign up for your ebook list. They might – even without a reader magnet – if they liked your book enough.
4. Prepare yourself for offering something as a reader magnet, preferably a free book, or a novella, or the first two books in a novella series. This needs to be something you can offer on an ongoing basis – different to give-aways and competitions where you might choose a more expensive and compelling prize to gain exposure. Make

these novellas or book exclusive to the mailing list; you have to sign up or you won't be able to read them – or make them an expensive buy on Amazon, but free for anyone signing up to your mailing list.

5. If you don't have a book or novellas to offer, create something else that is exclusive, and of interest to your target readership – insider knowledge, tips, resources, interesting research. Reference it to your book so it is clear it is derived from or related solely to the book.

6. Upload your book/novella/resource to the place you are going to send mailing list sign-ups to in order to claim it, and create a landing page on your website to act as a funnel to send interested parties to your sign-0up form. The autoresponder from the newsletter provider where your list is being hosted will deliver the link to download.

7. Set up a series of welcome emails and newsletters to welcome your new sign-ups, remembering that whilst the intention is to sell other books you have written to them; assist in launches/collect reviews etc, you will need to build a relationship with them first and this is best done by offering more of yourself or your books before asking anything of them.

8. Never spam anyone!

THE SERIES STRATEGY

I talk about offering novellas or the first/first two in a series and this is a strategy that many employ to grow a mailing list, and indeed a faithful readership. I read every single Enid Blyton book there was when I was a child, and when I moved on to adult books I did the same with my favourite adult fiction authors. You may regard writing a series as a marketing ploy, but it is also a wonderful way of developing characters beyond the limited parameters of just one novel, or expanding a story into an epic in a way that wouldn't be possible in a standalone book. My Patchwork People series started out as a standalone story but about half way into *Patchwork Man* I realised the story was already expanding far beyond what I could realistically put into just one book. It became three, and I was satisfied that was how it should be, so series and serials are not just to capture an audience, they are to tell a story in the most complete way you can. They do, of course, also provide wonderful reader magnets and upselling opportunities if the first in the series is offered free, because you hope the rest of the series will be ready-made sales if your readers enjoy their free book. You don't have to have a series to use the series strategy to good effect. What do you think Wattpad is if not a form of series strategy? A writer uploads a section of their book and having gained a following dribbles out the rest until it's published and the avid readership buys the book to be able to read the whole thing from start to finish. You can do this with a part-book, or even chapters of a book, offering the rest for free in exchange for entry onto your mailing list. Build some rapport in between by tailoring your auto-responders to deliver the next parts of the story instalment style, with requests for feedback. Even suggest tweets fans might like to share such as: *"Enjoying free chapters of [book title] by [author name/Twitter handle] right now. Click here to download them. [mailing list sign-up link]."* If you are determined to sell the book, withhold the last section and offer them a special deal (put the book down to 99c/99p for a limited time) plus a special bonus if they review it. Don't forget to tell them about the next book you're releasing either and invite them to follow you on Facebook/Twitter or whichever social media platforms you favour. Build your fan base as well as your mailing list.

Of course it's all very well for me to talk about offering free books/novellas/chapters/ information but how do you let people know that's what you're doing? After all, we've already agreed that the biggest hurdle to selling your books and getting readers to read them is visibility, haven't we? I'm afraid good old promotion and marketing kicks back in here – you see promotion and marketing can have a number of targets, and not just directly selling books. I'll look at targets, planning promotions and marketing strategy in Chapter 23 but here's some information about straightforward paid advertising, aside from direct selling in the form of Facebook, Twitter and Amazon advertising.

FACEBOOK AND TWITTER ADVERTISING

Can be very expensive if you don't get it right – by that I mean get the targeting and the aim right. Decide what you are targeting and stick with that so you are clear about what you are spending your advertising budget on. It's very easy to let it run away without getting what you intended from it. Basically are you advertising your books or building your mailing list? These are the two main targets of Facebook and Twitter advertising.

FACEBOOK ADS

Some things to consider when setting up your adverts:

- Use the Power Editor in Ads Manager to fine-tune audiences and targets.
- Direct ads at specific geographical areas, don't combine, for example the UK and the US. Tastes, time zones and ways of life are different.
- Split test ads with different imagery and content to see which works best. Regularly monitor which is performing best and with which parts of your target audience. Fine-tune the ad on the basis of results.
- Aim for the lowest CPC (cost per click) or conversion rates possible and check what your ROI (return on investment) is producing within your budget.
- Start with a low daily budget and build up if you find a good combination.
- With targeting start with the highest audience numbers and whittle it down. Facebook targets on an 'and/or' basis, not an 'and/and' basis, so by starting with the widest range of interests in terms of numbers and subsequently selecting other interest areas you will be reducing numbers rather than increase them (as you might otherwise assume you would be doing).
- Use bold imagery and beware you don't overshoot the no more than 20% rule of text to images although the text on book covers doesn't count.
- Facebook ads can be a wonderful way of promoting a reader magnet campaign because, remember, whilst you may not be selling anything directly with your ad, only gathering email sign-ups, your ROI comes good when you market another of your products to your sign-ups.
- There are some links to some great Facebook ad courses and information on my website amongst the documents available to download on signing up and I would recommend joining one of them because getting it right

with Facebook ads can be an expensive business whilst on the learning curve.

TWITTER ADS

42% of Twitter users follow brands or companies, apparently, so Twitter is potentially an important element in your marketing strategy. Twitter ads https://ads.twitter.com/ are an easy way to put tweets in front of a larger audience than just those who follow you. It is also therefore useful in generating new leads for your mailing list.

- Choose whether you wish to promote your account or your tweet. Promoting tweets will allow your tweets to appear in users' Twitter streams or in search results. Promoting your account will display your username under 'Who to Follow'. Promoting your account encourages growth of your follower base but promoting tweets enables you to take users away from Twitter, and – for example – onto your mailing list sign-up page or your book sales page on Amazon.
- Targeting is by interests or followers or keywords if you're promoting tweets. There is also a tailored audience option allowing you to use data taken from your website or database. Targeting by interests and followers allows you to create a basic list of Twitter usernames influential in the particular area you've picked and then create a larger 'lookalike' audience based on them.
- Targeting by keywords allows you to reach people searching, tweeting about, or engaging with specific keywords. This helps you find an audience that is actively interacting with the specific keywords relevant to you or your book/offer.
- Targeting 'Tailored Audiences' allows you to run retargeting campaigns through Twitter too. You'll need to work with a suitable Twitter ad partner to build audiences based on pixels placed on your site or by matching the list drawn off your database, such as Perfect Audience. This is a lot more complicated so try the more basic forms of targeting first.

- Targeting by interests and followers is better if you're looking for new audiences as you will reach a larger, but less specifically interested audience. Targeting by keywords will bring you a smaller but more focused audience – such as writers looking for a book about writing and self-publishing, for example.
- As with Facebook, try split testing to see which works best for you. You can also target your audience by location, gender and age – which may be relevant for you in specific genres; Romance, for instance – and which devices you'd like your promoted tweets to appear on (again like Facebook): desktop, mobile or a combination of all of them.
- As with Facebook, too, always set a budget and stick to it – unless your ROI suggests you should actually invest and promote more, not less. Also continue to tweak and change your tweets to optimise them based on results.

GIVEAWAYS, COMPETITIONS AND FREEBIES – HOW AND WHY

Giveaways, competitions and free offers are also part of the promotion game plan for many. Everyone loves a freebie, and everyone loves the chance to win something – and that something could be anything. It could be a signed copy of your book, or a bundle of them, a digital reader to read them on or something else completely unrelated to your books if it's going to arouse interest. There are two main competition sites. Kingsumo https://kingsumo.com/ has a life-time subscription charge, so it's not cheap but once you've paid your subscription fee, you can run as many competitions as you like. Rafflecopter https://www.rafflecopter.com/ has a free option and a monthly paid option, although to access the features that help maximise the appeal of your campaign (adding imagery, for instance), you will have to pay. What do they do? They allow people to enter your 'competition' in exchange for something, usually for an email address or a Facebook or Twitter or other social media follow. They are mainly to grow your mailing list, and can also be fine-tuned to encourage entrants to 'share' the competition with others, thereby organically increasing the reach of your potential audience, in exchange for more chances at winning. There are three things to remember when running a competition like this though:

- You will need to promote the competition. The service provider provides the competition entry and data handling, it doesn't provide the publicity for it. That is down to you – back to Facebook and Twitter ads!
- Make the prize something that will be of interest to your audience, even if it's not one of your books – maybe it's a signed book by a well-known author in your genre? At least you'll know you're reaching an audience interested in *the kind of thing* you write.
- You cannot require entrants to purchase or have to do something requiring a purchase to have taken place in order to enter, so your entry question can't be "Whose name appears on line 3 of page 79?" Better, basically to simply require entrants to provide an email address. You can go from there...

Don't forget that Amazon will also run a giveaway for you of your print book. You simply have to pay for the number of 'prizes', i.e. your book plus post and packaging to send to the winners, that you're prepared to provide, and you're away. The options for collecting data about your entrants are limited – a Twitter follow at most – but I've added well over 1,000 Twitter followers to my account using this strategy. They may not remain followers if they're not truly engaged with you or your books, but a percentage will remain, and your potential audience for sales has been increased again; now run a Twitter ad campaign to get them onto your mailing list...

The content comprising a series of auto-responders you could use is available on my website – yes, you've guessed it – if you'd like to sign up to receive them, alongside lists of free and paid promotion sites, useful marketing and social media software, Facebook, Twitter, Pinterest, LinkedIn, Reddit and other groups to join and more information and training on using Facebook, Twitter, Mailchimp and Rafflecopter. Don't worry, I won't spam you – I tell you not to, so why would I? But if you are interested in content and information I know about, why not join a mailing list where you might learn more? Makes sense, doesn't it? Apart from that, all I can say is: get yourself to the internet and get a mailing list, now!

Chapter 23:
Social Proof – Getting Reviews

If you've ever browsed Amazon, you'll see most products have reviews. Some have a lot of reviews – *Gone Girl* by Gillian Flynn has 42,218 reviews as I write this; the most in the book store on Amazon, averaging out at 3.9* – not bad by any standards! Others have only a few. Why are reviews so important? Because they are social proof; proof that your book is worth reading – and even if your book is free, some potential readers still need to be convinced it's worth being given house room on their Kindle. We are all very precious about what we like and dislike, do and don't do; we're creatures of habit, even the most spontaneous of us. As a new, debut or relatively unknown author, you need a lot of social proof to convince readers to find out what your books are like, which is why it's important you get all the other basic elements of publishing your book right: the style, plot, genre, quality, editing, formatting, presentation, description, keywords and categories. It's even more important to have social proof that you've done so by obtaining social proof confirming it: reviews.

Reviews are Credibility. And in case you need to be convinced about the credibility of that statement, here are some statistical reasons why it's true:

- Not a Gold Rush - The Taleist Self-Publishing Survey http://www.amazon.com/Not-Gold-Rush-Taleist-Self-Publishing-ebook/dp/B0085M7KIU showed that authors with books reviewed by Amazon's top reviewers (the top 5,000) enjoyed approximately 32% higher sales.
- As far back as 2012 a *Harvard Business Review* article https://hbr.org/2012/03/bad-reviews-can-boost-sales-heres-

why/ar/1 found that positive reviews increased sales between 32% to 52%; and even bad reviews increased sales of books by unknowns by up to 45%!

- Amazon's algorithms are an unknown but we do know that they work on signs of social trending – for example the continued and sustained boost in sales compared to the sudden but short-lived one. So the fact that even bad reviews triggered something is confirmation that the algorithms work on interaction – social signalling.
- Stanford University's Web Credibility Research Survey https://credibility.stanford.edu/ found that the biggest boost to a product or a service's credibility where consumers were concerned was whether it received 'third-party support' – in other words, comments and reviews.

Reviews are what tell potential readers your book is good. Reviews encourage comment and consideration. Reviews help sell books. If you don't have any reviews, and are a debut author, or a relative unknown, who is going to take a risk and pay good money for your book? Precisely. But if you have a range of 4* and 5* reviews, potential readers know your book could be worth reading. Price it right and you may have made a sale. For digital books, I would recommend no more than $4.99 or the UK equivalent (around £3.50). You'll get most sales at 99c or 99p. For print books, probably $11.99 or £7.99 will hit the right spot.

But how do you get reviews, apart from twisting everyone you know plus the dog's arm to write them for you? Lots of ways:

- Review swaps: I know of over 100 review swap groups – a willing source of reviews if you are prepared to reciprocate. Again time consuming, but good to participate in over a period of time as long as you are selective about what you review, and vice versa. The review swap list forms part of my workshop/mentoring content.
- Press releases, announcing anything newsworthy about your book: its release, winning an award, adding to the series, a successful event involving it. Choose the right press release agency and invite reviewers. You will have to make the book available free for reviewers so there is potentially a cost to factor in, and of course the cost of the

press release agency – hence the importance of finding the right one. Having tried several, I now know which agency is most productive for me, and will only use it. I know the cost is worth it for the results.

- Many promotional sites have options to submit books for review, and there also some sites that enable you to upload your book for free in return for readers reviewing it. I now have a list of over 30 book review sites specifically seeking books for review, and over 50 promotional sites I use to promote whatever I'm offering. I review my lists regularly and add to them as new sites rise in stature (check the Alexa score) and reach, and I include all of them in my workshop and mentoring content.

- Attend events, book clubs, give talks – recently I collected four avid fans from one small book club meeting I spoke to – well worth the time and effort later. Four good fans that might be potential reviewers are worth many half-hearted readers.

- Ask for reviews at the end of each book: ask nicely and explain why they're important to you as an author and you'll appeal to your readers' good nature. Better still, add an incentive to review the book in the front and back matter. Some authors have even asked readers to email them the link to their review by a set date in order to stand a chance of winning vouchers and prizes.

- And of course, encourage friends, family – and the dog – as well...

Size does matter in this case. For Amazon, apparently 50 is the magic number for them to take note of your book; the same with some of the bigger online promoters – for instance Bookbub https://www.bookbub .com/partners, the big daddy of all promoters.

The best way to approach a blogger or reviewer to ask if they would consider reviewing your book is to ask politely, individually – not as part of a mass mail-out.

- Amazon has a top 10,000 reviewers list – the reviewers whose reviews are most influential. You can find it here: http://www.amazon.com/review/top-reviewers and it can also be sorted into another list, located on the same page; the Hall of Fame reviewers, who are most active and most highly ranked most recently. Take time to look at each profile to identify those with interests in books similar to yours – bearing in mind some of these reviewers may be mainly general product reviewers, not necessarily book reviewers. Select the best 50 or so and work your way through them, with a polite request. Remember, these are not just your average "Liked it/Didn't like it" reviewer. They are thoughtful, thorough and influential. They write longer reviews and they generally receive more "Likes" from other users, pushing their review to the top of the list of reviews on your books page. Make sure it's a good one!

(An example template can be downloaded from my website, as can a ready-made list of reviewers to contact to start with to save yourself some time and effort.)

- Top Amazon reviewers often also have their own blogs where they will also post their review of your book – more publicity...
- There are numerous bloggers sites reviewing books in all genres. Some will accept self-published authors, some won't. Some useful places to look for bloggers and reviewers are here:

  - Book Blogger Directory https://bookblogger directory.wordpress.com/, a comprehensive, genre-organised alphabetical listing of book blogs.
  - YA Book Blog Directory http://yabookblog directory.blogspot.ca/; bloggers reviewing YA books.
  - Story Cartel https://storycartel.com/ where books are free in exchange for honest book reviews.
  - The Author Marketing Club also offers its members a tailor-made reviewer locator service, based on books in specific genres.

- Book review services can also be used, although bear in mind some may charge upwards of hundreds of pounds/dollars for the privilege. Kirkus https://www.kirkus reviews.com/ is one of these – and although well-respected, do ask yourself what real value you will be getting from one review when you could be obtaining twenty or thirty for the same price. Remember, social proof is quality and quantity. A list of paid book review services is included with the blogger and reviewer list on my website but here's Bookplex http://bookplex.com/pg/28/book-review-service for you to look at to see what kind of service they offer.

- Reviews you have paid for should not be posted up on Amazon as customer reviews as these are against Amazon's terms and conditions. But you can add excerpts in the editorial section of your book page via your author's page.

(A comprehensive list of bloggers and blog directories is available for download in the materials referred to in the Appendix.)

And to leave this section on a very important note: *never, never* respond to a bad review. Take note of any fair criticism, make adjustments and revisions where necessary and then rise above it and move on. Not everyone will like your books. Not everyone will review your books – average statistics suggest that no more than 1% of readers will actually do so. Value more the readers who do, and who do it positively.

Chapter 24:
Promotion Central Station

So let's recap, going back to my radical mnemonic:

...on to promotion in general, and what are the various types of promotional goals you might be aiming for?

TO GROW YOUR MAILING LIST:

- Select which book(s) you are going to offer for free/promote.
- Include an 'advert' to that effect, with a sign-up link in your lead book.
- Create a free download platform linked to your promotional tool (the book advert or a media campaign), and your mailing list sign-up page.
- Set up auto-responders linked to your sign-up page, delivering the bonus for signing up.
- Remember to follow up afterwards – stay gently in touch until you have something else you are promoting.
- You can also make a/your book free on a reader/review site in return for reviews and the reader joining your mailing list in order to access the free DOWNLOAD.

INCREASING SALES RANKINGS ON AMAZON AND OTHER SALES PLATFORMS:

- Currently this is easiest on Amazon because it offers two possible promotional services – *Kindle countdown*, where your book starts at a heavily discounted price and gradually increases over a period of time. Or *Kindle free* days, where you can offer your book free for up to 5 days in any 90. For both promotional services the 90 days referred to is the period you have to sign up to in order to sell your book exclusively through Amazon. And beware if you contravene this – the sanctions can be severe, including being banned from publishing future titles on Kindle.
- *What does the promotion do?* Because your book is either free or very cheap – and the countdown option creates a sense of urgency – the barriers to accessibility are virtually nil. It's free – what's the risk? As a result, you can potentially achieve many more hundreds of downloads than if it cost something. *Advantage*: increased discoverability.
- It also enables you to spread the news about your sign-up link to thousands of readers – via that advert you put in the front of the book in order to push your mailing list sign-up link, remember?
- More downloads means your book will rapidly rise up the Kindle category lists – maybe even to #1 or #2 like mine did (see below). *Advantage*: increased discoverability.

USING PERMA-FREE BOOKS:

Perma-free books are books that are the first in a series, or if you have a number of published books, you are happy to allow to be downloaded free to encourage interest in the rest of your work.

The advantages to having a perma-free book are these:

- You can place an advert in the front of your book – or an incentive to sign up to your mailing list, or any other action you'd like to encourage readers to take, and know it will be seen by thousands of potential readers, not a mere handful. Why? The book is free – it's a no-risk purchase.

- It's a way of enabling potential readers to read and become a fan, without risk to them. Why? The book is free – it's a no-risk purchase.
- Because the book is free and therefore will be attracting more downloads than books that a potential reader has to pay for, it will be higher up in the sales rankings than them. It will be seen more easily, you will be discovered more easily – and so will your other books.
- By having a perma-free book available on a number of platforms, you also increase your potential to be discovered by different types of readers. This is why I urged consideration of which platforms to use to sell your books, and also whether exclusivity is best for you or not. Of course, simply because you have one book perma-free and available on a number of sales platforms – not just Amazon – it doesn't mean you can't take advantage of Amazon's KDP exclusive package for other books; the best of both worlds, maybe? If you have a perma-free book, it will still need promoting from time to time though. Use all the promotional sites I've mentioned earlier to remind the reading public that it's there and FREE. So are a lot of other books, all employing the same strategy!

NEW RELEASE LAUNCHES:

- Use the books you already have out as leverage. *Advantage*: advertising and to increase discoverability. Offer them free, discounted or as part of a package including the new release.
- Use your mailing list to announce it. *Advantage*: sales on the day of release, and the more sales you have in the shortest period of time, the greater the impact on your sales ranking.
- Use your pre-release review team (gleaned from your most avid fans on your mailing list) to review before the release and be primed to post their review on the day of release or soon afterwards. *Advantage*: increased credibility for your book – remember, reviews = good book = sales.

OBTAINING REVIEWS:

See Chapter 23 above for the importance of reviews and:

- Offer a free book to your mailing list in return for a review.
- If your reviewers are enthusiastic, also enlist them onto your new release review team.
- Post your book onto review sites (see list referred to above) and invite reviews.
- Invite review swaps via review site swaps (see list referred to above).

There are a lot, aren't there? It's a bit like climbing a promotional mountain, isn't it? It needn't be, if you take a step at a time.

LET'S PLAN A CAMPAIGN AND SEE HOW THAT'S DONE

Step 1: Build your mailing list by:

- Setting up a free book to download for sign-ups.
- Creating a landing page on your website for sign-ups to funnel through. A landing page looks like this:

  - **A compelling headline**
  - **Interesting visuals**
  - **The benefits of your offer**
  - **A form to sign up** – or sometimes a link to click, leading to the form on your mailing list provider.

  Hubspot is all about marketing and it has some useful examples of good landing pages here: http://blog.hubspot.com/marketing/landing-page-examples-list. Have a look and play with design to create yours on your own website.

- Adding sign-up invitations to the front and back matter in all your books.
- Setting up your KDP promo – either a Kindle Countdown Deal or a series of KDP free days.

- You can add 'free book' as a keyword for the duration of the free promotion period but you must remove it as soon as you end the free promotion or you are being 'misleading' within Amazon's Terms and Conditions.
- Organise your promotion for the free days on promotional sites like Booksends, ENT, Bookbub (if you can get on it). Make sure at least one is a really big promoter and usually position it later in the overall promotion with smaller pushes earlier – remember how Amazon likes to build on an already increased rank? Well so do buyers; the higher the rank when they see the book, the more likely they are to buy it – social proof again. It's all cumulative in this game!
- Use the free sites for promotion too. Some sites are set up to promote free books and some will even do it for free, or a very small fee. The Author Marketing Club has a free sites submission tool allowing you to submit to a number of sites in one hit. So do some others, and the KDROI software package will do it for you for nothing if you've already bought it. *The downloadable information on my website includes a list of sites you can promote through, whether for free or via paid advertising. You can find the link to download it here: http://eepurl.com/bH8yEX*
- Set up your own social media posts to promote the offer too using Hootsuite or similar.
- Prepare your auto-responders on your mailing list service provider.

Step 2: Use your free days to sell:

- Put the price of your free book up 24 hours or so before it's free.
- Put the price down to 99p/99c a few hours before you are going to end the free days.
- End the free promotion between 1pm and 3pm EST to grab sales from those potential downloaders who respond to the free offer as latecomers but decide to buy anyway even though the book is now 99p/99c as it is high in the rankings.
- Follow through with some continued promotion on

promotional sites – maybe in the 99p/99c promotional options or Facebook/Twitter ads to maintain an upward trend in sales to trigger the Amazon algorithms.

OR, if you have chosen to run a Kindle Countdown Deal:

- Follow through with some continued promotion on promotional sites – maybe in the 99p/99c promotional options or Facebook/Twitter ads after the Countdown has ended to maintain an upward trend in sales to trigger the Amazon algorithms.

Step 3: Using your mailing list to sell:

- Put the price down of the next book in the series the free book was from, or another book you'd like to promote.
- You now have an increased mailing list following your promotion. Begin the relationship-growing process by sending out a newsletter/email asking what they thought of the free book – did they enjoy it?
- Follow up with a reminder about the free book and whether they have reviewed it yet. If you want to, add an incentive for reviews – respond positively to any incoming mail as a result.
- Thank everyone for their reviews and ask for them to keep on coming. Follow up the first email by telling them how you got the idea for the book/series. Ask if they've found out what happens next/had a look at anything else you've written yet if they enjoyed the free book. Offer information about where the next book in the series/another book you've written can be found ON OFFER. Now you're selling books – three messages down the line…

Step 4: Continue to sell your books/get sign-ups:

- Your mailing list messages/newsletter should always be chatty and interesting, never pushy – and never, "Buy my books, buy my books!" Keep building the relationship with your readers by telling them what you're working on, interesting snippets of news or information – related to books or the topic of your books, or just life in general. Keep gently asking for – and thanking readers for – reviews. Occasionally mention when a book is on offer or maybe when you've pulled together a boxed set.

- Create a sub-list of your most dedicated followers. Mention to them how much you value their input – would they be interested in reviewing in a slightly more formal way? This is the basis for your advance review team; the fans who love what you write and are willing to take time out of their day to write a review for you just because. When you next have a new book to release, these are the advance reviewers I referred to in Chapter 20 that you will call on to help you launch it.
- You can slowly do the same to create a beta readers list if you like. Ensure the people you include are stalwart fans, but also critical and clear-headed, avid readers.
- Make the free book you started your list with perma-free so you can use it as a permanent reader magnet. Here's how you make a book perma-free despite not being able to price a book for free on Amazon unless it's in a free promotion period:

  - Make sure your book is not signed up to KDP Select, or if it is, uncheck the automatic renewal box and wait for the current period to end.
  - Upload the book to Smashwords or Draft2Digital.
  - Make the book free on whichever platform you choose to draw readers – especially if it's the first in a series.
  - Once it's live on the other platform tell KDP by making contact through the 'help' section. Explain that the book is currently being made available free through whichever platform you are using as part of a promotional campaign currently – would Amazon like to price match it, referring to their price-matching statement here: https://kdp.amazon.com/help?topicId=A22DBITFA52 H1S
  "Any update to a list price is subject to the KDP pricing Terms and Conditions. For example, if you set

a list price higher than the list price in another sales channel, we may price-match your book." Amazon should pick up the ball and run from here, price-matching your book at zero. As long as your book remains free on the other platform, it will remain free on Amazon – perma-free. Note that it's not a good idea to have a perma-free book and the same book in use as a reader magnet book – why would someone give you their email address if they can already simply download the book for free elsewhere?

- Run competitions via Rafflecopter or similar to keep your list growing.
- Run Facebook and Twitter adverts for your reader magnet book to reach new audiences.

Step 5: Rinse and repeat.

- With a new book.
- With a boxed set.
- With a new promotion.
- Remember to add taster chapters of the next book in a series to the first or previous books.
- Use the data you've gathered from monitoring (and I've included a suggested Excel template for doing this in the downloads on my website) the campaigns you've previously run to adjust audiences, targets and promotional sites you use for future campaigns – for instance, which of the free sites you submitted to actually ran your ad; which paid sites produced most downloads, and so on.
- Add taster chapters and information about all the books you write, updating books you've previously written as they're released.
- Make sure your goals are clear: do you want mailing list sign-ups, do you want sales, are you launching a new release, are you seeking reviews. Each will require a slightly different approach, but nevertheless should still be strategically planned, bearing in mind how it could impact on other longer-term goals. Increasing your mailing list will

provide a bigger audience to promote to, so maybe this is a good first strategic goal to set...

- Plan ahead to the next campaign.

Finally; putting it all together:

I put all of this together in campaigns. On their own, individual aspects will make very little impact. Added together, and used with a specific target in mind, for instance – growing your mailing list, improving your books' rankings, increasing discoverability in a number of keywords or categories, improving review rates or launching a new release – the impact can be astonishing.

There are many different types of campaign you may wish to run, for many purposes, depending on the type of books you have on release, but ultimately they are all aimed at one thing: making you an author who is read. And that requires being discoverable so above all, with any campaign or strategy, make sure as many people as possible know about your promotion. This is where my last useful list comes into play – the list of sites and promoters who will help you do that. Apart from your own social media presence – Twitter, Facebook, Google+, Pinterest, Instagram, Tumblr – make use of online book promoters like Bookbub and the 100 or so on my list to push your message under as many noses as possible.

Below I've shown some of my results from running a combination of promotions:

File Size: 552 KB
Print Length: 253 pages
Publisher: IM Books; 1 edition (July 23, 2014)
Sold by: Amazon Digital Services, Inc.
Language: English
ASIN: B00M37OUPY
Text-to-Speech: Enabled
X-Ray: Not Enabled
Word Wise: Not Enabled
Lending: Not Enabled
Amazon Best Sellers Rank: #129 Free in Kindle Store (See Top 100 Free in Kindle Store)
  #1 in Kindle Store > Kindle eBooks > Mystery, Thriller & Suspense > Mystery > Series
  #1 in Kindle Store > Kindle eBooks > Mystery, Thriller & Suspense > Mystery > International Mystery & Crime

Here is Patchwork Man at #1 in both its Kindle categories on 20th May 2015. Notice the categories are different; a useful trick to remember – vary your choice of categories from time to time, depending on other books' performances in the genre.

This is a campaign in June 2015, where you can see *Patchwork People* shot up the rankings after only one day of promotion:

Product Details

File Size: 778 KB
Print Length: 259 pages
Publisher: I.M. Books; 1 edition (September 30, 2014)
Publication Date: September 30, 2014
Sold by: Amazon Digital Services, Inc.
Language: English
ASIN: B00NP4U55S
Text-to-Speech: Enabled ☑
X-Ray: Not Enabled ☑
Word Wise: Not Enabled
Lending: Enabled
Amazon Best Sellers Rank: #621 Free in Kindle Store (See Top 100 Free in Kindle Store)
    #2 in Kindle Store > Kindle eBooks > Mystery, Thriller & Suspense > Mystery > **Series**
    #5 in Kindle Store > Kindle eBooks > Mystery, Thriller & Suspense > Thrillers > **Conspiracies**

> Patchwork People had hit at #2 and #5 in its two Kindle categories on 26th June 2015, after only one day of promotion.

If you've followed through all the other steps in your campaign – you may end up with this:

> Here are Patchwork Man and Patchwork People at #1 and #2 of an Amazon bestseller list on 15th March 2015, as the result of a promotional campaign.

Chapter 25: The Last Word

These are the final elements of my marketing mnemonic:

ADDING VALUE: every reader you reach out to will be looking for added value. That means not only a good and professionally produced book, but the extras they hope will come with it – rewards for loyalty. There are many ways of rewarding loyal readers – free books, bonus books, collections of a series exclusive to them, advance knowledge of new releases, special discounts and offers – and personal contact. My own promotional strategies include a variety of these, and I have an automated system in place so that the rewards flow from my mailing list and the books themselves, which maintains continuity and contact. I teach the nuts and bolts of these strategies to my students, but I also encourage them to stay in touch with their readers and always reply personally to all fan mail. Give a little of yourself in the same way that you would give to a friend who has read and is now commenting on one of your books.

LETTING IT FLOW… In other words, keep writing! The more you have to offer, the more readers have to read. Some promotional strategies will work with just one book for sale, but if you have two – or more – the advantages are enormous. Series particularly lend themselves to promotional strategies, as well trilogies, follow-up books and collections.
    Writing is a tough business if you do it as a business or as a career. Writing as a career is 50% writing and 50% marketing. You will have to spend an equal amount of time on promoting your books as writing them. That's not to say don't plan to do it as a career, but plan to do it as a career without labouring under the illusion that you are immediately going to become a best-selling author as soon as your first book is published. Success – even in a modest way – is probably the third, fourth or maybe even the fiftieth book down the line. The stars of self-publishing you hear about – Amanda Hocking, Joe Konrath, Tracy

Bloom, Guy Kawasaki, Joanna Penn, Rachel Abbott, Hugh Howey, Bella Andre, Mel Sherratt and Mark Dawson – are stars in their own right as marketers too because they are more than just authors, they are authorpreneurs in the truest sense of the word. Joanna Penn's blog http://www.thecreativepenn.com/blog/ regularly dishes out more writing and publishing tips than you can find houseroom for in an upbeat, always optimistic manner. Mark Dawson offers expert online tuition free of charge on mastering Facebook advertising: http://www.selfpublishing formula.com/. They have learnt how to become marketers as much as they are authors, and to be successful, you will have to too. Their blogs contribute to the wealth of useful information that can be found online and in various forums, demonstrating a rather heart-warming characteristic of self-published authors and the self-publishing community in general. No matter how big and successful they are, there is still a desire to see others achieve success too. You can find support from all these sources:

- The Alliance of Independent Authors (ALLi): http://allianceindependentauthors.org/
- The forums on KindleBoards: http://www.kboards.com/
- Your local writers' group (join one as soon as you start writing!):

  - In the UK you can find the ones local to you here: http://www.nawg.co.uk/
  - In the US have a look here: http://freelancewrite.about .com/od/writingcommunities/a/List-Of-Writers-Associations.htm
  - And here: http://writersrelief.com/writing-groups-for-writers/

- The Society of Authors in the UK (protecting your rights as a writer): http://www.societyofauthors.org/
- Author's Licensing and Collecting Society in the UK (ALCS): http://www.alcs.co.uk/
- There are a whole host of Facebook Groups – download the list from my website.
- Also network with the like-minded, for example:

- The Crime Writers Association: www.thecwa.co.uk
- The Romantic Novelists Association: www.rna-uk.org
- Author Network: www.authornetwork.com/crime.html

And now also open to indie authors too:

- Thriller and Mystery Writers: http://thrillerwriters.org/
- Romance writers: https://www.rwa.org/
- Sci-fi and fantasy writers: http://www.sfwa.org/ 2015/02/sfwa-welcomes-self-published-small-press-authors/

Search online and you will find many more to help you ease your way forward in the world of writing and publishing, but above all else, write because you love writing, publish because you relish the success of seeing your book in print (or online) and promote it because you'd like others to read it. Write the best book you can, have it edited and proofed professionally, with proper formatting and a good cover design. Write a marketing plan and devote a reasonable amount of time to action it. In theory, you now have all the tools – in this book and the downloadable material – that you need to become a best-selling author. I cannot guarantee that you *will* become a best-selling author, just as I cannot guarantee that the world will still be spinning gaily on its axis next year, the year after or in a thousand years' time.

There are, without doubt, other elements that come into play in making a book sell in the hundreds of thousands. The people you have the luck to connect with, and luck itself have a lot to do with it too. It's like trying to work out what makes a trend go viral; we can determine a number of the relevant factors but never isolate the specific one that makes the real difference.

TO CONCLUDE: WHAT WOULD I DO NEXT (AND ACTUALLY HAVE DONE)?

I would connect with the authors who have yet more to say on the subject of writing and book promotion, such as:

- Joanna Penn: http://www.thecreativepenn.com/blog/ for her excellent hints, tips, general expertise and all her self-help writing books, and Jane Friedman: https://janefriedman .com/self-publish-your-book/ for her wonderful insight into the publishing industry as a whole, together with a variety of other independent authors I list in the Appendix for more of the same.

- Join ALLi: http://www.selfpublishingadvice.org/guide books-for-authors/ for advice and support from a great community of independent authors.
- And if you have a budget to spend, have a look at:

    - Nick Stephenson for a great initial course on list building and Matt Stone for a new twist on building the list,
    - Mark Dawson for an excellent course on mastering Facebook and Twitter advertising, and,
    - Tim Grahl for a comprehensive course on how to launch your books when they're ready for (or already on) release.

    All the links are in the downloadable material I refer to in the Appendix.

- Plus make wide and extensive use of all the other websites, tools and detailed in the downloadable material in the Appendix.

LASTLY, WHAT IS SUCCESS?

I believe success is whatever you see it as, and to my mind, the achievement of having written a good book IS success, whether it sells one copy or millions. Publishing it is also a phenomenal success, and readership of it, ultimate success. With that in mind I am going to conclude this book with a few comments on awards that you can enter, be it as a traditionally or self-published author. An award is added value for you, just as what you give to your readers, over and above the book(s) you've written, is the added value for them. No matter how many thousands of times your book has been downloaded, purchased and read, being formally given an award for it is like a birthday, Christmas, rubbing Aladdin's lamp and finding the genie has still all three wishes left to grant you, all rolled into one. My book, *Patchwork Man*, has won an award. It's one of the awards on the list I've included in the downloadable material, and I can still remember the glow I felt when I was notified. For me, that is success too.

Appendix

PLEASE READ THIS CAREFULLY:

Some of the links and sites/books I have referred to can be found in this Appendix. Most of the others can be found by signing up to my information download list here: http://eepurl.com/bH8yEX

The documents available for download are:

1. All the terminology you'll need to tackle publishing-world-speak
2. Advice from the pros: the best guides to publishing and selling books
3. Publishers accepting direct submissions
4. Book cover design and free image sources
5. The software the professionals use: software for writing, publishing and promoting books
6. Bloggers and reviewers list
7. Sites to promote your books on
8. Blog tours – the list
9. Facebook groups to join for support, marketing and reviewers
10. Twitter hashtags and more
11. Reviewer request template
12. Awards list

These documents are downloadable because they can be easily refreshed as and when information changes – as it does often in an evolving industry. It is easier to update a single document than a whole book! Below is information that is not likely to change often:

SOME BOOKS/INFORMATION TO READ TO DEMONSTRATE HOW IT'S DONE BY THE MASTERS

Text books and creative writing

1 *Monomyth – The Hero with a Thousand Faces* (the collected works of Joseph Campbell)
2 Jung's 12 archetypal characters: http://www.uiltexas.org/files/capitalconference/Twelve_Character_Archetypes.pdf
3 TV Tropes archetypal characters: http://tvtropes.org/pmwiki/pmwiki.php/Main/Archetypal Character
4 *On Writing* by Stephen King
5 *Save the Cat* by Blake Snyder
6 *Grammar Girl's Quick and Dirty Tips for Better Writing* by Mignon Fogarty
7 *The Complete Guide to Writing Fiction and Non-Fiction and Getting it Published* by Pat Kubis and Bob Howland (an American title, available on Amazon)
8 *Take off your Pants* by Libbie Hawker

Some fiction to read for ideas on brilliant plotting and structure, or the use of a theme or object to plot

1. *The Hare with the Amber Eyes* by Edmund de Waal
2. *The Conjuror's Bird* by Martin Davies
3. *Sophie's World* by Jostein Gaarder
4. *The Lord of the Rings* by J R R Tolkien
5. *The Beach* by Alex Garland
6. *The Life of Pi* by Yann Martel
7. *The Alchemist* by Paulo Coelho
8. *The Girl with the Dragon Tattoo* by Stieg Larsson
9. *The Go-Between* by L P Hartley
10. *Lolita* by Vladimir Nabokov
11. *A tale of Two Cities* by Charles Dickens
12. *Pride and Prejudice* by Jane Austen
13. *Nineteen Eighty-Four* by George Orwell
14. *Rebecca* by Daphne du Maurier

15. *Hamlet* by William Shakespeare
16. *Dark Matter* by Michelle Paver
17. *Jane Eyre* by Charlotte Bronte
18. *The Da Vinci Code* by Dan Brown
19. *Silence of the Lambs* by Thomas Harris
20. *Before I go to Sleep* by S J Watson
21. *Gone Girl* by Gillian Flynn
22. *The Night Following* by Morag Joss
23. *The Perks of Being a Wallflower* by Stephen Chbosky
24. *Herzog* by Saul Bellow
25. *Skin* by Mo Hayder
26. *Darkly Dreaming Dexter* by Jeff Lindsay
27. *One Day* by David Nichols
28. *Life After Life* by Kate Atkinson
29. *Cloud Atlas* by David Mitchell
30. *The Hunger Games* (the complete trilogy) by Suzanne Collins
31. *The Virgin Suicides* by Jeffrey Eugenides
32. *Possession* by A S Byatt
33. *Tokyo* by Mo Hayder
34. *We Need To Talk About Kevin* by Lionel Shriver
35. *The Good Soldier: A Tale of Passion* by Ford Maddox Ford
36. *Lolita* by Vladimir Nabokov
37. *A Tale of Two Cities* by Charles Dickens
38. *Nineteen Eighty-Four* by George Orwell
39. *The Fault in Our Stars* by John Green
40. *Game of Thrones* (series) by George R R Martin
41. *The Curious Case of Benjamin Button* by F. Scott Fitzgerald
42. *Brave New World* by Aldous Huxley

WHO WILL HELP YOU SELF-PUBLISH?

- **CreateSpace:** http://www.createspace.com/ for print distribution on Amazon (zero upfront cost)
- **IngramSpark:** https://ingramspark.com/ for print distribution to the universe outside of Amazon ($49 US/ £29 UK set-up costs)

- **Amazon KDP:** http://www.kdp.amazon.com/ for ebook distribution on Amazon; i.e. Kindle (zero upfront cost)
- **Draft2Digital**: https://draft2digital.com/ for ebook distribution to the universe outside of Amazon (zero upfront cost)
- **Smashwords:** http://www.smashwords.com/ also for ebook distribution to the universe outside of Amazon, but with slightly complicated file formatting (zero upfront cost)
- **eBook Partnership:** http://eBookPartnership. com also for ebook distribution to the universe outside of Amazon, but with upfront costs
- Crowd Funding e.g. **Unbound:** https://unbound.co.uk/
- **Lulu**: https://www.lulu.com/
- **BookTango**: http://www.booktango.com/
- **Bookbaby**: http://www.bookbaby.com/
- **Vook**: http://pronoun.com/
- **Pressbooks**: http://pressbooks.com/
- **eBookIt**: http://www.ebookit.com/index.php
- **Nook:** https://www.nookpress.com/ebooks
- **Gumroad:** https://gumroad.com/
- **Sellfy:** https://sellfy.com/

TECHNICAL TIPS AND LINKS

- The most up-to-date list of current BISAC codes can be found here https://www.bisg.org/bisac-subject-codes
- To be included in certain categories on KDP your keywords must include some specified for that category. You can find the lists here: https://kdp.amazon.com/help?topicId= A200PDGPEIQX41
- British Standard Institution – BSI – marks for proofreading are detailed here: http://www.cse.dmu.ac.uk/~bstahl/ CORRECTION_MARKS.pdf

AND SOME DEFINITIONS OF 'FAIR USE' RELATING TO PERMISSIONS

- *A Writer's Guide to Fair Use* http://www.mbbp.com/ resources/iptech/fair_use.html

- Or have a look at good old Wiki's definition: https://en.wikipedia.org/wiki/Fair_use
- Is something copyrighted or in the public domain? Check here: http://www.unc.edu/~unclng/public-d.htm

GOOGLE'S SEO GUIDE IS HERE

- http://static.googleusercontent.com/media/www.google.co m/en//webmasters/docs/search-engine-optimization-starter-guide.pdf

SOFTWARE/WEBSITES REFERRED TO

Mind mapping:

- **iThoughtsHD:** https://geo.itunes.apple.com/gb/app/ithoughts-mindmap/id866786833?mt=8&at=100118vT)
- **MindNode:** https://geo.itunes.apple.com/gb/app/mindnode-delightful-mind mapping/id312220102?mt=8&at=100118vT)
- **Creately**: http://creately.com/diagram/example/ggvrpcfo1/Harry+Pott er (The Harry Potter mind map as an example).

Idea generation:

- http://www.seventhsanctum.com/generate.php?Genname=q uickstory

Inspiration:

- **NaNoWriMo:** National Novel Writing Month in November. http://nanowrimo.org/

Writing:

- Scrivener

FACEBOOK GROUPS

A large list of Facebook Groups you could join is included in the downloadable material on my website under the document title *Facebook groups to join for support, marketing and reviewers*. You can also try identifying others in your genre by searching on Facebook, for example "Romance Novels" and you will bring up groups such as Romance Novels & Romantic Fiction Readers and Writers with nearly 3,000 members. Enter search terms relevant to your genre and join any groups that appear suitable.

Here are some examples of more general book groups that may be interesting to join:

- **All About Books**: https://www.facebook.com/groups/AllAboutBooks2009/ with over 22,000 members.
- **Books Gone Viral:** https://www.facebook.com/groups/booksgoneviral/ with nearly 25,000 members.
- **Authors, Reviewers and Book Lovers:** https://www.facebook.com/groups/BooksLuvers/ with over 21,000 members.
- **Book Marketing and Review Exchange:** https://www.facebook.com/groups/bookmarketingandreviews/ with nearly 34,000 members.
- **Book Junkie Promotions:** https://www.facebook.com/groups/bookjunkiepromotions/ with more than 23,500 members.

HERE ARE SOME USEFUL PLACES TO LOOK FOR BLOGGERS AND REVIEWERS

- **Book Blogger Directory:** https://bookbloggerdirectory.wordpress.com/), a comprehensive, genre-organised alphabetical listing of book blogs.
- **YA Book Blog Directory**: http://yabookblogdirectory.blogspot.ca/; bloggers reviewing YA books.
- **Story Cartel**: https://storycartel.com/ where books are free in exchange for honest book reviews.
- **The Author Marketing Club** also offers its members a tailor-made reviewer locator service, based on books in

specific genres.

- **The Book Blogger List**: http://bookbloggerlist.com/, a database of book bloggers organised by genre.
- **Directory of Book Bloggers on Pinterest:** http://www. mandyboles.com/2012/01/directory-of-book-bloggers-on-pinterest/ a list of book bloggers using Pinterest curated by Mandy Boles.
- **Kate Tilton's Book Bloggers**: http://katetilton.com/kate-tiltons-book-bloggers/ a listing of book bloggers who provide reviews.

AND SOME FREE RESOURCES ONLINE THAT AUTHORS CAN USE ARE HERE

- **Books Blog**: http://bookblogs.ning.com/ is a community of authors and book bloggers who work together at reciprocal promotion.
- **The Indie View:** http://www.theindieview.com/ is a vast list of book bloggers who specialise in reviewing independent authors. Some may charge a fee.
- **Story Cartel:** https://storycartel.com/ allows authors and reviewers to connect without charges. The author provides their book free in exchange for an honest review.
- **The Great Big Book Reviewer List:** http://readerswritersj ournal.com/the-great-big-book-reviewer-list/ provides links to the submission pages of many blogs, all in one place.
- **Bookplex:** http://bookplex.com/pg/28/book-review-service also provides a book review service. There is a charge for the service.
- **Author Key Book Marketing:** http://www.authorkey.com/ #!self-published-book-review-service/c1q35 sends free copies of your book to the readers on its database with an interest in your book's genre, as well as to top Amazon reviewers. There is a charge for the service.
- **Storyfinds:** https://storyfinds.com/ also connects reviewers and readers for a price.

PLACES TO FIND AN AUDIENCE TO TALK TO

- Literary festivals in the UK: http://www.literaryfestivals .co.uk/list_of_literary_festivals.html
- And internationally: http://www.novelicious.com/ 2014/01/ 25-of-the-best-annual-book-festivals-around-the-world.html

WHERE TO FIND A WRITERS GROUP TO JOIN

- In the UK, look on the National Association of Writers' Groups website: http://www.nawg.co.uk
- In the US, look on Writers and Editors: http://www. writersandeditors.com/local_and_regional_organizations_5 7451.html

AND A THANK YOU AND A MENTION FOR MY OWN PROOFREADER AND FORMATTER:

- Proofreading – Alison Farrell, who you can find on http:// www.sfep.org.uk/
- Formatting – Frank at http://www.bookformatting.co.uk/

ABOUT THE AUTHOR

Debrah Martin writes literary fiction as well as adult psychological thriller fiction as D.B. Martin. She also writes contemporary YA fiction, featuring a teen detective series, under the pen name of Lily Stuart. She chaired an Oxfordshire, UK literary festival 2014-2015 and also teaches creative writing and publishing. You can find more of her work on www.debrahmartin.co.uk. or sign up for updates on upcoming releases and special offers at: http://eepurl.com/3-965

She also loves reviews and feedback so if you've enjoyed this – or any of her books – please DO leave a review. Just click on the button that says 'WRITE A CUSTOMER REVIEW' after the section containing other reader's reviews and have your say!

Other books by this author:

WRITING THRILLER FICTION
AS D. B. MARTIN:

PATCHWORK MAN

Lawrence Juste is top of the British legal world; a paragon of justice in action…

But Lawrence Juste isn't all that he seems. Outside of the courtroom, he's another man with another past – one full of conspiracy and secrets. One that is about to catch up with him.

It's not just the blackmail note his wife leaves him just before her death, or the vengeful family he's forced to reconnect with that bring the past crashing into the present. There's someone with their own very specific agenda who's after Lawrence Juste; someone Lawrence tangled with a long time ago. Someone with a long and vindictive memory, and now they want their pound of flesh.

Patchwork Man is the first book in the Patchwork People mystery suspense trilogy, and the winner of an Indie B.R.A.G. Medallion award.

It's available on Amazon here:
http://smarturl.it/patchworkman

PATCHWORK PEOPLE

Previously the name in the news in UK courtrooms, now Lawrence Juste, QC, is making headlines of a different sort. Yet despite admitting to a murky history, he's still on the up. It's a PR triumph for the man with the patchwork past; until the first sinister black edged card arrives. It's followed by a parcel of evidence that puts Lawrence right in the middle of a deceit he helped create ten years ago. Not only that, when his hated sister is found dead in his house, he's prime suspect number one.

The black edged card is followed by others, and more damning evidence. They draw Lawrence deep into a pit of conspiracy and suspense, with the certain knowledge that the dead do tell tales; and there's no escaping revenge.

Patchwork People is the second book in the trilogy.

It's available on Amazon here:
http://smarturl.it/Patchwork People

PATCHWORK PIECES

When Lawrence Juste QC, gentleman and liar, originally championed the case of the boy who reminded him of himself, he couldn't have known precisely how much like him the boy would turn out to be. Or that the boy's past was already as entangled in murder and betrayal as his own.

Now the wheel has turned full circle. The past is the present, the betrayed are the betrayers and only the ultimate sacrifice can save both Juste and the boy. The only question ultimately remaining, as the patchwork completes:

Who will be sacrificed?

Patchwork Pieces is the final book in the trilogy.

It's available on Amazon here:
https://smarturl.it/PatchworkPieces

OR READ THE WHOLE TRILOGY HERE:
https:// smarturl.it/PPBoxSet

WRITING LITERARY FICTION AS DEBRAH MARTIN:

FALLING AWAKE

Some would say suffering has driven Mary mad, and the people and places she remembers all just dreams dreamt inside her insanity. But then how can her husband Joe remember them too?
Falling Awake is the story of Mary, Joe and a world populated by love, betrayal and obsession - and what it does to those who live in it.
Magic or madness? The impossible is only ever a breath away.
Just don't fall awake…

It's available on Amazon here: http://smarturl.it/FallingAwake

CHAINED MELODIES

"Chaos is about rejecting all that you have learnt, chaos is about being yourself." – Emile M. Cioran
   If chaos theory applied to anyone, it's Will and Tom. Best friends since childhood, life takes very different courses for them until they're thrown back together in the middle of their own individual chaos.
   Surviving the terrors of war in Northern Ireland and the heartbreak of childlessness and a broken marriage, Tom learns that courage isn't about daring death, it's about facing life, and he's never been good at that. For Will, it's about being yourself - in his case, a very different kind of self; a woman called Billie.
   As Will transitions from male to female, so the once-close friendship between Tom and Will changes too – from surprise to grudging respect, to admiration and eventually to love. But it takes more than love to face a world of prejudice and a life-time of stereotyping – it takes courage, and Tom has always had a problem with that, despite being the archetypal alpha male. And when an unexpected tragedy throws both Tom and Billie into the public eye, courage becomes more than an issue, it becomes the difference between life and death.

It's available on Amazon here: http://smarturl.it/ChainedMelodies

WRITING YA FICTION
AS LILY STUART:

WEBS

Deadly intrigue with a ton of teenage humour thrown in... Webs is the first book in the Lily S: Teenage Detective series.

Sixteen-year-old Lily's policeman Dad is trying to untangle a particularly nasty death and Lily's intrigued. She's even more intrigued when she proves to him it's actually murder. Perhaps she'd make a detective too? If only she could work out what would get Dad to dump awful Ange, grovel, and patch things up with Mum. Irritating isn't the word!

In retaliation, for awful Ange, Lily's mum resorts to the web for romance – the world-wide-web. Convinced she can get her parents back together, Lily resorts to her own bit of web-weaving to trip up the candidates for replacement daddy. Whilst her school friends are up to their usual tricks; Matt is alternately ignoring and chasing her. Melezz is being the worst best friend, and Jacob is up to no good with his nipple tassel pranks again, Lily's busy sleuthing. The trouble is, whilst Lily thinks she's a clever little spider, weaving clever little traps, one of her prey is smarter still – and deadly.

It's available on Amazon here: http://smarturl.it/Webs-book

MAGPIES

The second in the Lily S: Teenage Detective series - THE teenage detective is back, and looking for trouble!

Or rather trouble's looking for her. They find each other in the series of little mysteries that start cropping up as soon as Lily's back at school after her brush with death, and meets the new boy, Si. He's different, like Lily is now, with her occasional narcolepsy and frequent inclination to investigate everything. But whereas Lily watches and works things out, Si blurts it all out at the wrong time and in the wrong way. He has Tourette's.

He also has a way with rhymes; one in particular that increasingly makes sense to Lily as the mysteries mount up and a gang of drug pushers target the school and her friends with potentially lethal consequences.

One for sorrow, two for joy, three for -

But 'joy' isn't a girl's name nor the opposite of sad, and the magpies the rhyme is about aren't just black and white birds that like stealing treasure. They're far more deadly than that…

It's available on Amazon here: http://smarturl.it/Magpies

32046103R00165

Printed in Great Britain
by Amazon